The Life and Writings of Salmon P. Chase

Constitutional Discourse Series

Series Editor: Randy E. Barnett

GEORGETOWN
Center *for the* Constitution

Published by the Georgetown Center for the Constitution
Georgetown Law
Washington, DC

The Georgetown Center for the Constitution

The Georgetown Center for the Constitution was founded in 2012. It offers a variety of programs on constitutional law and theory at Georgetown Law, placing special emphasis on how best to remain faithful to the Constitution's text. Led by Professor Randy Barnett, the Center sponsors lectures, faculty colloquia, conferences, visiting scholars, post-graduate fellowships, and student fellows. All of its activities are designed to engage scholars, students, and even Supreme Court Justices in conversations about how to interpret and apply the document that sits under glass less than ten blocks away from Georgetown Law.

Georgetown Center for the Constitution
Georgetown Law
600 New Jersey Avenue, NW
Washington, DC 20001
lawconstitution@georgetown.edu
https://www.law.georgetown.edu/constitution-center/

Table of Contents

The Life and Writings of Salmon P. Chase

PREFACE

DISTINGUISHED LECTURE

Making Freedom National: Salmon P. Chase and the Abolition of Slavery

JAMES OAKES*

"Every man can read the Constitution." That's what Salmon P. Chase believed, or so he said on November 1, 1860, just before Abraham Lincoln was elected president. Chase was in Covington, Kentucky campaigning for the Republicans by spelling out one of the cardinal principles of the party's platform, and of the broader antislavery movement he had done so much to build. Not only can anybody read the Constitution, Chase went on, "every man can read the debates of the framers of the Constitution for himself, and I confess," he concluded,

> I do not see how any man can read either and come to the conclusion that property in slaves is anywhere recognized in that instrument . Not only is there no recognition, but there is careful avoidance of recognition of property in man. Whenever and wherever slaves are referred to in the Constitution, they are always mentioned as *persons*.[1]

Earlier in that same year, in February of 1860, Abraham Lincoln had used nearly identical language in the famous speech he gave at the Cooper Institute in Manhattan—the speech that helped secure him the Republican party's presidential nomination. "[N]either the word 'slave' nor 'slavery' is to be found in the Constitution," Lincoln said. On the contrary, "wherever in that instrument the slave is alluded to, he is called a 'person.'" This "mode of alluding to slaves

---

*James Oakes is a historian of nineteenth-century America at CUNY Graduate Center. This lecture was delivered on December 7, 2014.

1. *Governor Chase in Kentucky,* N.Y. TRIB., Nov. 7, 1860, at 6.

and slavery," Lincoln insisted, "was employed on purpose to exclude from the Constitution the idea that there could be property in man."[2]

Lincoln presented his case as the sober conclusion he arrived at after diligent research in the Illinois state library, where he had recently pored over the documentary record left by the Founders. Chase, by contrast, spoke as if it were all perfectly obvious—that anyone who read the Constitution could easily see that it did not recognize a right of property in slaves. Or that anyone who read Madison's published notes of debates at the Constitutional Convention in Philadelphia in 1787 could also see that the men who drafted the "instrument" were clearly, unambiguously, *obviously* determined to exclude any wording that recognized a property right in human beings.

But of course, what was obvious to Chase was not obvious to all those who read the Constitution. Not everyone read it the same way. In this case one particular man read it very differently, and that man happened to be the Chief Justice of the United States Supreme Court, Roger B. Taney. In 1857, only a few years before Lincoln's election, Taney had issued his explosive decision in the case of *Dred Scott v. Sandford*. It was and remains a notoriously difficult decision to unpack, in part because there were so many different concurring and dissenting opinions, in part because it's not always easy to disentangle which passages were—as Lincoln believed—mere dicta, and in part because Taney's opinion covered several different issues, each one riddled with complexity. But on one point Taney was clear and unmistakable. The "right of property in slaves," he ruled, "is distinctly and expressly affirmed in the Constitution."[3] As far as Taney was concerned, anyone who bothered to read the Constitution would see this. It is "done in plain words," he wrote, "too plain to be misunderstood."[4]

Plenty of scholars have leapt in to adjudicate this dispute, and though I'd just as soon stay out of it, if pressed I would likely conclude that Chase had the better argument. At the very least it is not obvious to me that *Dred Scott* was correctly decided. Still, I'm a historian, not a magistrate and what interests me about the disagreement over the constitutional property right in slaves is not who won or lost, but the terms of the debate itself. Because that's what has been missing from so many readings of the *Dred Scott*

---

2. THE COLLECTED WORKS OF ABRAHAM LINCOLN 544 (Roy P. Basler, ed., 1953) [Hereinafter *CW*].
3. Dred Scott v. Sandford, 60 U.S. 393, 451 (1856). 4.
4. *Id.* at 445.

decision, and indeed the entire sectional crisis over slavery. We have not fully grasped what was at stake in the conflict between the North and the South because we don't yet recognize the terms of the debate. We have been, rather surprisingly, blind to the way the *opponents* of slavery framed their arguments, especially their constitutional arguments. And until we've reconstructed the contours of antislavery constitutionalism, we will not fully appreciate what Roger Taney was doing in his *Dred Scott* decision. Think of it this way: Taney had set about to destroy the intellectual edifice that Salmon Chase had spent decades struggling to build.

This is one of the reasons Chase is so crucially important to the history of the United States in the middle of the nineteenth century. For no one person did more to translate the antislavery principles and precedents bequeathed by the Founders into a coherent political program for getting slavery abolished. Chase had carved out the building blocks of antislavery constitutionalism, and then used them to construct a politically viable antislavery platform. If it was plausible for him to claim, in November of 1860, that *anyone* could read the Constitution and plainly see that it did not recognize a property right in slaves, that was in large part because Chase had been successful in his generation-long struggle to make that *seem* obvious to anyone who read the Constitution. When Lincoln told the audience at the Cooper Institute that there was no such thing as a constitutional right of property in slaves he was not leading the way for Chase; he was following Chase's lead.

Historians need to do the same thing—follow Chase's lead, reconstruct the way he himself constructed his antislavery constitutionalism and, guided by those principles, proposed a practical antislavery platform with powerful appeal to northern voters, a platform that was implemented during the Civil War, even as the war radicalized and transformed Chase's platform. But we cannot even begin to appreciate what the war changed until we understand the project Chase himself had outlined decades before.

From his studies of the American founding Chase discerned several important antislavery precedents, the first and most obvious of which was the abolition of slavery in the northern states. That process had gotten started in Vermont in 1777 with a new state constitution that freed all slaves upon reaching adulthood. In one sense Vermont was unusual, for no other state abolished slavery by means of a new constitution—though Massachusetts came close. There, slavery was abolished by a series of court decisions declaring that property in man violated the principle enshrined in the state's revolutionary constitution, that all men are born free and equal. But in most states, beginning with Pennsylvania in 1780, slavery was abolished by the legislatures. In 1784 Connecticut and Rhode Island abolished slavery by legislative statutes. New York and New Jersey followed suit until, by 1804, every northern state had embraced abolition. This process is known as the "first emancipation."

Historians have been squabbling for some time about what this "first emancipation" actually accomplished, but for Salmon Chase abolition in the northern states was important for very specific reasons, some of which are so self-evident that we don't even notice them. Above all, the first emancipation established the presumption, accepted by nearly all Americans from the Revolution to the Civil War, that abolition was something *states* did. Indeed, one of the reasons the Americans originally rebelled against Great Britain was because they wanted each colony to be able to regulate slavery on its own—which is precisely what Americans proceeded to do. London had repeatedly vetoed every effort by individual colonies to restrict the importation of slaves, for example, but immediately upon declaring their independence every state quickly banned the importation of slaves from the Atlantic trade. In the north, as we've already seen, one state after another set about abolishing slavery. For Chase and like-minded opponents of slavery, the lesson of the Revolution was clear. Abolition was something individual states did, and would continue to do. Stimulated by the example of the northern states and inspired by the principle of the Declaration of Independence, Chase argued, "it was expected that all the States . . . would, at no distant day, put an end to slavery within their respective limits."[5]

Abolition could only be accomplished state by state because central government established by the Constitution could *not* interfere with slavery in the states. This was very different from revolutionary France, which abolished slavery in its American colonies by means of a directive sent out from Paris. Nor was it like the more conservative Great Britain, whose parliament in London likewise abolished slavery in its own Caribbean colonies a generation or two later. Americans, by contrast, assumed that

5. SOUTHERN AND WESTERN LIBERTY CONVENTION, ET AL., ADDRESS OF THE SOUTHERN AND WESTERN LIBERTY CONVENTION: HELD IN CINCINNATI, JUNE 11 AND 12, 1845, TO THE PEOPLE OF THE UNITED STATES (1845).

slavery was something established by the laws of individual states and that only states could repeal those laws. Because American leaders believed that Parliament had no business forcing individual colonies to keep the Atlantic slave trade open, it never occurred to those same leaders that the Continental Congress had the power to force states to import slaves, much less to abolish slavery in any state. Nor did the Congress under the Articles of Confederation assume that it had any power to regulate or interfere with slavery in the individual states. The Constitution of 1787 left that premise intact. Slavery was strictly a state institution, and the new federal government had no power to interfere with or abolish the institution in the states where it was legal.

So when Lincoln declared in his first inaugural address, "I have no purpose, directly or indirectly, to interfere with the institution of slavery in the States where it exists," he was reiterating a familiar principle subscribed to by nearly all Americans, including those dedicated to abolishing slavery.[6] It wasn't only the moderate Lincoln who disclaimed any intention of interfering with slavery in the states. Fervent abolitionists like William Lloyd Garrison and Theodore Dwight Weld said the same thing. So did antislavery politicians whose radical credentials are impeccable—Thaddeus Stevens, Benjamin Wade, Charles Sumner—all of them agreed that under the Constitution the federal government had no power to interfere with slavery in the states, and all of them said so openly. Which is to say, the *antislavery* position—including the radical abolitionist position—was a state's rights position. This point is worth emphasizing if only because of the inexplicably popular myth that the South seceded from the Union to defend state rights.

But this raises a fairly obvious question. If the federal government could not abolish slavery, how did abolitionists and antislavery politicians expect to get slavery abolished? What did it mean to be an *abolitionist* in Massachusetts or Ohio while declaring that the federal government had no power to abolish slavery? How could Lincoln say, on the one hand, that he had no intention of interfering with slavery in the states where it existed and, at the same time, declare, repeatedly, that he wanted the federal government to put slavery on the course of "ultimate

6. 4 *CW, supra* note 2, at 264

extinction?"[7]

For Chase a crucial part of the answer rested on a second legacy of the American Revolution, the relegation of slavery to a sectional institution. This was partly the unintended consequence of state-by-state abolition. We say all the time that in the late eighteenth century slavery was abolished in "the North." But that isn't quite right. Slavery was not abolished by an entity we can call "the North." It was the other way around. Beginning in 1777 one state after another began to abolish slavery, and when the process ended with the abolition of slavery in New Jersey in 1804, the accumulation of free states had come to constitute the entity we know as "the North." The *North* did not abolish slavery; rather, state by state abolition created a section we call the North. Almost by default, the states that retained slavery became the section we call "the South."

This process was not entirely unintended, however. In 1787 the sectional isolation of slavery became more deliberate when Congress, under the Articles of Confederation, passed the law commonly known as the Northwest Ordinance effectively thwarting the expansion of slavery into the Old Northwest. The ordinance was subsequently readopted by the first Congress meeting under the new Constitution, and although slaveholders in some northwestern states later tried to repeal the bans on slavery they were consistently beaten back. The result of the Northwest Ordinance, therefore, was the eventual creation of the free states of Ohio, Michigan, Indiana, Illinois, and Wisconsin. The federal government had thus facilitated the establishment of two sections, a "North" composed of free states and a South composed of slave states, both of them stretching from the Atlantic Ocean to the Mississippi River. Not surprisingly, Chase looked upon the Northwest Ordinance as one of the most important legacies of the Founders. It made slavery to purely sectional institution—sectional not simply because of the sequential abolition of slavery in the northern states, but as the consequence of the considered policy of the Founders who *intended* to make slavery sectional.

These two facts—that slavery was a state institution and that it was restricted to one section—carried no necessary antislavery implications. They merely described the situation as it was, certainly by the time Chase began thinking systematically about

---

7. 2 *id.* at 453, 461, 471, 491-4, 498, 514-5; 3 *id.* at 18, 82, 86-7, 89, 117, 181, 276, 305-8, 316, 407, 427, 438-9, 520.

the problem of slavery in the middle of the 1830s. But Chase also believed that the Founders intended to go further. They did not simply reserve slavery to the states, they *restricted* it to the states. And they didn't simply make slavery sectional, they also made freedom *national.* He could not have been clearer about this. "Freedom is National," Chase declared in 1850, "slavery is only local and sectional."[8]

The fact that slavery was strictly a state institution and that it was limited to one section of the country did not prevent the federal government from adopting policies that would promote freedom wherever it exercised sovereign jurisdiction. As one Congressman had put it in the buildup to the Missouri crisis in 1819, "Congress *within its sovereignty* has steadily maintained the truth 'that all men are born equally free,' but disclaims the power of applying this doctrine to *state* sovereignties." Here was the third and, for Chase, the most compelling legacy of the Founders. Beyond the borders of the states in which slavery was legal Congress was empowered, perhaps even morally obligated, to promote freedom and restrict slavery. If the founders "did not intend to authorize direct national legislation for the removal of the slavery existing in particular States under their local laws, they did intend to keep the action of the national government free from all connection with the system; discountenance and discourage it in the States; and to favor the Abolition of it by State authority."[9]

What did that mean? Was it a purely negative injunction that forbade the government from doing *anything* with regard to slavery? Was this call for the "denationalization" of slavery a variation on the familiar Jacksonian that called elsewhere for the absolute divorce of the federal government from banking? Or was the government empowered by a positive charge to "discourage and discountenance" slavery in the states, to pursue affirmative policies that would "favor the abolition of slavery by State authority?" Chase never resolved this philosophical ambiguity.

Consider the fact that the Constitution empowered Congress to ban the Atlantic slave trade within a generation. The slave trade clause of the Constitution, which looks to many historians today like a scandalous twenty-one year *delay* in banning the importation of slaves, looked quite different to many men at the time. For one

8. Salmon P. Chase, Union and Freedom, Without Compromise: Speech of Mr. Chase of Ohio, on Mr. Clay's Compromise Resolutions, March 26, 1850.

9. SOUTHERN AND WESTERN LIBERTY CONVENTION, ET AL., *supra* note 5.

thing, the state-by-state bans on the slave trade remained in place all through the 1790s, unaffected by the new Constitution. Yet the Constitution did represent a significant shift. In 1776 the colonists had rebelled against Great Britain in part because they *objected* to central government control over the slave trade, but little more than a decade later, in 1787, the Constitution empowered the new central government to eventually exercise such control.

This was more than mere federalism. Federalism might be enough to explain why slavery was local, but not why freedom was national. Were the Founders inconsistent when they argued, on the one hand, that slavery was purely a state institution and on the other that the federal government should ban slavery in the northwestern territories or make it a crime to import slaves into the United States? Maybe. But what if the Founders were not really *protecting* slavery in the states but were actually *restricting* slavery to the states? That's what Chase believed, and the clearest evidence he discerned for this reading of the Founders' legacy was their explicit refusal to recognize a constitutional a right of property in slaves.

Chase did not deny that slaves were property: Property in Man is what slavery was. But borrowing from the logic of Lord Mansfield's influential *Somerset* decision of 1772, Chase argued that slavery was such an "odious" violation of the natural right to freedom that it could only exist where "positive" local law overrode the natural right to freedom. The Founders agreed, Chase believed. They had embraced the principle that every human being was endowed with the natural right to freedom on the basis that principle they had deliberately refused to recognize property in man as a constitutional right. For the Founders slave property existed not as a natural or a constitutional right, but as what Chase called a "naked *legal* right"—a right that existed only where local, positive law created the right.

Here's how Chase summed it all up in the address he wrote for the proceedings of the first convention of the Ohio Liberty Party, which met at Columbus in December, 1841:

> By the convention which framed the [Federal] Constitution, the irreconcilable opposition of slavery to freedom, and of slave-labor to free labor, was well understood, and the solemn pledge given in the Declaration of Independence was freshly remembered . . . .
>
> It was impossible that this convention could recognize the principle of slavery in the frame of the national Government.

> In the emphatic language of Mr. Madison, 'they thought it WRONG to admit in the Constitution the idea that there could be property in man! Yet, as they had no power to change the personal relations of the inhabitants of any State to each other, but were charged with the duty of framing a general system of government for the people of all the States, leaving those relations untouched, it was equally impossible for them to abolish slavery in the States where it existed.'
>
> Accordingly, we find that the Constitution designates all the inhabitants of the States as persons, and nowhere recognizes the idea that men can be the subjects of property; at the same time it nowhere confers on Congress the right to abolish slavery in the States where it is recognized and sanctioned by the local constitutions . The Constitution found slavery and left it a State institution—the creature and dependent of State law—wholly local in its existence and character. It did not make it a national institution. It gave it no national character; no national existence.[10]

Beyond the reach of local law, the legal right to own slaves ceased to exist. This alone should have been enough to put slavery on a course of ultimate extinction. Instead, organized political opposition to slavery had become necessary, Chase concluded, "BECAUSE SLAVERY HAS OVERLEAPED ITS PRESCRIBED LIMITS AND USURPED CONTROL OF THE NATIONAL GOVERNMENT." To counteract this "Slave Power," Chase and the Liberty Party insisted that "THE WELFARE, THE SAFETY OF OUR COUNTRY imperiously require THE ABSOLUTE AND UNQUALIFIED DIVORCE OF THE GOVERNMENT FROM SLAVERY."[11] In short, all federal support for slavery must cease.

This did not mean that the federal government should do nothing, however. The negative proposition had a positive counterpoint. Chase would withdraw support for all federal legislation in *support* of slavery, but he would endorse a variety of policies that would sustain freedom wherever the federal government was sovereign. If Congress could not touch slavery in the states that legalized it, there were nevertheless a number of areas beyond the borders of the states where the federal government exercised jurisdiction, and in those areas, Chase

10. J.W. SCHUCKERS, THE LIFE AND PUBLIC SERVICES OF SALMON PORTLAND CHASE, 48-49 (1874).
11. *Id.* at 49-51.

believed, the Constitution virtually mandated policies that would suppress slavery and uphold the principal of universal freedom.

This was how antislavery northerners read their nation's history. The Founders had made slavery a purely state institution and restricted it to one section. But this was not merely a negative injunction against the use of federal power. By 1820 opponents of slavery were beginning to argue that the Founders were committed to affirmative policies that would make freedom *national.* In 1821 the pioneering abolitionist, Benjamin Lundy, spelled out a seven-point program by which the federal government would restrict slavery to the states where it existed and encourage those states to abolish the institution on their own. A decade later Lundy's protégé, William Lloyd Garrison, wrote Lundy's program into the "Declaration of Sentiments" announcing the formation of the American Anti-Slavery Society in 1833. Garrison had invited all those committed to "immediate" abolition to convene in Philadelphia to coordinate their state and local efforts within a new, nationwide campaign against slavery. Yet despite their sincere desire to abolish slavery "immediately," the Garrisonians clearly understood that slavery was a state institution. "We fully and unanimously recognize the sovereignty of each State, to legislate exclusively on the subject of slavery which is tolerated within its limits," Garrison wrote, adding that "we concede that Congress under the present compact, has no right to interfere with any of the slave States in relation to this momentous subject." It was at this point, however, that we can begin to discern the abolitionist answer to the question I raised earlier: What "immediate emancipation" mean if by Garrison's own account the slave states alone had the power to abolish slavery within their own borders? The answer can be found in the constitution endorsed by the American Anti-Slavery Society at the Philadelphia convention. We will "do all that is lawfully in our power to bring about the extinction of slavery," the delegates vowed. Article II was more specific. They would "endeavor, in a constitutional way

> to put an end to the domestic slave-trade, and to abolish slavery in all those portions of our common country which come under its control, especially in the District of Columbia—and likewise to prevent the extension of it to any state that may hereafter be admitted to the Union.[12]

12. WENDELL PHILLIPS GARRISON AND FRANCIS JACKSON GARRISON, 1 WILLIAM

Here was the practical application of the radical abolitionist project. The federal government should shut down the interstate slave trade, abolish slavery in Washington, D.C., ban slavery from all federal territories, and prevent the admission of any new slave states into the Union. With these policies in place the federal government would tilt the scales in favor of the expansion of freedom and toward the steady erosion of slavery.

Within a few years Garrison became persuaded that the U.S. Constitution was so hopelessly proslavery that it did not even allow Congress to implement the policies endorsed by his own American Anti-Slavery Society. Nothing short of constitutional amendments would be required to abolish slavery in the District of Columbia and ban it from the territories. In his denunciation of a pro-slavery Constitution Garrison parted company with his fellow immediatists, most of whom continued to believe that Congress already had the constitutional authority to enact their program.[13] As Garrison drifted away from direct involvement in partisan politics, Chase moved in the opposite direction. With his embrace of the Liberty Party in 1841 Chase became the leading voice of the rapidly emerging mainstream of the antislavery movement. Yet his agenda remained faithful to the principles of the American Anti-Society. "When I say that we [of the Liberty Party] are against slavery wherever it exists without constitutional warrant," Chase explained,

> I mean that we are against Slavery in the District of Columbia, in Florida [still a federal territory] & on the seas: in short, we hold that no man can be constitutionally held as property in this country except *in a state* where the local constitution maintains slavery.[14]

Chase went on to write the platform for the Free Soil Party in 1848—which garnered far more votes than the Liberty Party but scarcely enough to win a national election. For several years after 1848 Chase advocated "fusion" with any major party that endorsed the Freedom National platform, a tactic that one again failed at the national level but which did score some impressive

---

LLOYD GARRISON, 1805-1879 380-419 (1894).

13. *See* W. CALEB MCDANIEL, THE PROBLEM OF DEMOCRACY IN THE AGE OF SLAVERY (2013) (discussing the essentially political nature of Garrison's project).

14. THE SALMON P. CHASE PAPERS 98 (John Niven, ed 1994) (1841).

successes in individual states—among them Chase's own election as governor of Ohio as well as the election of Charles Sumner as U.S. Senator from Massachusetts. Though Sumner was hardly a mainstream politician, his election was a symptom of the growing influence of the antislavery movement in national politics. This became clear in August of 1852 when Sumner delivered his inaugural speech to the Senate, entitled "Freedom National, Slavery Sectional." Though framed as a demand for the repeal of the Fugitive Slave Act of 1850, the speech also revealed the consistency of the antislavery agenda. Like every opponent of slavery from Garrison to Lincoln, Sumner readily acknowledged that under the Constitution the federal government had no power to abolish slavery in a state. But there were still many things the federal government could do to thwart slavery, and Sumner was not shy about spelling them out:

> In all national territories Slavery will be impossible.
>
> On the high seas, under the national flag, Slavery will be impossible.
>
> In the District of Columbia Slavery will instantly cease.
>
> Congress can give no sanction to Slavery in the admission of new Slave States.
>
> Nowhere under the Constitution, can the Nation, by legislation or otherwise, support Slavery, hunt slaves, or hold property in man.[15]

Sumner went on to become a leading spokesman for the radical wing of the Republican Party, the first major party to bear the imprint of the antislavery movement. State and local Republican organizations across the North drafted platforms and issued resolutions that would have been familiar to the abolitionists in attendance at the first meeting of the American Anti-Slavery Society in Philadelphia back in 1833. In the mid-1850s a local Republican organization in Aurora, Illinois, for example, vowed to

> to repeal and entirely abrogate the fugitive slave law; to

15. The Honorable Charles Sumner, Senator of Massachusetts, Speech before the United States Senate: Freedom National; Slavery Sectional 31 (1852).

> restrict slavery to those States in which it exists; to prohibit the admission of any more slave States into the Union; to abolish slavery in the District of Columbia; to exclude slavery from all the territories over which the general government has exclusive jurisdiction; and to resist the acquirements of any more territories unless the practice of slavery therein forever shall have been prohibited.[16]

This was more than a mere hodge-podge of policies that antislavery activists glommed onto in a desperate scramble for anything they could justify under a Constitution that banned outright abolition. There was, in fact, a larger logic to this antislavery platform. For together these policies were designed to build what the opponents of slavery called a "cordon of freedom" around the states where slavery already existed. Confined within those state limits, unable to expand, deprived of all federal support—in the territories, on the high seas, or in the north—a slave system thus hemmed in would eventually shrivel and die. The cordon of freedom could be built immediately but abolition itself would be gradual as the slave states succumbed, one by one, to the pressure from the federal government to abolish slavery on their own. Wherever the federal government was sovereign—in the western territories, and in the nation's capital—slavery would be abolished by the national government. When slaves rebelled on the high seas, the federal government would no longer support southern demands for suppression and re-enslavement. When slaves escaped to the northern states, the federal government would do nothing to assist slave catchers. Federal officials would not be compelled to hunt down and re-enslave a species of "property" that existed only under the law of the southern states. No new slave states would be admitted to the Union, while the number of free states continued to grow—steadily tightening the federal noose, further isolating an already isolated section.

What the federal government would not do, what it could never do, was directly abolish slavery in a state where it was legal. "The question of slavery in the States may be safely left to the States themselves," Chase freely acknowledged. Nevertheless, he argued, whatever "can be constitutionally done by the national Legislature to promote their progress and improvement, should be unhesitatingly and ungrudgingly done." If the federal government builds its cordon of freedom around the slave states, Chase

16. 3 *CW*, *supra* note 2, at 4.

predicted, "the wisdom of the people will, I trust, so dispose of it that in the not far distant future a day will come, when the sun in all his course over our broad land, from the Atlantic to the Pacific, shall not behold a slave."[17] Thaddeus Stevens made the same point in less poetic terms. Confining slavery "within its present limits," Stevens explained in 1850, "will bring the *States themselves* to its gradual abolition." Encircle slavery within "a cordon of freedom so that it cannot spread," he predicted, "and in less than twenty-five years every slaveholding State in the Union will have on its statute books a law for the gradual and final extinction of slavery."[18]

The cordon of freedom was not the end, but the means to an end—the resumption of abolition, one state at a time. Even the most radical Republicans assumed that this would be the policy pursued by the Lincoln administration in the wake of the 1860 presidential election. As Charles Sumner explained, Lincoln's victory established several things:

> that it is wrong to admit into the Constitution the idea that there can be property in man . . . . that Slavery is sectional and freedom national . . . that all the outlying Territories of the Government, so enormous in extent, and destined to be inhabited by an immense population, shall be consecrated to Freedom; that the soil shall never be pressed by the footstep of the slave . . . . that the slave trade, which it is now proposed to open with increased activity, shall in reality be suppressed, and that all the force of this Government shall be directed in that way.[19]

Sumner was proved right. As soon as the Republicans got the chance, they did all that he predicted and more. In the first regular

---

17. SCHUCKERS, *supra* note 10, at 167.

18. Thaddeus Stevens, Speech of Thaddeus Stevens, of Pennsylvania: In the U.S. House of Representatives, Wednesday, Feb. 20, 1850, in the committee of the whole on the state of the Union, on the reference of the president's annual message 7 (1850).

A small but articulate faction within the abolitionist movement, led by William Goodell, Lysander Spooner, Gerrit Smith, and Frederick Douglass, came to believe that the Constitution not only allowed Congress to abolish slavery in the states but virtually required it. Few abolitionists shared this view, and virtually no one outside the antislavery movement adopted it. *See* William M. Wiecek, *The Sources of Antislavery Constitutionalism in America, 1760-1848* (Ithaca, 1977) (describing the origins of this interpretation).

19. *The Hon. Charles Sumner on the Result of the Election*, N.Y. TRIB., Nov. 12, 1860, at 7.

session of Congress they ever controlled, between December, 1861, and July, 1862, Republicans abolished slavery in Washington, D. C., prohibited the Union Army from enforcing the Fugitive Slave Law, banned slavery from the western territories, forced West Virginia to abolish slavery as a condition for admission to the Union, and ratified a treaty with Great Britain to suppress the Atlantic slave trade. No one hid the fact that these policies were inter-connected, that their larger goal was to surround the slave states with a "cordon of freedom" until, "like a scorpion surrounded by fire," Republicans commonly declared, slavery would sting itself to death—one state at a time.[20]

Abraham Lincoln was no less committed to the goal of getting the states to abolish slavery. He signed all the antislavery legislation Congress passed and it was his own Secretary of State who swiftly negotiated the slave trade treaty with Great Britain. But because he was the President, and because there was a war on, Lincoln was in a unique position to press for abolition in individual slave states much more aggressively than he could have done in peacetime. But Lincoln's sustained effort to implement Chase's platform has all but disappeared from histories of the Civil War and biographies of the sixteenth president. Historians spend so much time focusing on his Emancipation Proclamation that they either ignore most of what he was doing about slavery most of the time, or else they're completely baffled by his policies. To be more precise, they are confused by the fact that throughout most of the war Lincoln was pursuing two distinct policies—the cordon of freedom was one, and military emancipation was another.

Military emancipation was an ancient practice in which belligerents offered freedom to their own (as a reward for military service) or their enemies' slave in an effort to win a war or suppress a rebellion. Both sides freed slaves during the American War of Independence. The British freed slaves during the War of 1812 and the Americans did the same thing during the Seminole wars. Though abolitionists certainly endorsed it during the Civil War, military emancipation was not in itself an abolitionist policy. It freed slaves individually, often in large numbers, but it was not designed to abolish slavery anywhere and it never resulted in

---

20. JAMES OAKES, FREEDOM NATIONAL: THE DESTRUCTION OF SLAVERY IN THE UNITED STATES, 1861-1865, 256-300 (2013). *See also*, JAMES OAKES, THE SCORPION'S STING: ANTISLAVERY AND THE COMING OF THE CIVILWAR (2014).

abolition. The federal government began emancipating slaves as a "military necessity" in the earliest months of the Civil War, and the Emancipation Proclamation represented a radical expansion of that policy. It offered freedom to all slaves in areas still in rebellion as of January 1, 1863.

But Lincoln himself was skeptical of military emancipation. Before he issued it Lincoln repeatedly expressed doubts that an Emancipation Proclamation was enforceable, and he never believed that it would be enough to get slavery abolished. This is not to say that Lincoln thought the proclamation was point-less, or that it would have no effect at all. He clearly understood that proclaiming emancipation would enable the Union army to free a substantial number of slaves, and he also hoped that systematic emancipation would help subdue the southern rebellion. But for Lincoln the Emancipation Proclamation, especially the enlistment of black soldiers, would work chiefly by adding to the pressure he was already putting on the states to abolish slavery on their own. Throughout the Civil War Lincoln's most enduring commitment was to the longstanding antislavery policy of state-by-state abolition.

By the time Lincoln issued the proclamation the cordon of freedom was already in place, and months before Congress had put it there Lincoln was already pressuring individual states to abolish slavery on their own. In November 1861, he drafted two proposals for gradual, compensated abolition in Delaware, proposals he viewed as models for all the Border States to follow. On March 6, 1862, frustrated by Delaware's peremptory refusal to consider his proposal, Lincoln went public with a speech urging Congress to "co-operate with any state which may adopt gradual abolishment of slavery" and offering federal compensation to any state that did so. This was same basic offer Lincoln had made to Delaware, now stripped of specific timetables, but available to "any state" that set about abolishing slavery on its own. Border State congress- men reacted angrily to the president's proposal, and in standard accounts of the war that hostile reaction from the Border States is said to have precipitated Lincoln's shift from gradual abolition to immediate emancipation.

But there was no such shift. In his annual message to congress on December 1, 1862—*after* he had announced his intention to release the Emancipation Proclamation—Lincoln renewed his proposals for federal aid to any state that abolished slavery on its own. Six months after that, the proclamation having long since been issued, Lincoln began firing off series of letters to civil and military officials—in Missouri, in Arkansas, in Tennessee, Louisiana, and Maryland, even Florida—urging, nudging, pressuring, insisting that their loyal legislatures restore their states' normal relations with the Union by passing laws or adopting new constitutions that would abolish slavery in their own states.

This is a point that requires some emphasis: Lincoln's efforts to get states to abolish slavery became more aggressive than ever *after* he issued the Emancipation Proclamation. Yet it was the proclamation that made all the difference. For besides offering the states carrots—a gradual timetable, federal compensation, and subsidies for voluntary colonization—Lincoln now waved the big stick of universal military emancipation in front of them, warning the states of the consequences if they failed to abolish slavery on their own.

That threat applied even to the four loyal Border States—Delaware, Maryland, Kentucky, and Missouri. Though formally exempt from the emancipation provisions of the proclamation, for example, the Border States were *not* exempt from the radical new policy of enlisting blacks—including slaves—into the Union Army. It was no accident that the largest numbers of slave enlistments came from the very states Lincoln was putting the most pressure on to abolish slavery. He was using the proclamation to weaken slavery on the ground in those states, making them more likely to abolish slavery on their own. In December 1863, Lincoln went still further, declaring that no seceded state would be readmitted to the Union until it endorsed the Emancipation Proclamation.

Within weeks, however, Congress came up with an even better proposal—a Thirteenth Amendment to the Constitution, abolishing slavery everywhere. But amendments are not easy to ratify, and this one was no sure thing. Not only does it take two-thirds of both houses of Congress to send an amendment to the states, it then takes three-quarters of the *states* to ratify it. Now let's assume that as a general rule free states were likely to ratify an abolition amendment and slave states were likely to reject it. In 1860 there were eighteen free and fifteen slave states, a proportion that made such an amendment all but impossible. If after 1860 the federal government stopped admitting any new slave states to the Union, ratification would still depend on an inconceivably dramatic increase in the number of free states, from eighteen to forty-five, for a total of sixty states. Only then would three-fourths of the states be free states. That's simply unimaginable. The simple truth is that for ratification of an abolition amendment to be feasible, a number of slave states would have to become free states. And that's what began to happen in 1864.

On March 4 of that year Arkansas abolished slavery, the first state to do so in sixty years. In September eligible voters in Louisiana endorsed a new free state constitution, under intense pressure from Lincoln to do so. A few weeks later, in October, Maryland held a referendum on a proposed constitution declaring simply that "[h]ereafter, in this State, there shall be neither slavery nor involuntary servitude."[21] The constitution narrowly lost in the initial count, but when the soldiers' votes came in from the field the free-state constitution of Maryland was safely ratified. Missouri and Tennessee were not far behind. In the November 1864 elections, radicals who endorsed the Thirteenth Amendment won control of both houses of the Missouri state legislature and immediately called for a convention to meet in early 1865. On January 11 the Missouri convention overwhelmingly endorsed immediate, unconditional abolition. Meanwhile in Tennessee, Andrew Johnson had finally succeeded in gathering delegates to a constitutional convention in Nashville where, on January 9, they proceeded to abolish slavery in the state.[22]

No doubt none of this would have happened without the war, but it's important to understand exactly what this particular war did, because there is nothing in all of human history suggesting that that wars inevitably lead to abolition. Usually it's the other way around. Over the millennia war has enslaved far more people than it liberated. The Civil War was different—because it was presided over by northern politicians committed to abolishing slavery, and to using the war to accomplish that goal. Those policymakers unleashed the revolutionary potential of slave resistance, first by forcing the army to accept any slaves escaping to Union lines to claim their freedom, and second by enlisting slaves in the Union army and thereby turning tens of thousands of southerners—black southerners—against the Confederacy. And the goal was not simply to emancipate as many slaves as possible, but to get slavery abolished in as many states as possible. In a sense, the Civil War put the abolitionist project on steroids. In

21. The Debates of the Constitutional Convention of the State of Maryland, Assembled at the City of Annapolis, Wednesday, April 27, 1864, at 579 (1864).
22. OAKES, *supra* note 20, at 456-470.

particular, Lincoln and the Republicans took advantage of the conflict to dramatically increase the number of free states and just as dramatically decrease the number of slave states.

Barely had the Deep South congressmen and Senators resigned their seats in late January 1861, before Congress finally admitted Kansas to the Union as a free state. Congress then required West Virginia to abolish slavery as a condition for admission to the Union, which it did in 1863. In 1864 Nevada was admitted to the Union as a free state as well. But these merely increased the number of free states by three. Far more important was the sustained campaign for state-by-state abolition. In the last year of the war five slave states—Arkansas, Maryland, Missouri, Louisiana, and Tennessee—abolished slavery on their own.

These state abolitions were decisive. By the time the House of Representatives finally voted to send the Thirteenth Amendment out for ratification the 1860 ratio of eighteen free to fifteen slave states was long gone. Now there were twenty-six free and ten slave states. Abolition in *one more state* would have made the ratio 27 to 9, or three quarters, the proportion necessary for ratification. The campaign for state abolition had shifted the balance of power between slave and free states enough to make ratification of the Thirteenth Amendment—inconceivable in 1860—feasible five years later.

Precisely how feasible became clear shortly after February 1, 1865, the day Congress sent the amendment to the states for ratification. West Virginia, the first state ever required to abolish slavery as a condition for admission to the Union, ratified the amendment on February 3. The two free states admitted to the Union since Lincoln's election—Kansas and Nevada—ratified the amendment on February 7 and February 16, respectively. Then there were the votes of the five states that had abolished slavery during the war itself. The Maryland House of Delegates was first off the mark, ratifying on February 1, the same day Congress endorsed the joint resolution. The Maryland state senate approved it two days later. By a joint resolution of its own two houses, the Missouri legislature ratified the amendment on February 10. Within a week both houses of the Louisiana legislature did the same. Next came Tennessee's state senate, on April 5, followed by its House of Representatives two days later. Finally, Arkansas—the first state to abolish slavery on its own in more than half a century—ratified the thirteenth amendment on April 20, 1865.[23] By contrast, not one of the ten remaining slave states ratified the amendment until they were all but forced to do so by President Andrew Johnson in late 1865.

State abolition had worked. Not by itself and not in the way Salmon P. Chase had imagined it would work—gradually, in peacetime—but it did work. Having done so much to formulate the antislavery platform back in the 1830s Chase could be forgiven if, in 1865, he took a fair share of the credit for the destruction of slavery in the United States. For he had done more than anyone to develop a viable antislavery project that would re-start the long-stalled process of state-by-state abolition. Thanks to that project, any one of us today can read the Constitution and plainly see that slavery is no longer legal anywhere in the United States.

23. UNITED STATES BUREAU OF ROLLS AND LIBRARY, 2 A DOCUMENTARY HISTORY OF THE CONSTITUTION OF THE UNITED STATES OF AMERICA 530-601 (1894).

From Antislavery Lawyer to Chief Justice: The Remarkable but Forgotten Career of Salmon P. Chase

RANDY E. BARNETT

ABSTRACT

THE NAME SALMON P. CHASE IS BARELY KNOWN AND HIS CAREER IS LARGELY FORGOTTEN. IN THIS ARTICLE, I SEEK TO REVIVE HIS MEMORY BY TRACING THE ARC OF HIS CAREER FROM ANTISLAVERY LAWYER, TO ANTISLAVERY POLITICIAN, TO CHIEF JUSTICE OF THE UNITED STATES. IN ADDITION TO EXPLAINING WHY HIS IS A CAREER WORTH BOTH REMEMBERING AND HONORING, I OFFER SOME POSSIBLE REASONS WHY HIS REMARKABLE ACHIEVEMENTS HAVE LARGELY BEEN FORGOTTEN.

TABLE OF CONTENTS

INTRODUCTION: CONSTITUTIONAL ABOLITIONISM

For several years, I have been studying a long-forgotten band of constitutionalists who, in the 1830s, '40s, and '50s, denied that the U.S. Constitution was proslavery.[1] They advocated enforcing the text of the Constitution without any gloss put upon it by intentions, understandings, or deals that were not expressly included therein. They contended that Congress not only had the power to ban the international slave trade, it also had the power to ban the interstate slave trade and to abolish slavery in the District of Columbia, in the territories under its jurisdiction, and in any states formed from these territories. They also contended that the Fugitive Slave Acts of 1793 and 1850 were unconstitutional. These positions put them at odds with the Garrisonian abolitionists who claimed that the Constitution was "a covenant with death, and an agreement with hell"[2] because it sanctioned slavery.

When I finally began writing this Article, I wanted to include biographical information about each member of this forgotten group. Gradually, I came to realize that most of them had something in common. Unlike the Garrisonians, many of whom became anarchists,

---

[1] See, e.g., Randy E. Barnett, Whence Comes Section One? The Abolitionist Origins of the Fourteenth Amendment, 3 J. Legal Analysis 165 (2011) (highlighting the contributions and tactics of key abolitionist constitutionalists).

[2] Resolution Adopted at the Annual Meeting of the Massachusetts Anti Slavery Society, in Faneuil Hall, January 26, 1843, in The Liberator, Apr. 21, 1843, at 63. ("Resolved, That the Compact which exists between the North and the South is a 'covenant with death, and an agreement with hell,' —involving both parties in atrocious criminality,—and should be immediately annulled.").

these antislavery constitutionalists favored political action. Most were involved in organizing the expressly antislavery Liberty Party as an alternative to the proslavery Democrats and the compromising, equivocating Whigs.

To learn more about the Liberty Party, I turned to historian Richard Sewell's *Ballots for Freedom: Antislavery Politics in the United States 1837–1860.*[3] In his book, Sewell describes what he calls "political abolitionism" that, unlike the Garrisonians, favored political action to attack what was then called the Slave Power.[4] Sewell relates a very clear chronology: the Liberty Party, founded in the 1840s by these political abolitionists, soon led to the Free Soil Party, which led briefly to the Free Democrat Party, and finally in the mid-1850s to the founding of the Republican Party.

Like many other historians of the period, Sewell gave very short shrift to the constitutional theorizing of these political abolitionists. What my study showed, however, is that this very same group of political activists advanced a powerful constitutional case against slavery—a case that was based on the protection of natural rights, the original meaning of the text of the Constitution, the limits on the enumerated powers of Congress, and the Due Process Clause of the Fifth Amendment. What is more, their constitutional arguments are remarkably persuasive compared to those advanced by the Supreme Court in cases such as *Dred Scott v. Sandford.*[5]

The constitutional approach of this group deserves its own label: constitutional abolitionist, a term actually used by some at the time or shortly thereafter to describe this movement.[6] Like the radical

---

[3] Richard H. Sewell, Ballots for Freedom: Antislavery Politics in the United States 1837–1860 (1976).

[4] *See id.* at ix (describing "political abolitionists" as those "who, though never attached to an antislavery society or insistent on *immediate* emancipation, nonetheless embraced non-extension in part because they thought it a perfectly constitutional way to hasten slavery's downfall"). Indeed, Sewell did not invent the term "political abolitionist." In June of 1855, a convention of "Radical Political Abolitionists" was called by Lewis Tappan, W.E. Whiting, William Goodell, James McCune Smith, Gerrit Smith, George Whipple, S.S. Jocelyn, and Frederick Douglass and held in Syracuse, New York. *See* Proceedings of the Convention of Radical
Political Abolitionists 3–4 (1855).

[5] Scott v. Sandford, 60 U.S. 393 (1857).

[6] *See* Benjamin F. Shaw, *Owen Lovejoy, Constitutional Abolitionists and the Republican Party, in* 111 Transactions of the McClean Cnty. Historical Soc'y 60, 62 (Ezra M. Prince ed., 1900) ("[T]he fight for liberty in this land was begun by the Radical Abolitionist long before the final battle. . . . They were, however, followed by a class known as the Constitutional Abolitionists; equally bold and brave, but more practical. It was the labor of the latter that accomplished glorious results; fought the good battle to a finish and destroyed

abolitionists, constitutional abolitionists desired the complete abolition of slavery. But unlike some radical abolitionists, like Garrison and his legal compatriot Wendell Philips, who believed that the Constitution was a covenant with death and an agreement with hell and who favored disunion,[7] the constitutional abolitionists believed that the Constitution was fundamentally antislavery.

Yet, the constitutional abolitionists were divided among themselves on one key issue. Some like Lysander Spooner, William Goodell, Joel Tiffany, and Gerrit Smith contended that slavery was unconstitutional anywhere in the United States. Others believed that, while slavery should be abolished everywhere, as a matter of positive law, slavery was constitutional within those of the original thirteen states that retained the practice.

The leading figure in this second camp was Salmon P. Chase. Of all the figures I surveyed, none was more important than he. Indeed, in a previous article I considerably underestimated his influence.[8] In this Article, I seek to rectify that error. My goal is to help revive the memory of Salmon P. Chase to its rightful place in our constitutional history.

Whether they know it or not, all those reading this Article have heard Chase's name, many have used it, and most see it every day. Yes, that's right. Chase Bank, originally founded in 1877, some four years after his death, was named in his honor.[9] As one drives down the street in most cities, one sees Chase's name prominently displayed, even illuminated in the darkness. But, though some readers have also heard the name Salmon P. Chase, if these readers are like me, they

---

the slave power. They were among the organizers of the Republican Party."); Doris Kearns Goodwin, Team of Rivals: The Political Genius of Abraham Lincoln 676 (2005) (quoting Lincoln's Attorney General James Speed as saying "I am a thorough Constitutional Abolitionist").

[7] *See generally* Lewis Perry, Radical Abolitionism: Anarchy and the Government of God in Antislavery Thought (1973) (reviewing radical antislavery movements and their respective weaknesses in execution); William M. Wiecek, The Sources of Antislavery Constitutionalism in America, 1760–1848 (1977) (tracking shifts in Constitutional attitudes and movements regarding slavery).

[8] Because I neglected Chase's argument in the *Matilda* case, he entered my chronology in mid-1840s, rather than the 1830s. *See* Barnett, *supra* note 1, at 210. As a result, my account failed to notice the degree to which he influenced the constitutional analysis of others I discuss in the late 1830s and early 1840s. In short, Chase was far more influential than I gave him credit for being.

[9] J.P. Morgan Chase & Co., The History of JPMorgan Chase & Co. 4 (2008).

may not remember exactly who he was and what he did to earn this posthumous honor.

Perhaps they know that he was Chief Justice of the United States. Perhaps they even know he was a politically ambitious rival of Lincoln who also wanted to be president. But what he stood for throughout his accomplished career has largely been forgotten. Long before he was Chief Justice of the United States, Salmon P. Chase was among the most prominent, brilliant, and ultimately politically effective members of this group of constitutional abolitionists. By forgetting them, we have also forgotten him.

I. CHASE'S RISE TO THE CHIEF JUSTICESHIP

A. Chase's Early Years

Salmon Portland Chase was born in New Hampshire in 1808, the year Congress abolished the slave trade.[10] He was nine when his father died, and, by the time he was twelve, his mother found herself unable to support him and his siblings. She prevailed upon her brother-in-law and Chase's uncle, Philander Chase, to take him into his care. Philander had just become the Protestant Episcopal bishop of Ohio and was running a boy's school in Worthington, Ohio, just north of Columbus.

The trip to the Western Reserve was an adventure for the young boy. His twenty-three-year-old brother and a neighbor, who were both joining an expedition to Michigan and Wisconsin, would take him by steamship as far as Cleveland. In 1820, Cleveland "was not much to see: a hamlet with a population of about 500 people, dwellings straggled across the heavily wooded bluffs that rose abruptly from the lake."[11] As there was no harbor, small boats conveyed the party to the mouth of the Cuyahoga River.

In Cleveland, Chase boarded with a local judge named Barber until someone could be found to take the boy to Worthington. Eventually, an Episcopal minister took him as far as Medina, where two other clergymen got him to his uncle's place. Chase lived with his uncle there for two years until, no longer able to sustain the school,

---

[10] Unless otherwise noted, the facts in the next several paragraphs are taken from the excellent biography, John Niven, Salmon P. Chase: A Biography (1995). This is the biography of Chase that is sold in the U.S. Supreme Court's gift shop.
[11] *Id.* at 11.

Philander accepted the presidency of Cincinnati College, which brought Salmon to the city where his legal and political career would begin.

But first Chase went back east for college at Dartmouth very near his boyhood home. After graduating in 1826, he moved to Washington, D.C. He first tried his hand as a school teacher, before deciding to study law with Attorney General William Wirt. Studying in Washington gave Chase the opportunity to watch cases argued before the Supreme Court. His association with Wirt and Wirt's family enabled him to meet many of the most prominent political and legal figures of his day.

When, after two years of study, Chase applied for the bar, his examination by the judges went well until he was asked about the length of his legal training. When he admitted it was not the required three years, the presiding judge instructed him he would need to study another year. Chase pleaded with the court. "Please your honors . . . I have made arrangements to go to the Western country and practice law" there.[12] After a brief conference, the judges decided to swear him in as a member of the bar.

By a strange coincidence, Lysander Spooner, perhaps the leading figure of abolitionist constitutionalism, also achieved bar membership prematurely after two years of study. At the time, Massachusetts required three years of apprenticeship for college graduates, while those who, like Spooner, had not gone to college had to study for five. Spooner defied the rule by opening his own practice in Worchester after apprenticing for just two years with two prominent Massachusetts political and legal figures: John Davis and Charles Allen. A few months later, he published a lengthy petition to the Massachusetts legislature in the *Worchester Republican*, in which he urged it to end the restriction on bar admission. Among his many arguments, Spooner maintained that

> The Courts were made for and by the people, and not the people for or by the Courts. Suitors, when in Court, are the people, and it is their right to present their causes to their own Courts, by whatever counsel they may think it for their interest to present them . . . .[13]

---

[12] *Id.* at 27.

[13] Lysander Spooner, *To the Members of the Legislature of Massachusetts*, Worchester Republican—Extra 4 (Aug. 26, 1835), *reprinted in* 2 The Collected Works of Lysander

During its 1836 session, the legislature agreed, and Spooner was allowed to become a member of the bar.[14]

Chase's law license secured, in 1830, he returned to Ohio, where he practiced law in Cincinnati. In those days, Cincinnati was a political cauldron. Its proximity to the slave state of Kentucky enmeshed it in the slavery economy, and much of its citizenry was sympathetic. But Cincinnati's location also made it a nearby refuge for antislavery Southerners who no longer felt welcome in their home states. One such refugee was James G. Birney, a former Kentucky slave owner—and Princeton educated lawyer—who turned against slavery and left his state for Cincinnati. There, Birney founded an abolitionist newspaper called the *Philanthropist*.

In 1836, Chase was drawn into antislavery activities when a mob attacked Birney's paper, destroying his press. At the time, Chase had yet to take any public stance on the slavery question. But when he heard that the mob was heading to the Franklin House to tar and feather Birney, Chase raced to the hotel to warn the publisher.

> As the mob surged forward, Chase braced his arms against the door frame, blocking the hotel's entrance with his body. Six feet two, with broad shoulders, a massive chest, and a determined set to his jaw, Chase gave the rioters pause. The crowd demanded to know who he was. "Salmon P. Chase," the young lawyer replied. "You will pay for your actions," a frustrated member of the mob told him. "I [can] be found at any time," Chase said.[15]

In fact, it was members of the mob who were made to pay damages when Birney retained Chase to bring a successful tort action against them for the property damage they had caused.

Spooner (1971). *See also id.* at 1 ("Any man, who is allowed the management of his own affairs, has the right to decide for himself whom he will employ as counsel. . . .").

[14] Charles Shively, *Biography*, *in* 1 The Collected Works of Lysander Spooner 17–18 (1971). Like Chase, Spooner had an Ohio connection. Having gone West to seek his fortune, Spooner purchased the land that now constitutes Grand Rapids, Ohio, as a speculative venture. *Id.* at 20–21. When the speculation failed, Spooner returned to his family's home in Athol, Massachusetts, to turn his attention to the issue of slavery. *Id.* at 24.

[15] Goodwin, supra note 6, at 109.

B. Chase as an Antislavery Lawyer

In 1837, Birney also enlisted the twenty-nine-year-old Chase to represent a young runaway slave named Matilda, who had been seized by slave catchers. Matilda was the light-skinned daughter of her owner, who had brought her with him on a long trip through free territory passing as his white daughter. Having tasted freedom, she pleaded with her father for a certificate of emancipation, but he refused. She then fled to the small neighborhood of free blacks in Cincinnati where she found refuge before coming into Birney's employ as a maid.[16]

Chase brought a writ of habeas corpus for her freedom and argued the case before the local judge. Based in part on ideas developed by Birney in the *Philanthropist*, Chase's hastily prepared argument was multifaceted.[17] The Fugitive Slave Act of 1793[18] authorized a slave owner to seize a fugitive slave in a free state and return her to bondage after obtaining a certificate of removal from a federal judge or a state magistrate in the free state. One of Chase's principal claims was that the Fugitive Slave Act was unconstitutional because it was beyond the delegated powers of Congress to enact. Article IV says that

> No Person held to Service or Labour in one State, under the Laws thereof, escaping into another, shall, in Consequence of any Law or Regulation therein, be discharged from such Service or Labour, but shall be delivered up on Claim of the Party to whom such Service or Labour may be due.[19]

Chase asked,

> Does this clause confer any power on government, or on any officer or department of government?—Clearly not. It says nothing about the government, or its officers, or its departments. It declares that the citizens of no state in the Union, legally entitled to the service of any person, shall be

---

[16] The events surrounding the Matilda case and Chase's involvement are discussed in Niven, supra note 10, at 50–54. See also Frederick J. Blue, From Right to Left: The Political Conversion of Salmon P. Chase, 21 N. Ky. L. Rev. 1, 9–12 (1993).

[17] Salmon P. Chase, Speech of Salmon P. Chase in the Case of the Colored Woman, Matilda, Who was Brought Before the Court of Common Pleas of Hamilton County, Ohio, by Writ of Habeas Corpus (Mar. 11, 1837) [hereinafter Matilda Speech].

[18] Ch. 7, 1 Stat. 302, repealed by Act of June 28, 1864, ch. 166, 13 Stat. 200.

[19] U.S. Const. art. IV, § 2, cl. 3.

> deprived of that right to service, by the operation of the laws of any state into which the servant may escape; and it requires such state to deliver him up, on the claim of the lawful master.[20]

But it gives no power of enforcement to Congress.

According to Chase, the provisions of the first three articles of the Constitution create, define, and empower the national government, with Congress's powers defined primarily in Article I. In contrast, Article IV constitutes a compact among the states themselves. "[T]he creation of a government and the establishment of a compact, are entirely distinct in their nature."[21] Most importantly, "clauses of compact confer no powers on the [national] government: and the powers of [that] government cannot be exerted, except in virtue of express provisions, to enforce the matters of compact."[22]

Article IV, Chase contended, provides articles of compact among the several states, amounting to treaty obligations to be enforced like other treaties by the parties themselves, not by the federal government.

> The clause has nothing to do with the creation of a form of government. It is, in the strictest sense, a clause of compact. The parties to the agreement are the states. The general government is not a party to it, nor affected by it. If the clause stood alone in the constitution, it would mean precisely what it does now, and would be just as obligatory as it is now. Nothing can be plainer, then, than that this clause cannot be construed as vesting any power in the government, or in any of its departments, or in any of its officers; and this is the only provision in the constitution which at all relates to fugitives from labor.[23]

To further support his "compact" interpretation of Article IV, Chase contrasted the Fugitive Slave Clause with Article IV's Full Faith and Credit Clause.[24] After imposing a duty on each state to give "Full Faith and Credit . . . to the public Acts, Records, and judicial Proceedings of every other State," Article IV there, and only there, gives Congress a power to "by general Laws prescribe the Manner in

---

[20] Matilda Speech, supra note 17, at 20.
[21] Id. at 19.
[22] Id.
[23] Id. at 20–21 (footnote omitted).
[24] Id. at 21–22.

which such Acts, Records, and Proceedings shall be proved, and the Effect thereof."[25] Chase then posed the following challenge to the court: "Am I not right in saying that the framers of the constitution were aware, that without this special provision, congress would have no power to legislate upon the subject of the section?"[26]If the first clause, by its own force, "confers on Congress legislative power," he asked, "why add the second? Why add it, if legislative power is conferred by the general grant, or by any other provision in the constitution?"[27]

Nor could the Necessary and Proper Clause be used to support the Fugitive Slave Act. "[T]he general grant of legislative power is expressly confined to the enactment of laws, necessary and proper to carry into execution" only those enumerated powers that are vested in Congress. [28]

> The constitution restrains the operation of the state constitutions and the state laws, which would enfranchise the fugitive. It also binds the states to deliver him up on the claim of the master, and by necessary inference, it obliges them to provide a tribunal before which such claim may be asserted and tried, and by which such claims may be decided upon, and, if valid, enforced: but it confers no jot of legislative power on congress.[29]

Chase quoted the Tenth Amendment as authority for his claim that the power to enforce the duty to return runaway slaves is reserved to the states.[30]

Chase proceeded to connect his textual argument to the founders.

> The framers of the constitution were men of large experience, comprehensive knowledge, sound judgment, and great ability. Among them were Hamilton, and Madison, and Washington. Such men, in framing such an instrument would avoid all needless repetition. They would not incorporate into the constitution a special provision upon any subject

---

[25] U.S. Const. art. IV, § 1.
[26] Matilda Speech, supra note 17, at 22.
[27] Id.
[28] Id. at 21.
[29] Id.
[30] Id.

> unnecessarily. To them, therefore, the second clause of the section under consideration, must have appeared not only fit, but necessary. But if a special provision was necessary to enable congress to legislate in regard to the authentication and effect of records, why is not a special provision necessary to enable congress to legislate in regard to fugitive servants? [31]

Chase's argument failed to convince the local judge who remanded Matilda to the slave catchers. She was swiftly taken "down the river" to be sold at auction in New Orleans, her fate then lost to history.[32] Birney was then prosecuted and convicted on the charge of harboring a fugitive slave in violation of Ohio's black code.[33] The Supreme Court of Ohio reversed his conviction on the narrow ground that Birney lacked knowledge of Matilda's legal status, rather than the constitutional grounds asserted by Chase in his appeal of Birney's conviction.[34]

Chase's argument in the *Matilda* case was published as a pamphlet and distributed widely throughout the country where it elevated his visibility and provided the legal basis for other challenges to the constitutionality of the Fugitive Slave Act. In Wisconsin, for example, it constituted the main line of Byron Paine's successful defense of editor Sherman Booth, who had been charged under the Fugitive Slave Act of assisting in the escape of a captured slave.[35] Payne's challenge was successful[36] that is, until the ruling was reversed by the U.S. Supreme Court in *Abelman v. Booth* in an opinion by Chief Justice Taney.[37]

Chase's legal defense of Matilda and other fugitives earned him the nickname the "attorney general for runaway negroes" from his

---

[31] Id. at 22. Chase made his argument in Matilda well before Spooner shifted the interpretive methodology of constitutional abolitionism from focusing on framers' intent to the legal or objective meaning of the text. See Barnett, supra note 1, at 199–205 (describing Spooner's interpretive approach). When, after Spooner's book was published, Chase made his argument in Van Zandt the next year, his methodology had changed. See infra text accompanying notes 40–61.

[32] Blue, supra note 16, at 11.

[33] Id.

[34] Id.; see also Harold M. Hyman, The Reconstruction Justice of Salmon P. Chase 45 (Peter Charles Hoffer & N. E. H. Hull eds., 1997).

[35] Byron Paine, Unconstitutionality of the Fugitive Act: Argument of Byron Paine, Esq., and Opinion of Hon. A. D. Smith 5–6, 18 (1854); see also Barnett, supra note 1, at 240–43 (discussing Payne's defense of Booth).

[36] In re Booth, 3 Wis. 13, 18 (1854) (opinion of Smith, J.); id. at 67 (opinion of the court).

[37] Ableman v. Booth, 62 U.S. (21 How.) 506, 526 (1859).

critics in Kentucky.[38] "Chase soon was using the title with pride, although it was not meant as a compliment, for 'I never refused my help to any person black or white.' "[39]

His enumerated powers argument, like so many of the abolitionist constitutional claims, seems powerful and almost obvious when first encountered. Yet these arguments, and the men who developed them, are largely unknown today. They are rarely mentioned in law schools, even when the topic of slavery and the Constitution arises. In Part III of this Article, I will consider possible explanations for this widespread neglect.

Years later, in 1846, Chase would present a more developed version of this argument to the United States Supreme Court in the case of *Jones v. Van Zandt.*[40] In his *Van Zandt* brief, Chase renewed his structural objection to the Fugitive Slave Act as outside the enumerated powers of Congress. "[N]o power to legislate on the subject is conferred, unless by very remote implication, upon Congress, by the constitution."[41] To this he added a Due Process Clause objection of the sort that had become popular among constitutional abolitionists beginning with the writings of Theodore Dwight Weld in 1838.[42]

"Now, unless it can be shewn that no process of law at all, is the same thing as due process of law," Chase contended, "it must be admitted that the act which authorizes seizures without process, is repugnant to a constitution which expressly forbids it."[43] Slaves were entitled to the protection of the Clause, he argued, because they were persons. "It is vain to say that the fugitive is not a person: for the claim to him can be maintained only on the ground that he is a person."[44]

---

[38] Blue, supra note 16, at 12.

[39] Id. (referencing Chase's language a letter he sent to John T. Trowbridge in 1864).

[40] Jones v. Van Zandt, 46 U.S. (5 How.) 215 (1847). The lawyer filing the formal appearance in the case was William Seward, who would serve with Chase in Lincoln's cabinet as the Secretary of State.

[41] S.P. Chase, An Argument for the Defendant, Submitted to the Supreme Court of the United States, at the December Term, 1846, In the Case of Wharton Jones v. Vanzandt 72 (1847). In this pamphlet the defendant's name is spelled "Vanzandt," unlike in the United States Reports where it is spelled "Van Zandt."

[42] Compare id. at 88–89 ("I submit, further, that the act is unconstitutional . . . [because i]t authorizes seizure and confinement, by private force, without legal process."), with Theodore Dwight Weld, The Power of Congress over the District of Columbia 37–41 (4th ed. 1838). See generally Barnett, supra note 1, at 176–83 (discussing Weld's argument and situating it against Due Process Clause arguments on behalf of slave owners).

[43] Chase, supra note 41, at 89.

[44] Id.

Chase was here referring to the wording of the Fugitive Slave Clause, which begins, "[n]o *Person* held to Service or Labor in one State . . . ."[45] To show that fugitive slaves were considered persons under the Due Process Clause, Chase noted that, while the Virginia ratification convention had proposed a clause reading, "no free man shall be deprived of life, liberty, or property, but by the law of the land," Congress changed its scope to "[n]o person."[46]

Chase's Due Process Clause challenge rested on the "summary manner" by which slaves were to be recaptured under the Act.[47] Suppose an owner of a horse should find the animal in the possession of his neighbor and, "instead of resorting to due process of law, and the old fashioned replevin," were to simply seize the animal and "take him before *his own hired magistrate*, and prove his claim by affidavits."[48] Or if he claims a failure to provide services, "instead of suing him for breach of contract, let him drag his reluctant neighbor before his magistrate, establish his claim, and then remove him to his task."[49] Chase then asked, "How long would society hold together, if this principle were carried into general application?"[50]

Near the end of his brief, which in pamphlet form runs 107 pages, citing *Calder v. Bull*,[51] Chase identified "certain great principles of natural right and justice," which were intended "to establish as written law" in the Constitution, but "which exist independently of all such sanction."[52] These great principles are:

> No Legislature is omnipotent. No Legislature can make right wrong; or wrong, right. No Legislature can make light, darkness; or darkness, light. No Legislature can make men, things; or things, men. Nor is any Legislature at liberty to disregard the fundamental principles of rectitude or justice. Whether restrained or not by constitutional provision, there are acts beyond any legitimate or binding legislative authority.[53]

---

[45] U.S. Const. art. IV, § 2, cl. 3 (emphasis added).
[46] Chase, supra note 41, at 89.
[47] Id. at 96.
[48] Id.
[49] Id.
[50] Id.
[51] Calder v. Bull, 3 U.S. (3 Dall.) 386 (1798).
[52] Chase, supra note 41, at 93.
[53] Id.

Such acts beyond legislative authority include:

> The Legislature cannot authorize injustice by law; cannot nullify private contracts; cannot abrogate the seeurities [sic] of life, liberty and property, which, it is the very object of society, as well as of our constitution of government, to provide; cannot make a man a judge in his own case; cannot repeal the laws of nature; cannot create any obligation to do wrong, or neglect duty. No court is bound to enforce unjust law; but, on the contrary, every court is bound, by prior and superior obligations, to abstain from enforcing such law.[54]

Chase then allowed that it "must be a clear case, doubtless, which will warrant a court in pronouncing a law so unjust that it ought not to be enforced; but, in a clear case, the path of duty is plain."[55]

Chase also made some methodological claims about constitutional interpretation. He countered a proslavery construction of the Constitution based on "the intention of [the] framers" by appealing to what he called the "plain import" of the text.[56] In today's parlance, he rejected framers' intent originalism in favor of public-meaning originalism. It is likely no coincidence that just the year before, Lysander Spooner made the case against reliance on framers' intent in his widely read book, *The Unconstitutionality of Slavery.*[57] Also like Spooner, Chase contended that natural rights should govern the

---

[54] Id. at 93–94.
[55] Id. at 94.
[56] Id. at 105.
[57] See Lysander Spooner, The Unconstitutionality of Slavery (1845). Spooner developed his interpretive approach in response to abolitionist Wendell Phillips's use of James Madison's recently disclosed notes of the Philadelphia convention in his book, Wendell Phillips, The Constitution: A Pro-Slavery Compact; or, Extracts from the Madison Papers, etc. (1844). See Barnett, supra note 1, at 203– 05 (discussing how Spooner formulated his constitutional argument and the link between the arguments of Spooner and Phillips). Spooner was hopeful of Chase. "I have been in the habit of considering him the most important anti-slavery man in the west, and therefore I am anxious he should be on the right ground." Lysander Spooner, Letter to George Bradburn (December 7, 1846). But the cantankerous Spooner was also disappointed in Chase's failure to embrace some of Spooner's substantive arguments. "As to Chase, if I had him within arm's length, I would break every bone in his body, if I could not otherwise make him understand, and either yield to, or answer the arguments in my book." Id. A year later, Spooner assumed that a respectful but unsigned review of his book in the Cincinnati Herald was by Chase. See Lysander Spooner, Letter to George Bradburn (December 5, 1847) ("Did you see the Cincinnati Herald's review of my book? It was respectful towards me, and complimentary of the ability of the book. It was such a farrago of absurd crotchets! It appeared as editorial—but I conjecture it was from Chase.").

construction of positive laws.[58] If there is a conceivable construction that would harmonize positive and natural law, it should be adopted by the courts. Indeed, Chase adopts a "presumption in favor of liberty."[59]

In addition to this methodological claim, Chase employed a standard abolitionist technique of meeting claims about the supposed intentions of the framers with an opposite supposition. Given that the preexisting state constitutions had "guarantied the absolute, inherent and inalienable rights of all the inhabitants or citizens," it could "hardly be supposed that any state, especially any non-slaveholding state, would have agreed to a constitution which would withdraw, from any of these rights, the ample shield of the fundamental law, and leave them exposed to the almost unlimited discretion of Congress."[60] As authority for this claim, Chase quoted the words of the Tenth Amendment.[61]

Notice here another forgotten fact. Before the Civil War, it was the Slave Power who enlisted the power of the federal government to impose the Fugitive Slave Acts. And it was the Northern states who complained about the interference with their rights to protect their free blacks from being kidnaped by slave catchers and sold down the river. "States' rights" was as much an antislavery doctrine as it was a proslavery doctrine.

Chase's argument in *Van Zandt*, however, came four years after the Court had rejected similar arguments in the case of *Prigg v. Pennsylvania*.[62] In *Prigg*, Justice Story upheld the constitutionality of the Fugitive Slave Act by adopting an expansive interpretation of the Necessary and Proper Clause.

---

[58] Spooner's emphatic use of this language from Chief Justice Marshall's opinion in United States v. Fisher was picked up and emulated by other constitutional abolitionists: Where rights are infringed, where fundamental principles are overthrown, where the general system of the laws is departed from, the legislative intention must be expressed with irresistible clearness to induce a court of justice to suppose a design to effect such objects. United States v. Fisher, 6 U.S. (2 Cranch) 358, 390 (1805).

[59] Chase, supra note 41, at 97 ("It is certainly incumbent, then, on those who claim, that, by the constitution, the general law and presumption in favor of liberty are set aside to give room for this right of recaption, to make out a clear case, and produce express words.").

[60] Id. at 106.

[61] See id. ("Am I mistaken, then, in thinking that the whole argument establishes the proposition, that the power to legislate, in reference to escaping servants, is 'a power not delegated to the United States by the Constitution, nor prohibited by it to the states, and is, therefore, reserved to the states respectively, or, to the people?'").

[62] Prigg v. Pennsylvania, 41 U.S. (16 Pet.) 539 (1842).

> No one has ever supposed that Congress could, constitutionally, by its legislation, exercise powers, or enact laws beyond the powers delegated to it by the Constitution; but it has, on various occasions, exercised powers which were necessary and proper as means to carry into effect rights expressly given, and duties expressly enjoined thereby. The end being required, it has been deemed a just and necessary implication, that the means to accomplish it are given also; or, in other words, that the power flows as a necessary means to accomplish the end.[63]

Though widely condemned at the time by abolitionists, some constitutional abolitionists like Joel Tiffany would later assert that the precedent provided by *Prigg* empowered Congress to legislate against slavery.[64] Later still, some Republicans in Congress would also claim *Prigg* as authority for its Reconstruction legislation. None of this later use of *Prigg* undermines the weakness of Story's analysis of the enumerated powers.

Chase's argument in the *Matilda* case in the 1830s shows that Story's capacious reading of the Necessary and Proper Clause was far from inevitable.[65] Story's analysis only seems compelling when the arguments on the other side are omitted. We are accustomed to hearing that a sweeping interpretation of the Necessary and Proper Clause is needed to ensure, for example, the constitutionality of Civil Rights laws. Yet, Story's use of the Necessary and Proper Clause in *Prigg* shows that a broad reading of congressional power can also be used to uphold evil.

Because Chief Justice Taney had previously adopted a rule that denied oral argument on matters that had already been adjudicated by the Court, Chase's challenge in the *Van Zandt* case was dismissed on the pleadings and he never appeared before the Court to present his argument in person.[66] But his *Van Zandt* brief was also published as a

---

[63] Id. at 618–19.

[64] See Joel Tiffany, A Treatise on the Unconstitutionality of American Slavery: Together with the Powers and Duties of the Federal Government In Relation to That Subject 99–100 (1849). I discuss Tiffany's views in Barnett, supra note 1, at 221–31.

[65] See supra Part I.B.

[66] See, e.g., Jules Lobel, Success Without Victory 61 (2003) ("Chief Justice Roger B. Taney objected to hearing oral argument [in Van Zandt], for he thought the constitutional question was already settled."); see also Jones v. Van Zandt, 46 U.S. (5 How.) 215, 229–30 (1847) ("This court has already, after much deliberation, decided that the act of February 12th, 1793, was not repugnant to the constitution. . . . We do not now propose to review at length the reasoning on which this act has been pronounced constitutional. . . . That this act of

pamphlet and received a wide circulation. The case "added considerable luster to Chase's national reputation," as both a principled opponent of slavery and a defender of the Constitution.[67]

C. Chase as an Antislavery Political Leader

Unlike the Garrisonian abolitionists who eschewed political action,[68] Chase engaged in electoral politics to pursue his antislavery agenda. In the 1840s, together with Birney and others, Chase helped form the Liberty Party, and became one of its leaders. Chase came to the Liberty Party after a less than successful initial association with the Whig Party.[69]

Even as he was working to build the Liberty and then the Free Soil parties, Chase came to view himself as a Democrat. Like others, he sometimes called himself an "Independent Democrat" or a "Free Democrat," a movement he hoped would one day capture the heart of that party.[70] Part of his motivation was practical as "Cincinnati was solidly Democratic . . . ."[71] But principle also played a major role. Chase was of the "belief, confirmed after years of intense study, that Jeffersonian idealism was basically much more appropriate to the abolitionist objective than the Whig program of economic development through national planning, which a strong central government would devise and execute."[72] "I do not concur in Whig views of public policy," he wrote, "either as an antislavery man or as simply a citizen."[73] Chase "opposed a high tariff, a recharter of the now defunct Bank of the United States, (a Whig priority), or any system of government support for corporate banking."[74] Moreover, even Chase's "views on slavery comported with Jeffersonian states'

Congress, then, is not repugnant to the constitution, must be considered as among the settled adjudications of this court." (citing Prigg, 41 U.S. 539)).

[67] Goodwin, supra note 6, at 113.

[68] See generally Perry, supra note 7.

[69] Chase was elected to the Cincinnati city council as a member of the Whig Party in 1840, but, despite Whig triumphs in most of the states, he lost reelection due to his refusal to support liquor licenses. See Niven, supra note 10, at 58–59.

[70] Id. at 146

[71] Id. at 88.

[72] Id.

[73] Id. at 96 (noting that Chase's comments were made when he turned down an invitation to an antislavery conference in Columbus, Ohio).

[74] Id.

rights doctrine. His arguments on fugitive slave cases consistently proclaimed slavery to be the creature of local custom and law."[75]

That Chase came from a Democratic background will explain much about his political sympathies: his strict constructionist views of the Constitution, his belief in laissez-faire, his opposition to economic (as opposed to revenue) tariffs, and his support of hard money over paper. It also explains the antipathy that later developed towards him by the Whigs who dominated Northern Ohio, and, later, by the former Whigs who joined the new Republican Party. Indeed, in the 1850s, he initially opposed adopting the name "Republican" for the new antislavery party in favor of what he sometimes called himself, an independent or free Democrat. This background also helps to explain the tensions that arose between former-Democrat Chase and ex-Whig Abraham Lincoln.

In 1845, Chase addressed the Southern and Western Convention of the newly formed Liberty Party on the question of the constitutionality of slavery. No less than one hundred thousand copies of Chase's speech were printed and circulated in pamphlet form.[76] In his speech, Chase declined to adopt the view expressed by other abolitionists "that no slaveholding, in any State of the Union, is compatible with a true and just construction of the Constitution,"[77] but favored instead "its removal from each State by State authority."[78] On the other hand, like every constitutional abolitionist I have surveyed, Chase "would have it removed at once from all places under the exclusive jurisdiction of the National Government"—meaning the District of Columbia and the territories—pursuant to the "true sense and spirit" of the "Constitution rightly construed and administered."[79]

In sum, Chase contended that Congress had the power to outlaw slavery in the District of Columbia and in the territories. Once again, given that Congress has a police power in these places akin to the police powers of states within their territories, this would seem like an obvious proposition. And, yet, it was vehemently denied by proslavery Democrats in Congress, beginning with an 1836 report of a special

---

[75] Id. at 88.

[76] Charles Dexter Cleveland, Prefatory Remarks to Salmon Portland Chase, The Address of the Southern and Western Liberty Convention (June 11, 1845) [hereinafter Liberty Convention Address] in Salmon Portland Chase & Charles Dexter Cleveland, Anti-Slavery Addresses of 1844 and 1845, at 72 (1867).

[77] Chase, Liberty Convention Address, supra note 76, at 101.

[78] Id. at 121.

[79] Id.

committee of the House of Representatives that claimed abolishing slavery would deny slaveholders their property rights in violation of the Due Process Clause of the Fifth Amendment.[80] Twenty years later in *Dred Scot*, Chief Justice Taney would extend the same Due Process clause reasoning to the territories.[81]

Yet, if Chase and the other constitutional abolitionists were right in their reading of the Constitution, and Story and Taney were wrong, then this means that, while the Constitution accommodated slavery in the states in which it already existed, the Constitution was otherwise an antislavery document. And, if this is so, then the persistent criticism of the Founders for having ratified slavery is, at best, an exaggeration.

In his 1845 Cincinnati address, Chase reiterated the standard abolitionist positions that "slaveholding is contrary to natural right and justice" and therefore "can subsist nowhere without the sanction and aid of positive legislation."[82] From the fact that the Constitution, "expressly prohibits Congress from depriving any person of liberty without due process of law,"[83] Chase derived the following antislavery political program:

(1) "repealing all legislation, and discontinuing all action, in favor of slavery, at home and abroad;"
(2) "prohibiting the practice of slaveholding in all places of exclusive national jurisdiction, in the District of Columbia, in American vessels upon the seas, in forts, arsenals, navy yards;"
(3) "forbidding the employment of slaves upon any public work;"
(4) "adopting resolutions in Congress, declaring that slaveholding, in all States created out of national territories, is unconstitutional, and recommending to the others the immediate adoption of measures for its extinction within their respective limits;" and
(5) electing and appointing to public office only those who "openly avow our principles, and will honestly carry out our measures."[84]

---

[80] See Barnett supra note 1, at 179–80 (discussing the Due Process Clause reasoning of the House select committee report and the antislavery response developed by Theodore Dwight Weld).
[81] Scott v. Sandford, 60 U.S. (19 How.) 393 (1856).
[82] Chase, Liberty Convention Address, supra note 76, at 101.
[83] Id.
[84] Id. at 100.

Chase maintained that the "constitutionality of this line of action cannot be successfully impeached."[85]

Chase's program was enormously influential. Historian Harold Hyman described Chase as "the antislavery crusaders' premier legal strategist."[86] Historian Eric Foner has observed that, in these and other strenuous efforts, "Chase developed an interpretation of American history which convinced thousands of northerners that anti-slavery was the intended policy of the founders of the nation, and was fully compatible with the Constitution."[87] Within a few years, it provided the core position of a new antislavery political party that would supplant the Whigs and capture the presidency and Congress. "Chase's interpretation of the Constitution," wrote Foner, "formed the legal basis for the political program which was created by the Liberty Party and inherited in large part by the Free Soilers and Republicans."[88] "[B]ecause of Chase's efforts," this antislavery interpretation of the Constitution "eventually came to form the constitutional basis of the Republican Party program."[89]

That the Republican Party's national platforms for the elections of 1856 and 1860 largely adopted Chase's constitutional views on slavery helps explain why Lincoln's victory in 1860 provoked the Southern states to secede. Though Lincoln insisted he would not interfere with slavery where it existed—a doctrine on which Chase also insisted over the vigorous dissent of Lysander Spooner and some other constitutional abolitionists—Southerners apparently feared that the Republican program would hasten the extinction of slavery throughout the United States.

The Liberty Party included many who, like Spooner, believed slavery to be unconstitutional within the existing slave states. Its strategy was to take enough votes away from the Whigs and Democrats that they would have to accommodate its antislavery demands.[90] When the single-issue, antislavery Liberty Party failed to provide the leverage between the Whigs and Democrats its founders were seeking, they attempted to broaden their appeal by founding the

---

[85] Id.

[86] Hyman, supra note 34, at 168.

[87] Eric Foner, Free Soil, Free Labor, Free Men: The Ideology of the Republican Party Before the Civil War 73 (1970).

[88] Id. at 87.

[89] Id. at 75.

[90] See Sewell, supra note 3, at 43–79 (describing the formation and strategy of the Liberty Party). Spooner himself remained apolitical, though he generally kept these views quiet lest he alienate his fans among the political abolitionists.

Free Soil Party around an antislavery program that conceded the power of existing states to perpetuate slavery within their borders—as Chase had long maintained.[91] (Because of this, the Liberty Party continued in greatly diminished form.[92]) Chase coined its motto: "Free Soil, Free Labor and Free Men."[93]

Because he conceded that slavery was constitutional in the original slave states, today Chase is considered to be an "antislavery" moderate, with the term "abolitionist" reserved to those "radicals" who would see slavery abolished throughout the Union. But Sewell makes clear that this "dispute was one among friends, since both sides equally desired the overthrow of slavery everywhere."[94] As Sewell puts it, "the great mass of Free Soilers were as much committed to uprooting slavery everywhere as were the most dedicated Garrisonians."[95] Indeed, given that the Garrisonian abolitionists maintained that the Constitution was a proslavery document because they too believed it authorized slavery in the South, the distinction between abolitionist and antislavery becomes considerably muddy when the interpretation of the Constitution is at issue.

From 1849 to 1855, Chase served as a United States Senator from Ohio as a member of the Free Soil Party.[96] The manner by which he attained this position would haunt him politically for the rest of his career. When the Free Soilers successfully obtained the balance of power in the 1848 election for the state legislature, Chase struck a deal with the Democrats whereby they would agree to abolish the black codes that imposed legal discrimination on Ohio's free blacks, and they would vote to name Chase a U.S. Senator.[97] The Democrats agreed to, and fulfilled, both conditions.

This deal infuriated the disappointed Whigs from the Northern part of the state and they would never forget or forgive Chase for what they said was his ruthless ambition. "It lost to him at once and forever the confidence of every Whig of middle age in Ohio," said one fellow politician.[98] "Its shadow never wholly dispelled, always fell upon him, and hovered near and darkened his pathway at critical places in his

---

[91] See id. at 170–201 (describing formation of the Free Soil Party).
[92] See id. at 247.
[93] See Niven, supra note 10, at 110.
[94] Sewell, supra note 3, at 90.
[95] Id. at 189.
[96] Id. at 204–06.
[97] Id. at 180.
[98] Goodwin, supra note 6, at 136.

political after life."[99]Twelve years later, the Whig enmity towards the ex-Democrat Chase lingered. In part because the Ohio delegation to the 1860 Republican presidential convention in Chicago was divided, with some of his nominal Ohio supporters working against him behind the scenes, Chase's candidacy for President was fatally undermined, eventually allowing the former-Whig Abraham Lincoln to capture the nomination.[100]

In Washington as a Free Soiler, Chase was marginalized in the Senate. Still, he forged lasting bonds with the few other antislavery senators he met there, most notably Massachusetts Senator Charles Sumner, the only other Free Soiler, who in 1851, like Chase two years before, had been sent to the Senate in a deal struck with Democrats. Sumner considered Chase to be among his closest and most principled allies in the fight against the Southern Slave Power.[101] In one lengthy floor speech, Democrat Senator Stephen Douglas of Illinois repeatedly condemned Sumner and Chase together as the "abolitionist confederates," saying they were "the pure, unadulterated representatives of Abolitionism, Free Soilism, Niggerism in the Congress of the United States."[102]

In opposing the repeal of the Missouri Comprise, "Chase assumed the leadership of the antislavery forces."[103] In collaboration with Sumner and Joshua Giddings, he drafted an "Appeal of the Independent Democrats in Congress to the People of the United States," which was "a brilliantly effective piece of antislavery propaganda."[104] "[T]he Appeal was reprinted in pamphlet form to organize opposition to the Kansas-Nebraska Act."[105] Chase's past connections to the more radical elements in Congress would be a potent source of his clout during the Lincoln presidency.

After the formation of the Republican Party, Chase was elected the governor of Ohio in 1855 on the Republican ticket, making him the first Republican governor in any state and the highest Republican

---

[99] Id.
[100] See id.
[101] Chase's close relationship with Sumner is discussed throughout David Herbert Donald, Charles Sumner and the Coming of the Civil War (Sourcebooks, 2009). Chase comes off better in Sumner's biography than he does in his own, most likely reflecting Sumner's high regard for his Free Soil antislavery colleague.
[102] Id. at 210.
[103] Goodwin, supra note 6, at 161
[104] Donald, supra note 101, at 210. It was the "Appeal" that provoked the wrath of Douglas who was sponsoring the repeal of the Compromise. Id.
[105] Goodwin, supra note 6, at 162.

office-holder in the country at that time.[106] After successfully dealing with a financial crisis involving the embezzlement by the outgoing Democratic treasurer of some half a million dollars, Chase was reelected Governor in 1857. The Ohio governorship was a largely powerless position, but Chase was responsible for shepherding several antislavery resolutions through the legislature.

After he failed in his bid for the Republican presidential nomination, the Ohio legislature returned Chase to the Senate, this time as a Republican, in 1861. When Lincoln appointed him secretary of the treasury, Chase vacated his Senate seat after serving all of two days. (He was replaced by Clevelander and former-Whig John Sherman, the future author of the Sherman Antitrust Act and brother of Union General William Tecumseh Sherman.)

Chase's "appointment of thousands of Treasury agents, many of whom were black and/or female, was an important step toward the nationwide implementation of one of his major goals: broadening opportunities for segments of society usually neglected in midnineteenth-century urban America."[107] Chase was "alone among cabinet heads [when he] hired thousands of blacks and females as civil servants and even placed an impressive number of black males in supervisory positions over white females."[108] Also, "[a]lone among Lincoln's cabinet, Chase openly called for the abolition of slavery as early as 1862 and privately criticized the president for being so dilatory on the subject."[109]

At the beginning of the war when Union casualties overwhelmed the hospitals in Washington, Secretary Chase, like others, opened his large house at Sixth and E as a hospital ward. Among the gravely wounded soldiers who were nursed there was future Justice Oliver Wendell Holmes, Jr.[110]

As treasury secretary, Chase was charged with the herculean task of financing the Civil War, preferably without raising taxes. His success at this endeavor made him invaluable to Lincoln's administration. "Chase had been indispensable to the war effort. More than any other member of Lincoln's cabinet, he realized the need for fiscal solvency as well as military supremacy if the Union was to

---

[106] Niven, supra note 10, at 175–76. Except where noted, the biographical details in the next several paragraphs are taken from this source.
[107] Jonathan Lurie, The Chase Court 22 (2004).
[108] Hyman, supra note 34, at 81.
[109] Lurie, supra note 107, at 23.
[110] Niven, supra note 10, at 269.

survive."[111] Eventually, and reluctantly given his views of hard money, Chase acquiesced to the Republicans' plan for paper money. But never shy about promoting himself politically, Chase saw to it that his picture appeared on the one dollar bill,[112] earning him the new nickname of "Old Mr. Greenbacks"—a title that, as we will see, later became ironic.

Chase's supreme competence in financing the war, along with his close ties to the radical Republicans in Congress, gave him political leverage with Lincoln, the former Whig, who came late in his career to the antislavery cause and who was distrusted by the radicals. Initially, Chase's working relationship with Lincoln was warm. Early in the war, they sojourned together on a treasury cutter off the coast of Virginia, where, with Secretary of War Edwin Stanton, they would plan a military invasion to secure the port of Norfolk. The three men even personally went ashore to survey possible sites for landing troops.[113]

Over time, however, Chase's often stiff and prickly personality, his incessant criticisms of Lincoln's vacillation, coupled with his public political maneuvering for the Republican presidential nomination in 1864, put Chase at odds with the President.[114] As Lincoln became increasingly close to his Secretary of State, William Seward, his relationship with his Secretary of Treasury deteriorated. In June of that year, after Chase protested Lincoln's appointment of someone to the Treasury department without his approval, Chase tendered his resignation (as he had done several times before). Chase expected Lincoln to yield, but he miscalculated. By this time, Lincoln's Emancipation Proclamation, as well as the success of the military campaign, had greatly raised Lincoln's own standing with the radicals in Congress. He could now afford to be rid of his difficult secretary.

So, to Chase's surprise, Lincoln accepted Chase's resignation with considerable relief.[115] When a number of Chase supporters protested privately to Lincoln, knowing his words would get back to Chase, he reassured them that, "if I have the opportunity, I will make him Chief

---

[111] Lurie, supra note 107, at 22.

[112] Goodwin, supra note 6, at 510. Chase's picture later adorned the $10,000 bill.

[113] For two accounts of this remarkable tale, see Niven, supra note 10, at 287–89, and Goodwin, supra note 6, at 436–39.

[114] Chase's relationship with Lincoln is vividly described at length in Goodwin, supra note 6, at 280–639.

[115] See id. at 631–39 (describing the events surrounding Chase's resignation).

Justice of the United States."[116] Perhaps in part because of this, when Chase's bid for the 1864 Republican presidential nomination quickly collapsed, he nevertheless actively campaigned for Lincoln and the Republicans, traveling by train, boat, and horseback throughout Ohio, Kentucky, Pennsylvania, Michigan, Illinois, and Missouri.[117] Such travel was arduous under the best of circumstances, but these were dangerous times. "En route to Toledo Chase was recognized and several McClellan Democrats tried to force him off the train. He held his ground and reached his destination safely."[118]

Among the towns at which Chase spoke during the 1864 campaign was Covington, Kentucky, where he had previously spoken on Lincoln's behalf in 1860, and where the Northern Kentucky University's Salmon P. Chase College of Law is now named after him. On that day in October when Chase spoke in Covington, Chief Justice Roger Taney died.[119] When Lincoln came under pressure by several of Chase's powerful rivals for the Chief Justiceship, he characteristically delayed his decision. But as soon as his reelection was secured, Lincoln nominated Chase, his political nemesis, to be the sixth Chief Justice of the United States.

In a remarkable turn of events, the racist author of *Dred Scott* was succeeded as Chief Justice by Salmon Portland Chase, the "attorney general for fugitive slaves."[120] Lincoln assured critics of his pick that "[h]e trusted that Chase would help secure the right of the black man, for which he had fought throughout his career, a belief that outweighed concerns about Chase's restless temperament."[121]

II. THE CHIEF JUSTICESHIP OF SALMON P. CHASE

A. Chase's Duties as Chief Justice

On March 4, 1864, Chief Justice of the United States, Salmon P. Chase, administered the oath of office to his political rival Abraham Lincoln, inaugurating Lincoln's second term. The evening before, Chase was visited in his Sixth Street home by the radical abolitionist orator, and future U.S. Marshall of the District of Columbia, Frederick

---

[116] Id. at 635.
[117] Id. at 657.
[118] Niven, supra note 10, at 373.
[119] Id.
[120] Foner, supra note 87, at 77.
[121] Goodwin, supra note 6, at 681.

Douglass. Douglass recalled helping Chase's dynamic daughter Kate "in placing over her honored father's shoulders the new robe then being made in which he was to administer the oath to the reelected President."[122] Douglass recalled the "early anti-slavery days" of their first meeting, when Chase had "welcomed [Douglass] to his home and his table when to do so was a strange thing."[123]

Douglass's faith in Chase was not to be disappointed. Chase readily agreed to the proposal by his friend Charles Sumner that Massachusetts attorney John Rock be admitted to the Supreme Court bar. The previous year, Rock, a black, had been denied admission by the Taney Court on the basis of his race. Now, upon Sumner's formal motion, Rock was sworn in as the first black lawyer admitted to the Supreme Court bar. *Harper's Weekly* observed that this event represented an "extraordinary reversal" of *Dred Scott*, and would "be regarded by the future historian as a remarkable indication of the revolution which is going on in the sentiment of a great people."[124]

When Lincoln was murdered by the Maryland-born actor and Southern sympathizer John Wilkes Booth on April 14, 1865, Chief Justice Chase administered the oath of office to Vice President Andrew Johnson, a Democrat from Tennessee. Two years later, when Johnson was impeached by the Republican House of Representatives for resisting its efforts to "reconstruct" the South, Chase presided over his trial in the Senate.

Without any precedent to guide him, the physically imposing Chase swept into the Senate chamber in his flowing judicial robes, dramatically dominating the scene.[125] Chase assumed control of the proceedings and insisted on them being administered as a judicial rather than a political tribunal. In part because of this, Johnson escaped conviction and removal from office by a single vote.

Chase conducted Johnson's trial "in a manner that diminished public anxiety about a rigged judgment either way and so fended off possibly recrudescing mob violence."[126] But it also cost him political support among congressional Republicans. "[O]ld comrades of the antislavery crusade berated him for his scrupulously neutral conduct during the impeachment. His relative evenhandedness at the trial . . .

---

[122] Id. at 697.
[123] Id.
[124] Id. at 681 (quoting John H. Rock, Colored Counselor, 9 Harper's Wkly. 124 (February 25, 1865)).
[125] Niven, supra note 10, at 3–4.
[126] Hyman, supra note 34, at 167.

helped to kill his chances to be either party's 1868 presidential candidate . . . ."[127]

B. Chase's Opinions on Reconstruction

As Chief Justice, Chase had two opinions affecting Reconstruction that vindicated Lincoln's confidence in him. One, *Texas v. White*, is well known, though criticized. The other, *In re Turner*, a case he decided while riding circuit, is now forgotten.[128]

1. *In re Turner*

In re Turner[129] involved Elizabeth Turner, a "young person of color" in Maryland who was freed after the passage of its new Constitution.[130] After her emancipation, she and others were gathered by local authorities and pressed into apprenticeships, typically to their previous owners. The century-long fight by Southern Democrats to reimpose the subordination of the freed blacks after the abolition of slavery was just beginning. Turner's apprenticeship to her former master had been entered into by her mother on her behalf. After she came of age, Turner brought suit for her freedom.

In 1867, Chase heard the case as a circuit court judge in the same courtroom in which Chief Justice Taney delivered his circuit court opinion in *Ex Parte Merryman*.[131] Turner's lawyer argued that Turner's apprenticeship contract, entered into by her mother, violated the Thirteenth Amendment and the Civil Rights Act of 1866.

In a case of first impression, Chase agreed and issued a writ of habeas corpus for Turner. Chase ruled that the apprenticeship contract constituted involuntary servitude in violation of the Thirteenth Amendment.[132] He also ruled that, because it did not conform to

---

[127] Id. at 138.
[128] See generally Hyman, supra note 34 (discussing the significance of In re Turner and Texas v. White); Lurie, supra note 107, at 26–27, 67–68 (same).
[129] In re Turner, 24 F. Cas. 337 (C.C.D. Md. 1867) (No. 14,247).
[130] Hyman, supra note 34, at 124. The facts surrounding Turner related in the following paragraphs are taken from id. at 124–26 unless otherwise noted.
[131] Ex parte Merryman, 17 F. Cas. 144 (C.C.D. Md. 1861) (No. 9,487) (holding that Congress, and not the President, has the power to suspend habeas corpus). President Lincoln disregarded this decision.
[132] In re Turner, 24 F. Cas. at 339 ("The first clause of the thirteenth amendment to the constitution of the United States interdicts slavery and involuntary servitude . . . . The

Maryland regulations concerning indentures of whites, the indenture was also in violation of the Civil Rights Act.[133] He then went on to rule that the Civil Rights Act was constitutional under Congress's enforcement powers under the Thirteenth Amendment—a then-controversial position, even among some Republicans in Congress.[134] Notably, his decision affirmed that a woman such as Turner was among those protected by both the Thirteenth Amendment and by the reference to "all persons" in the Civil Rights Act. As we will see, this assumption about the legal equality of women will reappear at the end of Chase's life.

Harold Hyman tells us that Chase hoped that the *Turner* case would make it to the Supreme Court to provide a national platform on which "to clarify in concrete, workaday terms the ways that the Thirteenth Amendment and the Civil Rights Act had altered federalism."[135] To Chase, "even a black female juvenile who as a slave had almost no legal rights was [now] a national citizen, according to the Civil Rights Act,"[136] a proposition that was not completely accepted until the ratification of the Fourteenth Amendment. Chase believed that his *Turner* decision "resolved inarguably not only the issue of blacks' legal rights and status of both in the former slave states and throughout the nation but also of all Americans' basic civil rights."[137] According to Hyman, "Elizabeth Turner's situation caught Chase's conscience because slavery, though illegal, was regenerating under covert guises provided by states' black codes."[138]

Turner never made it to the Supreme Court. But Chase's 1867 ruling protecting the citizenship rights of blacks, and other like actions, contributed to his failure to capture the Democratic presidential nomination in 1868.[139] Some Democrats hoped, with the

---

alleged apprenticeship in the present case is involuntary servitude, within the meaning of these words in the amendment.").

133 Id. ("[T]he indenture set forth in the return does not contain important provisions for the security and benefit of the apprentice which are required by the laws of Maryland in indenture of white apprentices, and is, therefore, in contravention of [the Civil Rights Act] . . . .").

134 Id.

135 Hyman, supra note 34, at 131

136 Id.

137 Id.

138 Id. at 135.

139 See id. at 133 ("[In re Turner] imposed federal standards on private labor contracts sanctioned by a state and on behalf of a black woman. . . . [Such a ruling] made Chase politically unacceptable as a presidential candidate in 1868 to white social conservatives in both parties, North and South, but particularly unacceptable to Democrats.").

antislavery activist Chase as its standard bearer, "the party could advertise itself as purged of Copperheadism, a reformed and penitent new party."[140] But "Chase and his supporters failed adequately to gauge the passion with which unregenerate Democrats viewed his antislavery past, wartime record, role in the Johnson impeachment, and postwar rulings on the legal status of emancipated blacks like Elizabeth Turner."[141] At the same time, his impartial conduct while presiding over Johnson's impeachment trial in the Senate in 1867 alienated him from some of his former radical Republican allies.[142]

Whatever else can be said about Chase's presidential ambitions, he always expected the presidency on his terms, rather than deviate from his core principles to acquire his coveted prize. Perhaps this fact undercuts to some degree the harsh assessments of his character discussed below.

2. *Texas v. White*

In *Texas v. White*[143] the Court considered a claim by the provisional reconstruction government of Texas that United States bonds owned by Texas since 1850 had been illegally sold by the Confederate state legislature during the American Civil War.[144] The Court ruled that Texas had remained a state ever since it first joined the Union, despite its joining the Confederate States of America and its being under military rule at the time of the decision in the case. For this reason, the ordinances of secession, and all the acts of the legislatures within seceding states intended to give effect to such ordinances, were "absolutely null."[145]

The case was politically tricky. By the time the suit was filed, Republicans in Congress were opposing President Johnson's reconstruction policy of extending swift recognition of southern state governments upon their ratification of the Thirteenth Amendment. Some Republicans began to abandon the position adopted by Lincoln and others that the states had never left the Union. Instead, they

---

140 Id. at 142.
141 Id.
142 See id. at 138 (noting that Chase's "evenhandedness at the [impeachment] trial . . . helped to kill his chances to be either party's 1868 presidential candidate").
143 Texas v. White, 74 U.S. (7 Wall.) 700 (1869).
144 The facts surrounding Texas v. White are taken from Hyman, supra note 34, at 140–50. See also Lurie, supra note 107, at 67–68.
145 White, 74 U.S. at 726.

considered the South as legally similar to conquered provinces over which they could exercise the same authority as they had to regulate territories. On this theory, the Supreme Court should reject jurisdiction in the case because Texas, as yet, had no legally recognized government.

Conversely, Democrats wanted the Court to acknowledge the existence of an official state government in Texas. Such a ruling would have the effect of accepting Texas as fully restored to its place in the Union and thus render unconstitutional the Military Reconstruction Act, which listed Texas as a "rebel State[]" with reduced status.[146] Wall Street was also concerned with the case, being opposed to any actions that threatened bondholders and investors. For this reason, as Hyman observes, Chase's decision to assign himself the writing of the majority opinion, rather than dodge the task, was not one that "a truly driven would-be presidential candidate or mere placeholder" would have made.[147]

In his opinion upholding the jurisdiction of the Court, Chase began by identifying what is meant by "state." He distinguished the territory and people of a state, which remained in the Union, from its government, which was hostile to the United States and therefore properly unrepresented in Congress. In the text of the Constitution, wrote Chase, "a plain distinction is made between a State and the government of a State."[148]

Chase then affirmed Lincoln's position that the Southern states, properly defined, had never legally left the Union. Although the states continued to maintain their separate existence, they were bound in perpetuity to the Union until they received its consent for them to secede. The Articles of Confederation, said Chase, had "solemnly declared" this union to "be perpetual."[149] And the Constitution was created "to form a more perfect Union."[150] "What can be indissoluble," he asked, "if a perpetual Union, made more perfect, is not?"[151] In what may be the most famous line of any Chase opinion, he wrote: "The Constitution, in all its provisions, looks to an indestructible Union, composed of indestructible States."[152]

---

[146] Hyman, supra note 34, at 146.
[147] Id. at 147.
[148] White, 74 U.S. at 721.
[149] Id. at 725.
[150] Id.
[151] Id.
[152] Id.

So, when Texas became one of the United States, she entered into an indissoluble relation. All the obligations of perpetual union, and all the guaranties of republican government in the Union, attached at once to the State. The act which consummated her admission into the Union was something more than a compact; it was the incorporation of a new member into the political body. And it was final. The union between Texas and the other States was as complete, as perpetual, and as indissoluble as the union between the original States. There was no place for reconsideration or revocation, except through revolution or through consent of the States.[153]

Because the government of the state of Texas was acting unconstitutionally and illegally when it refused its obedience to the Constitution, it could properly be denied representation in Congress until it was reconstructed to establish a republican form of government for all its citizens, including those persons who had been emancipated from bondage. But because both presidential and congressional reconstruction policies had resurrected its government, that provisional government had standing to sue.

Having affirmed that the state of Texas had remained within the Union, what was the legal status of the actions taken by its government while it was in open rebellion against the United States? Chase answered that there were two categories of state action. First were those acts that are "necessary to peace and good order among citizens, such for example, as acts sanctioning and protecting marriage and the domestic relations, governing the course of descents, regulating the conveyance and transfer of property, real and personal, and providing remedies for injuries to person and estate . . . ."[154] These and other similar acts, "would be valid if emanating from a lawful government," and therefore "must be regarded in general as valid when proceeding from an actual, though unlawful, government."[155]

In contrast were acts "in furtherance or support of rebellion against the United States, or intended to defeat the just rights of citizens."[156] These "and other acts of like nature, must, in general, be regarded as invalid and void."[157] Because the particular act of the rebellious government of Texas in selling the bonds, unlike many of its other actions of maintaining the peace, was done in aid of treason and

---

[153] Id. at 726.
[154] Id. at 733.
[155] Id.
[156] Id.
[157] Id.

insurrection, it was null and void. "It follows that the title of the State was not divested by the act of the insurgent government in entering into this contract."[158]

Chase's distinction between the territory and people of a state and its government harkened back to the Supreme Court's first great constitutional decision in *Chisholm v. Georgia*,[159] where the Court found that, because sovereignty resided in the people as individuals rather than in the government of their state, individuals of one state may sue the government of the other, as apparently authorized by the Constitution, and that state governments cannot plead sovereign immunity in defense.[160]

Chase's opinion also harkened back to his ruling in *Turner* that blacks were now citizens of the United States. After grounding the authority of Congress to suppress the rebellion in "the power to suppress insurrection and carry on war," he derived the power to reconstruct the governments of the rebellious states from "the obligation of the United States to guarantee to every State in the Union a republican form of government."[161] Because "[t]he new freemen necessarily became part of the people, and the people still constituted the State," he concluded, "it was the State, thus constituted, which was now entitled to the benefit of the constitutional guaranty."[162] In other words, the freeman were part of the people who deserved representation in any republican government, and it was Congress's constitutional duty to guarantee to them that form of government by means of reconstruction.[163]

Had Chase been guided solely by his political ambition, he would have attempted to please either the Republicans, by denying jurisdiction, or the Democrats, by upholding the sale of the bonds and vindicating the legal status of the existing government of Texas, which would then entitle it, and all other states with provisional governments, to immediate representation in Congress. Instead, his decision in

---

[158] Id. at 734.

[159] Chisholm v. Georgia, 2 U.S. (2 Dall.) 419 (1793).

[160] See Randy E. Barnett, The People or the State?: Chisholm v. Georgia and Popular Sovereignty, 93 Va. L. Rev. 1729 (2007) (discussing the significance of Chisholm despite being infrequently taught in law schools).

[161] White, 74 U.S. at 727.

[162] at 727–29.

[163] Other more radical constitutional abolitionists had contended that this had always been the case, and therefore the Guarantee Clause empowered Congress to protect blacks even in states that authorized slavery. See William M. Wiecek, The Guarantee Clause of the U.S. Constitution 136–37 (1972).

Texas v. White pleased no one entirely, while remaining true to his vision of the Union, which he shared with the murdered President who had nominated him to be Chief Justice.

C. Chase on the Enumerated Powers of Congress

Chase decided two cases concerning the scope of Congress's power under the Necessary and Proper Clause that continue to resonate today. The first is still good law, and is consistent with the majority in *NFIB v. Sebelius*[164] who found that the Affordable Care Act's individual insurance mandate was beyond the power of Congress under the Commerce and Necessary and Proper Clauses. The second was quickly reversed by the Court itself after the completion of what amounted to a court packing scheme by Congressional Republicans.

1. United States v. Dewitt

The very first Supreme Court decision invalidating an act of Congress for exceeding its powers under the Commerce Clause was *United States v. Dewitt.*[165] In 1867, Congress enacted a law prohibiting both the interstate and intrastate sale of a mixture of "naphtha and illuminating oils" or "oil made from petroleum for illuminating purposes, inflammable at less temperature or fire-test than 110 degrees Fahrenheit."[166] The violation of this prohibition was a misdemeanor punishable by fine or imprisonment.[167] In his opinion for the Court, Chief Justice Chase posed the question presented as whether "Congress [has] power, under the Constitution, to prohibit trade within the limits of a State?"[168]

Chase began his analysis by affirming the following first principle: The "express grant of power to regulate commerce among the States has always been understood as limited by its terms; and as a virtual denial of any power to interfere with the internal trade and business of the separate States."[169] Notice that Chase referred not merely to the internal *commerce* of a state, but also to its "trade and

---

[164] NFIB v. Sebelius, 132 S. Ct. 2566 (2012).
[165] United States v. Dewitt, 76 U.S. (9 Wall.) 41 (1870).
[166] Id. at 42.
[167] Id.
[168] Id. at 43
[169] Id. at 44.

business," which is a broader category.[170] The only exception to the prohibition on congressional interference with the internal trade and business of states, Chase said, is when doing so is "a necessary and proper means for carrying into execution some other power expressly granted or vested."[171]

First, he rejected the analogy to a statute that uses the tax power to regulate "the business of distilling liquors, and the mode of packing various manufactured articles."[172] The analogy fails because, with the statute under consideration, "no tax is imposed on the oils the sale of which is prohibited."[173] In short, Chief Justice Chase distinguished between penalizing conduct and taxing it. Here the statute (a) expressly prohibited the conduct in question and (b) punished violations of the prohibition with fine or punishment or both. Hence, the statute itself was not an exercise of the tax power.

Chase then considered the argument that the prohibition of the sale of the illuminating oil described in the statute "was in aid and support of the internal revenue tax imposed on other illuminating oils."[174] By this reasoning, prohibiting these oils would lead people to use the other illuminating oils that were being taxed, thereby "increasing the production and sale of other oils, and, consequently, the revenue derived from them."[175] He dismissed this assertion of Congress's power under the Necessary and Proper Clause as "too remote and too uncertain to warrant us in saying that the prohibition is an appropriate and plainly adapted means for carrying into execution the power of laying and collecting taxes."[176] And he reached this conclusion notwithstanding that the prohibition was included in "an act imposing internal duties."[177]

"Standing by itself," wrote Chase, this "is plainly a regulation of police."[178] To this he added that it was so considered, if not by the

---

[170] Id. For a discussion of the original meaning of "commerce," see Randy E. Barnett, The Original Meaning of the Commerce Clause, 68 U. Chi. L. Rev. 101 (2001); Randy E. Barnett, New Evidence of the Original Meaning of the Commerce Clause, 55 Ark. L. Rev. 847 (2003); Randy E. Barnett, Jack Balkin's Interaction Theory of "Commerce," 2012 U. Ill. L. Rev. 623.

[171] Dewitt, 76 U.S. at 44.

[172] Id.

[173] Id.

[174] Id.

[175] Id.

[176] Id.

[177] Id.

[178] Id.

Congress which enacted it, certainly by the succeeding Congress, may be inferred from the circumstance, that while all special taxes on illuminating oils were repealed by the act of July 20th, 1868, which subjected distillers and refiners to the tax on sales as manufacturers, this prohibition was left unrepealed.[179]

Chase ended his opinion by invoking the same theory of federalism that, years before, had led him to contend that, while Congress could ban slavery in the District of Columbia and the territories under its control, it could not prohibit the practice within the original states. Because the law in question is "a police regulation, relating exclusively to the internal trade of the States," he reasoned, "it can only have effect where the legislative authority of Congress excludes, territorially, all State legislation, as for example, in the District of Columbia. Within State limits, it can have no constitutional operation."[180] For Chase, this proposition was "so frequently declared by this court, results so obviously from the terms of the Constitution, and has been so fully explained and supported on former occasions, that we think it unnecessary to enter again upon the discussion."[181]

The relevance of *Dewitt* to the constitutional challenge to the Affordable Care Act[182] did not go unnoticed during that litigation. The case was relied upon by the National Federation of Independent Business in its brief to the Court.[183] But, although this precedent by his predecessor went unmentioned by Chief Justice Roberts in his opinion for the Court in *NFIB v. Sebelius*,[184] his reasoning about the tax power takes at least some of *Dewitt*'s holding into account.

In his *NFIB* opinion, Chief Justice Roberts adopted what he called a "saving construction" by rewriting the individual insurance mandate to eliminate the "requirement" that everyone purchase private health insurance.[185] Section 5000A of the Affordable Care Act "reads more naturally as a command to buy insurance than as a tax," he wrote, and he "would uphold it as a command if the Constitution allowed it. It is only because the Commerce Clause does not authorize such a command that it is necessary to reach the taxing power question."[186]

---

179 Id.
180 Id. at 45.
181 Id. (citations omitted).
182 Patient Protection and Affordable Care Act, Pub. L. No. 111-148, 124 Stat. 119 (2010).
183 Brief for Private Respondents on the Individual Mandate at 43, NFIB v. Sebelius, 132 S. Ct. 2566 (2012) (No. 11-398).
184 NFIB v. Sebelius, 132 S. Ct. 2566 (2012).
185 Id. at 2600–01.
186 Id. at 2600.

Although the statute expressly speaks of a "requirement" to purchase qualifying health insurance,[187] like Chief Justice Chase concluded of the prohibition in *Dewitt*, Chief Justice Roberts flatly affirmed that "Section 5000A would . . . be unconstitutional if read as a command" under both the Commerce Clause and the Necessary and Proper Clause.[188]

Discarding the "requirement" in the statute, Roberts adopted the saving construction that "[t]hose subject to the individual mandate may lawfully forgo health insurance and pay higher taxes, or buy health insurance and pay lower taxes."[189] He then upheld the "penalty" in § 5000A standing alone as a tax, in part because it is not so punitive as to coerce people to purchase health insurance, which would render the mandate an unconstitutional command. "[W]e need not here decide the precise point at which an exaction becomes so punitive that the taxing power does not authorize it."[190]

Chief Justice Roberts's opinion, however, skirted the issue that Chase squarely considered in *Dewitt*: Did Congress consider § 5000A to be a Commerce Clause regulation or a tax? In *Dewitt*, Chase considered the question and answered in the negative. Roberts elided the question by rejecting the "more natural[]"[191] reading of the statute, which would best evidence congressional intent, and then adopting his "saving construction" without regard to whether or not Congress intended the "penalty" to be a tax.

On the basis of his opinion in *Dewitt*, I think there is little question that Chief Justice Chase would agree with Chief Justice Roberts that the more natural reading of § 5000A is as a penalty enforcing a prohibition, which is beyond the enumerated power of Congress. Although it went uncited, *Dewitt*, therefore, both supports this aspect of Chief Justice Roberts's opinion and remains good law.

The *Dewitt* case is noteworthy in another respect. Having been decided in 1869, it undermines the narrative that the judicial enforcement of limits on the Commerce power—beginning 1895 with *E.C. Knight*[192] and continuing up until 1935 in *Schechter Poultry*[193]—was a judicial invention reflecting the more conservative Justices'

---

[187] § 5000A, 124 Stat. at 244.
[188] NFIB, 132 S. Ct. at 2601.
[189] Id. at 2600 n.11.
[190] Id, at 2600.
[191] at 2600–01.
[192] United States v. E.C. Knight Co., 156 U.S. 1 (1895).
[193] A.L.A. Schechter Poultry Corp. v. United States, 295 U.S. 495 (1935).

disapproval of progressive and populist legislation. If the judicial enforcement of the limits on Congress's power under the Commerce and Necessary and Proper Clauses is a judicial invention, it is one that began some eighty years after the adoption of the Constitution, and well before the rise of the Progressive and Populist movements, which sought to label the Supreme Court activist for enforcing the enumerated powers scheme.

2. The *Legal Tender Cases*

Chase's stance in the *Legal Tender Cases* is much better known. In the 1869 case of *Hepburn v. Griswold*,[194] he wrote the majority opinion that laws compelling contracting parties to accept paper money in settlement of debts—called "legal tender laws"—were unconstitutional. After the appointment of two additional Justices by President Grant, this decision was reversed just two years later in *Knox v. Lee*.[195]

Hepburn and *Knox*—like *Prigg* and *Dewitt*—are actually Necessary and Proper Clause cases. In *Hepburn*, Chase began by reaffirming the first principle he had enunciated in *Dewitt*: "[I]t is generally, if not universally, conceded, that the government of the United States is one of limited powers, and that no department possesses any authority not granted by the Constitution."[196] Chase never questioned the existence of implied powers, though he noted that "the extension of power by implication was regarded with some apprehension by the wise men who framed, and by the intelligent citizens who adopted, the Constitution."[197] He found evidence for this concern in the wording of both the Necessary and Proper Clause and the Tenth Amendment.[198]

Sometimes the *Legal Tender Cases* are loosely described as involving the power to issue paper money. But Chase identified the power being asserted by Congress, not as the power to issue paper notes, a power he says was held by Congress under the Articles of Confederation, but as the power to make these notes a "legal tender."[199] This requires that they be accepted as settlement of debts

---

194 Hepburn v. Griswold, 75 U.S. (8 Wall.) 603 (1870).
195 Knox v. Lee, 79 U.S. (12 Wall.) 457 (1871).
196 Hepburn, 75 U.S. at 613.
197 Id.
198 See id. at 613–14.
199 Id. at 616.

even by those who stipulated in their contracts for payment in specie. Is this power both necessary and proper for carrying into execution an enumerated power?

As he did in *Dewitt*, Chase then sought to apply the standard provided by *McCulloch v. Maryland*.[200] After identifying the power in question, Chase first considered whether it is "implied in, or incidental to" any enumerated power, such as the power to coin money.[201] The power to make paper notes a legal tender "is certainly not the same power as the power to coin money. Nor is it in any reasonable or satisfactory sense an appropriate or plainly adapted means to the exercise of that power."[202] Neither is the power claimed "implied in, or incidental to, the power to regulate the value of coined money of the United States, or of foreign coins."[203] Chase defined this as "a power to determine the weight, purity, form, impression, and denomination of the several coins, and their relation to each other, and the relations of foreign coins to the monetary unit of the United States."[204]

Much like the Court in *NFIB v. Sebelius*, Chase distinguished between the concepts of "necessary" and "proper." Unlike the modern doctrine that largely defers to Congress's assessment of "necessity," Chase addressed this issue. "[W]hatever benefit is possible from that compulsion to some individuals or to the government," Chase recognized that "there is abundant evidence" that this benefit "is far more than outweighed by the losses of property, the derangement of business, the fluctuations of currency and values, and the increase of prices to the people and the government, and the long train of evils which flow from the use of irredeemable paper money."[205]

Applying the standard from *McCulloch*, Chase considered whether this measure is "plainly adapted" to any enumerated power. As to the power to declare and carry on war, because "it adds nothing to the utility of the notes, it cannot be upheld as a means to the end in furtherance of which the notes are issued."[206] Further, "while facilitating in some degree the circulation of the notes, it debases and

---

200 McCulloch v. Maryland, 17 U.S. (4 Wheat.) 316 (1819).
201 Hepburn, 75 U.S. at 616.
202 Id.
203 Id.
204 Id.
205 Id. at 621.
206 Id.

injures the currency in its proper use to a much greater degree."[207] For the same reason, Chase found this measure is not justified under the powers to regulate commerce or to borrow money. "Both powers necessarily involve the use of money by the people and by the government, but neither, as we think, carries with it as an appropriate and plainly adapted means to its exercise, the power of making circulating notes a legal tender in payment of pre-existing debts."[208]

Although the modern Court might shy away from so fact bound an inquiry into the "necessity" of a law, Chase's approach resembles the view expressed by Justice Kennedy in his concurring opinion in *United States v. Comstock.*[209] The Court's modern Commerce Clause precedents, he wrote, "require a tangible link to commerce, not a mere conceivable rational relation, as in *Lee Optical*."[210] For Justice Kennedy, "[t]he rational basis referred to in the Commerce Clause context is a demonstrated link in fact, based on empirical demonstration. While undoubtedly deferential, this may well be different from the rational-basis test as *Lee Optical* described it."[211]

Like the majority in *NFIB*, Chase then separately assessed the issue of the law's propriety. Quoting Chief Justice Marshall in *McCulloch*, he asked whether the means employed, however plainly adapted they may be, are "not prohibited, but consistent with the letter and spirit of the Constitution."[212] He then did a broad survey of how the power to compel the acceptance of paper money in satisfaction of debts violate the "cardinal principles"[213] embodied in the Contracts, Takings, and Due Process Clauses—an analysis that is too lengthy to summarize here.

With respect to the Due Process Clause, he offered the following analogy: "No one probably could be found to contend that an act enforcing the acceptance of fifty or seventy-five acres of land in satisfaction of a contract to convey a hundred would not come within the prohibition against arbitrary privation of property."[214] Yet he was then "unable to perceive any solid distinction between such an act and an act compelling all citizens to accept, in satisfaction of all contracts

---

[207] Id. at 622.
[208] Id.
[209] United States v. Comstock, 130 S. Ct. 1949 (2010).
[210] Id. at 1967 (Kennedy, J., concurring).
[211] Id.
[212] Hepburn, 75 U.S. at 622.
[213] Id.
[214] Id. at 625.

for money, half or three-quarters or any other proportion less than the whole of the value actually due, according to their terms."[215] For this reason, he said, it "is difficult to conceive what act would take private property without process of law if such an act would not."[216]

In this way, Chase adopted what today would be called a "substantive" reading of the Due Process Clause, years before the socalled *Lochner* Court is said to have invented the concept for political reasons. Chase used the Due Process Clause to protect what would later be characterized as an "economic" liberty. And he found that a law that violates due process is not a proper means of carrying into execution the enumerated powers.

Both because of a lack of sufficient means-end fit, and because it violates the letter and spirit of the Constitution, Chase concluded that the legal tender law is unconstitutional. Requiring creditors to accept paper money as payment for debts "is not a means appropriate, plainly adapted, really calculated to carry into effect any express power vested in Congress; that such an act is inconsistent with the spirit of the Constitution; and that it is prohibited by the Constitution."[217]

Before ending his opinion, however, Chase implicitly acknowledged his own role as Treasury Secretary in promoting the use of paper money, including the making of it a legal tender. The "tumult of the late civil war" when "apprehensions for the safety of the Republic [were] almost universal," was "not favorable to considerate reflection upon the constitutional limits of legislative or executive authority. If power was assumed from patriotic motives, the assumption found ready justification in patriotic hearts."[218] Perhaps referring to himself, he wrote, "Some who were strongly averse to making government notes a legal tender felt themselves constrained to acquiesce in the views of the advocates of the measure."[219] Now "since the return of peace, and under the influence of the calmer time," many "who then insisted upon its necessity, or acquiesced in that view, have . . . reconsidered their conclusions, and now concur in those which we have just announced."[220]

---

[215] Id.
[216] Id.
[217] Id.
[218] Id.
[219] Id.
[220] Id. at 625–26.

Notwithstanding this explanation, Chase has sometimes been criticized for the inconsistency of his stances on legal tender laws as the Secretary of the Treasury and as Chief Justice. Yet another Justice is not similarly rebuked for a similar switch. In 1952, during the height of the Korean conflict, President Truman took control of the Youngstown Sheet and Tubing company facilities by an executive order. As Attorney General, Robert Jackson had previously advised President Roosevelt that such a seizure would be allowed as an exercise of the President's war power. Yet later as a Justice in *Youngstown Sheet & Tube Co. v. Sawyer*,[221] Jackson voted to invalidate the seizure by Truman as unconstitutional.

Like Chase, Jackson obliquely acknowledged his change of heart. "That comprehensive and undefined presidential powers hold both practical advantages and grave dangers for the country will impress anyone who has served as legal adviser to a President in time of transition and public anxiety."[222] History has been kinder to Jackson than to Chase for his switch in opinion from war-time cabinet member to Supreme Court Justice. But, if consistency is a virtue, then perhaps we too should be consistent in our praise or condemnation of Justices who find decisions they once approved as members of the executive branch in time of national emergency to be unconstitutional when they are confronted with the same question as a Justice in peacetime.

In any event, Chase's decision was not to survive. Considerable intrigue surrounds the reversal. During the Johnson administration, the Republicans in Congress employed the first court-packing scheme, reducing the number of Justices to eight, to deny Johnson any nominations to the Court.[223] The *Hepburn* case was heard by the full complement of eight Justices, and the initial vote in conference on November 27, 1869, was 4–4. Shortly thereafter, claiming confusion, Justice Grier changed his vote to make the count 5–3 in favor of declaring legal tender unconstitutional.

In December, Congress enacted a law restoring the number of Justices to nine, giving President Grant an additional vacancy to fill. The law also gave full salary to any Justice who had served for ten years and was over the age of seventy. Grier met both of these qualifications and was in failing health. Upon the urging of his colleagues, he resigned effective January 29, 1870. Chase hoped to

---

[221] Youngstown Sheet & Tube Co. v. Sawyer, 343 U.S. 579 (1952).
[222] Id. at 634 (Jackson, J., concurring).
[223] Lurie, supra note 107, at 73.

announce the majority decision on January 31 while Grier was still sitting, but, perhaps to prevent this, the dissenters asked for more time to prepare their dissenting opinion.[224] Consequently, by the time the decision was announced in February, there were two vacancies on the Court, and the vote to invalidate the law was reduced to 4–3,[225] a fact the dissenters would exploit when they formed a new majority to reverse.

The very day that *Hepburn* was announced, President Grant appointed William Strong and Joseph Bradley to fill the vacancies created, directly and indirectly, by the December statute. Strong had upheld the constitutionality of a state legal tender law as a Pennsylvania Supreme Court justice,[226] and Bradley too had voiced his support for that position.[227] To the charge that Grant had engaged in court packing, Jonathan Lurie replies that "[t]here is no evidence that he intentionally sought out nominees in favor of paper money as legal tender."[228] Still he acknowledges that "the government moved for reconsideration of Chase's decision only *after* Grant's two nominations had been confirmed."[229]

Be this as it may, in his motion for rehearing, Grant's Attorney General Rockwood Hoar stressed that the case had hinged on the vote of one man, Justice Grier, whose switch in votes created the 5–3 majority.[230] The motion created much consternation among the Justices. Justice Miller, a dissenter in *Hepburn*, wrote his brother-inlaw of the "desperate struggle in the secret conference of the Court," and that "the fight has been bitter."[231] In the end, rather than rehear *Hepburn*, a majority instead decided to revisit the issue in the new case

---

[224] Id. at 73–74.

[225] In his opinion, Chase dealt with that situation by noting the following:

> It is proper to say that Mr. Justice Grier, who was a member of the Court when this cause was decided in conference, [November 27, 1869] and when this opinion was directed to be read, [January 29, 1870] stated his judgment to be that the legal tender clause, properly construed, has no application to debts contracted prior to its enactment, but that upon the construction given to the act by the other judges he concurred in the opinion that the clause, so far as it makes United States notes a legal tender for such debts, is not warranted by the Constitution.

Hepburn, 75 U.S. at 626. Chase included the dates in brackets in footnotes.

[226] See Lurie, supra note 107, at 48.

[227] See id. at 50.

[228] Id.

[229] Id.

[230] Id. at 75–76.

[231] Id. at 76 (quoting Letter from Justice Miller to his Brother-in-Law (Apr. 21, 1870)).

of *Knox v. Lee.*[232] The new majority opinion in *Knox*, which reversed *Hepburn*, stressed the fact that *Hepburn* had been decided by less than the full complement of Justices.[233]

Judicial intrigue aside, what is especially noteworthy about *Knox* is its capacious and deferential approach to Congress's powers under the Necessary and Proper Clause. In his opinion for the new majority, Justice Strong stressed that the Constitution must have granted to the national government the "power of self-preservation."[234] It would "be a most unreasonable construction of the Constitution which denies to the government created by it, the right to employ freely every means, not prohibited, necessary for its preservation, and for the fulfilment of its acknowledged duties."[235] Nor need the power being claimed "be found specified in the words of the Constitution, or clearly and directly traceable to some one of the specified powers."[236] It is enough that its "existence may be deduced fairly from more than one of the substantive powers expressly defined, or from them all combined." Indeed, it "is allowable to group together any number of them and infer from them all that the power claimed has been conferred."[237]

Of course, if Congress is the sole judge of necessity, then this gives Congress a power limited only by express prohibitions, not by the "spirit of the Constitution," as Marshall had said and Chase had stressed. Sure enough, the new majority adopted a highly deferential approach to the issue of "necessity." The choice of means, wrote Strong, was "*left to the discretion of Congress*, subject *only to the restrictions that they be not prohibited*, and be necessary and proper for carrying into execution the enumerated powers given to Congress."[238] This deference was also emphasized in Strong's summary of the legal issue confronting the Court:

> Before we can hold the legal tender acts unconstitutional, we must be convinced they were not appropriate means, or means conducive to the execution of any or all of the powers of Congress, or of the government, *not appropriate in any degree*

---

[232] Knox v. Lee (Legal Tender Cases), 79 U.S. (12 Wall.) 457 (1871).
[233] Id. at 553–54.
[234] Id. at 533.
[235] Id. at 533–34.
[236] Id. at 534.
[237] Id.
[238] Id. (emphasis added).

> (*for we are not judges of the degree of appropriateness*), or we must hold that they were prohibited.[239]

Under this deferential standard, Congress apparently has any power it deems to be appropriate that is not expressly prohibited to it by the Constitution. This means that Congress's Article I powers are essentially plenary so long as they satisfy something like the modern rational-basis test. That they may only be trumped by *other* express prohibitions in the Constitution underscores the proposition that, on this reading of the Necessary and Proper Clause, the enumerated powers in Article I, in and of themselves, provide little or no constraints on the power of Congress.

Today, it is considered retrograde to question the constitutionality of legal tender laws. Yet, Chase's opinion in *Hepburn* shows just how problematic the case for such laws is, provided one takes seriously the enumerated powers scheme. Equally problematic is the expansionist reading of the Necessary and Proper Clause adopted by the Court in *Knox* combined with its highly deferential stance toward Congress to define the scope of its own power.

But wait, there's more. One fair reading of *Knox* is that it limited its finding of the unlimited choice of congressional means to emergency situations involving the "self-preservation" of the government itself. After all, both *Hepburn* and *Knox* involved the implementation of legal tender laws in wartime. In 1884, however, the Court in *Juilliard v. Greenman*[240] held that legal tender laws were also constitutional in peacetime. "[W]hether at any particular time, in war or in peace, the exigency is such . . . that it is, as matter of fact, wise and expedient to resort to this means," wrote Justice Gray, "is a political question, to be determined by Congress when the question of exigency arises, and not a judicial question, to be afterwards passed upon by the courts."[241] Yet, it would only be a few years later that the Court managed to march back up the slippery slope.

If *Dewitt* shows that the judicial policing of the enumerated powers scheme long predates the so-called "*Lochner* era," *Knox* and *Juilliard* show that a highly expansionist reading of the Necessary and Proper Clause adopted by the New Deal Court can be traced back as far as the Reconstruction era. Indeed, as mentioned above, it can be

---

239 Id. at 539 (emphasis added

240 Juilliard v. Greenman, 110 U.S. 421 (1884).

241 Id. at 450

traced still further back to Justice Story's reasoning upholding the constitutionality of the Fugitive Slave Act in *Prigg.*[242]

Whichever of these stances is correct, it is quite clear that, as Chief Justice, Salmon P. Chase was on the side of construing Article I to provide judicially enforceable limits on the legislative power of Congress, beginning with his enumerated powers objection to the Fugitive Slave Act and ending with his same objection to legal tender laws.

As we saw in *In re Turner*, Chase did not abandon his stance on the equality of civil rights that he had advocated for thirty years when he became Chief Justice.[243] After his decision in *Turner*, in response to Southern denials of the economic and personal liberties of freed blacks, as well as of white Republicans, Republicans in the Thirty-Ninth Congress enacted the Fourteenth Amendment. One key provision of this amendment was the Privileges or Immunities Clause, which reads: "No state shall make or enforce any law which shall abridge the privileges or immunities of citizens of the United States,"[244] language that was drafted by Ohio Republican Congressman John Bingham.[245]

In 1873, in the *Slaughter-House Cases*,[246] the Supreme Court gutted this Clause by limiting it to only those rights that stem from the federal government, such as the protection of life, liberty, and property while on the high seas, or the right to access the American embassy—as though these were the privileges or immunities that Republicans in Congress amended the Constitution to protect. In his opinion for the majority, Justice Miller (who had so vehemently clashed with Chase in the *Legal Tender Cases*) claimed that the basic economic liberties of property and contract were to be protected solely by state governments,[247] a conclusion that was hotly contested in three dissenting opinions by Justices Bradley, Swain, and Field.

Slaughter-House is well known to be a five-to-four decision. Yet, likely because he wrote no opinion in the case and because the name of the Chief Justice was not included in the Supreme Court Reports, it is generally overlooked that the fourth dissenter was Salmon P. Chase.

---

[242] See supra Part I.C.
[243] See supra Part II.B.
[244] U.S. Const. amend. XIV, §1.
[245] See Barnett, supra note 1, at 166–67 (describing Bingham's role in the drafting of Section 1 of the Fourteenth Amendment).
[246] Slaughter-House Cases, 83 U.S. (16 Wall.) 36 (1873).
[247] Id. at 74–79.

That same day, the Supreme Court also announced its decision in *Bradwell v. Illinois*,[248] a lawsuit in which Myra Bradwell contested the state's refusal to allow her to practice law because she was female. Bradwell, forty-three, "had been editing one of the country's best law periodicals, the *Chicago Legal News*, for some years, meanwhile studying law under the tutelage of her husband, a regionally prominent attorney and later a judge."[249] She clearly fit the statutory requirement specifying "that any adult person of good character and having the requisite training, was eligible for admission to the bar."[250]

For Justice Miller, *Bradwell* was an easy case. If the privileges or immunities of citizens of the United States did not include the economic liberty to pursue a lawful occupation, it protected neither butchers nor lawyers. But because Justice Bradley had strongly asserted that the Privilege or Immunities Clause *did* protect this liberty, he was obligated either to justify the discrimination against women as reasonable, or invalidate the restriction.[251] He opted for the former. In a now notoriously misogynistic concurring opinion, he explained why the legal incapacities of married women, coupled with "the paramount destiny and mission" of women "to fulfil the noble and benign offices of wife and mother" justified the legislative classification.[252] In sum, whereas Miller found the Fourteenth Amendment inapplicable, Bradley found that the amendment applied, but the classification by the state was a reasonable one. In this opinion he was joined by Justices Swain and Field, the two Justices who had joined Bradley in filing dissenting opinions in *Slaughter-House*.

Only the frail and ailing Salmon P. Chase (in the words of the reports) "dissented from the judgment of the Court *and from all the opinions*."[253] Chase was too weak and ill from a series of previous

---

[248] Bradwell v. Illinois, 83 U.S. (16 Wall.) 130 (1873).

[249] Hyman, supra note 34, at 163.

[250] Lurie, supra note 107, at 84.

[251] Lysander Spooner's defense in 1835 of his own bar admission would have supported Bradwell's too.

> If the admission be to anyone a privilege, all, who desire that privilege, have as good a right to it as any one can have. None of us are entitled to exclusive privileges: and therefore, if this privilege be granted to one, the obligations of equity are imperative that be also granted to each and every other one, who may desire it.

Spooner, supra note 13, at 2.

[252] Bradwell, 83 U.S. at 141 (Bradley, J., concurring).

[253] Id. at 142 (emphasis added). It is reasonable to surmise that Chase, who lost three wives to illness, was influenced by his close working relationship with his brilliant and politically savvy daughter, Kate, who managed both his social and political life. Indeed, some of

stokes to write opinions in either case. Three weeks after the decisions on *Slaughter-House* and *Bradwell* were announced, a final stroke took his life.

Robert Kaczorowski wonders how the outcome of *Slaughter-House* might have been different if Chase had retained some of his early vigor. "Would he have been able to persuade one justice to transform the dissenters into the majority?"[254] Kaczorowski thinks Chase might very well have succeeded.

> Just weeks before the Court announced its decision in *SlaughterHouse*, Justice William Strong issued an opinion as circuit justice for Delaware in which he, and the district court judge, Edward Bradford, ruled that the Reconstruction amendments affirmatively secured the fundamental rights of citizens. Strong's opinion in this circuit court case would have placed him with the dissenters in *Slaughter-House*. We do not know how and why he changed his understanding of the Reconstruction amendments. Had a healthy Chase been able to hold him with the dissenters, American legal and constitutional history very likely would have been very different.[255]

Regardless of whether a healthy Chase might have changed the outcome of *Slaughter-House*, most certainly he could not have assembled a majority in *Bradwell* in which he alone "stood on the far broader ground of race-free and gender-free access to life's

---

Chase's wellknown political ambitions might be attributable to her influence. See Frederick J. Blue, Salmon P. Chase: A Life in Politics, at xi, 245 (1987). But female activists made up an important contingent of the abolitionist movement and, both for this reason and because of its natural-rights and free-labor ideology, it was closely aligned with the women's movement. See Ruth Bogin & Jean Fagan Yellin, Introduction to The Abolitionist Sisterhood: Women's Political Culture in Antebellum America 3 (Jean Fagan Yellin & John C. Van Horne eds., 1994).

[254] Robert J. Kaczorowski, The Chase Court and Fundamental Rights: A Watershed in American Constitutionalism, 21 N. Ky. L. Rev. 151, 191 (1993). I sometimes wonder the same thing about another Chief Justice. William Rehnquist was ill from cancer such that he was unable to attend oral argument in the medical marijuana case of Gonzales v. Raich, 545 U.S. 1 (2005), and he had to participate in the conference on the case by telephone. In Raich, the Court upheld the constitutionality of applying the Controlled Substances Act to the possession and distribution of marijuana for medical purposes as authorized by state law. The vote was six to three with Rehnquist, together with Justices O'Conner and Thomas, in dissent. Had he been in his prime, could the Chief Justice have held Justice Kennedy's and Scalia's votes to make a majority for invalidating the CSA? As with the Slaughter-House Cases, we will never know.

[255] Kaczorowski, supra note 254, at 191..

opportunities, benefits, and hazards."[256] Given its beginning in the fight to emancipate blacks held in bondage, to its very ending to vote to uphold the equal civil rights of women, the long career of Salmon P. Chase deserves to be remembered, and remembered fondly.

III. WHY HAS CHASE'S CAREER BEEN FORGOTTEN?

I hope I have told you enough about the remarkable career of Salmon P. Chase to lead you to ask the question: So why don't we all know the story of Salmon P. Chase? The most obvious answer lies in the thing for which Chase is most known today, if he is remembered at all: his life-long political ambition, which has diminished his memory. In other words, it is not Chase's deeds that account for his neglect, but his alleged deficiencies of character.

Chase's later successor as Governor of Ohio and Republican President Rutherford Hayes wrote in his diary that Chase "possessed noble gifts of intellect" as well as "great culture and commanding presence." But, "[w]hen this is said, about all that is favorable has been said. He was cold, selfish, and unscrupulous . . . . Political intrigue, love of power, and a selfish and boundless ambition were the striking features of his life and character."[257] Rockwood Hoar, who as Grant's Attorney General moved for the reversal of *Hepburn*, was even more critical, calling Chase "insincere, selfish and intriguing."[258] Justice Miller, with whom Chase contended in the *Legal Tender Cases*, the *Slaughter-House Cases*, and *Bradwell*, wrote that Chase's strengths were "warped, perverted and shrivelled by the selfishness generated by ambition."[259]

So, truth be told, there was much to dislike about the personality of Salmon P. Chase that affected his contemporaries and, through them, his memory. But this cannot be a sufficient explanation for Chase's neglect by history. For one thing, ambition is rampant among persons in public life who achieve what Chase achieved—even if we limit our focus to Chase's contemporary political rivals. Doris Kern Goodwin's book, *Team of Rivals*, makes evident the enormous

---

[256] Hyman, supra note 34, at 165

[257] Lurie, supra note 107, at 85.

[258] Id.

[259] Id. For what is worth, "Miller blamed his opinion [in Slaughter-House] and the intrigue of Bradley and Swayne for being passed over to replace Chase as chief justice." Kaczorowski, supra note 254, at 188.

political ambitiousness of Chase's competitors: William Seward, Edward Bates, and Abraham Lincoln himself.

What emerges from Goodwin's fascinating treatment is that Chase was simply not as gifted as the others in concealing his ambitiousness in an age when ambition was so frowned upon that presidential candidates were not even supposed to campaign on their own behalf. In the end, despite his many political accomplishments, try as he might, Chase was simply not a very good politician. Especially in contrast to Abraham Lincoln, Chase was not, we might say, a people person, which even then was extraordinarily important both to achieve high office, and to succeed in the offices one achieves.

Remember as well, that Chase was a former Democrat whose core political convictions put him at odds with the more numerous formerWhigs who formed the Republican Party. In many respects, then, Chase had much more intellectually in common with Thomas Jefferson's small government republican party than he did with the political successor to Alexander Hamilton's big government Federalist Party. So Chase was condemned to be distrusted and resented by both his Democratic enemies and his Republican friends. Although he helped found at least three political parties—the Liberty, Free Soil, and Republican parties—in the end, he was truly a man without a party in an age of violent partisanship. In a sense, Salmon Chase was simply his own man for better, but also for worse.

This brings me to another of Chase's character traits that comes through his various biographies. Chase, both consciously and unconsciously, aspired to be a man of great principle, and he largely achieved this aspiration. In very few instances can he be found betraying these principles for the purpose of attaining the offices he held or the one office that eluded his grasp.[260] No, as we have seen in various contexts, he always tried to win while championing his principles, something we might consider admirable rather than deficient.

Chase was what we today would call a "conviction politician." "He won elections as rewards for his activism and because he understood early the need to match existing means with antislavery ends."[261] As even his harsh critic Justice Miller conceded, Chase "was

---

[260] See Foner, supra note 87, at 75 n.7 ("Chase's views on the constitutional relations of slavery remained relatively constant throughout his career.").

[261] Hyman, supra note 34, at 55.

a great man and a better man than public life generally leaves one."[262] Or as George Templeton Strong eulogized: "He leaves an honest record behind him, though in [public] office nearly all his days."[263]

Strong's observation that Chase "was an anti-slavery man long ago when anti-slavery opinions seemed an absolute bar to all hope of social or political advancement"[264] is also telling. And what this tells us is that, however personally ambitious he was, ultimately Chase put his principles ahead of even those powerful ambitions. This must mitigate the charge that Chase was all about ambition and nothing more.

Indeed, it is ironic that, to some extent, Chase's very public proclamation of his principles might well have contributed to his negative reputation. For one thing, some reacted to this character trait as phony, arrogant, or self-righteous. But, more importantly, how does one politically attack a conviction politician who justifies what he does on the ground of such great and noble principles as liberty and equal rights? One way is to attack his character. Say he does what he does, not because of the principles he espouses, but because of his naked ambition. That way, we are free to disregard the principles along with the man who is advocating them. In short, you counter a conviction political figure with an ad hominem argument that undermines his apparent commitment to principle, which is all the more effective if there is a basis in fact in his character that even his friends would acknowledge.

Such ad hominem arguments should not be used to conceal the career of a man who contributed so importantly to the end of chattel slavery. But this very accomplishment may also figure among the possible reasons why we don't remember the story of Salmon P. Chase. For that matter, why don't we know the story of the constitutional abolitionists and their role in establishing the Republican Party? Why don't we know the names of the Republicans in the Thirty-Ninth Congress who, like John Bingham, wrote and approved the Fourteenth Amendment the way we know the names of the Founders? Why don't we know that the Justice Department of Republican President Ulysses S. Grant obtained convictions of Southern terrorists from Southern juries only to have the Republican enacted Civil Rights laws under which they were prosecuted held

---

[262] Lurie, supra note 107, at 85.
[263] Hyman, supra note 34, at 167.
[264] Id

unconstitutional by the Supreme Court? Why don't we know that Grant's administration successfully wiped out the Ku Klux Klan (until it was revived in the twentieth century)?

Chase's political ambitiousness is no answer to these questions, so let me offer another. The early twentieth century saw the rise of a revisionist Southern historiography that retold the nineteenth-century battles for freedom. In this retelling, abolitionists became crazed extremists, congressional Republicans became dangerous radicals, and Reconstruction became a period of Northern oppression of the South and black fecklessness at self-governance. And Ulysses S. Grant became one of the worst presidents in American history.

This narrative certainly fit the need of both the North and South for a story that would contribute to national reconciliation. So the fight to perpetuate slavery became the great Lost Cause for states' rights. But, not coincidentally, the narrative also fit the needs of the defeated and morally discredited Democratic Party—the same Democratic Party that, under Woodrow Wilson, would formally segregate the federal government.

It was not until the 1960s and '70s that revisionist historians—most notably Eric Foner—began to reexamine antebellum abolitionism, the Civil War, and Reconstruction, including the life and achievements of one of its founders, Salmon P. Chase.[265] But even forty years later, their revisionist accounts have yet to permeate the popular culture. Despite their efforts, far more Americans know the term "carpet-baggers" than know the names John Bingham or Salmon P. Chase.

CONCLUSION

With all this in mind, let me close my account of Salmon P. Chase with the assessment of him rendered by his greatest political rival, Abraham Lincoln. As we saw, if anyone had a complaint about Chase, it was he. Yet, as was his wont, Lincoln adamantly refused to let his judgment of Chase's personality cloud his assessment of Chase's abilities and his principled commitment to the equal protection of civil rights.

On the morning Lincoln intended to reveal his choice of Chase to replace Roger Taney as Chief Justice, Lincoln was visited by Chase's

---

[265] See generally Foner, supra note 87 (reexamining this biased historical account

supporter John Alley of Massachusetts. When Lincoln informed Alley of the news he knew would make his visitor happy, Alley responded,

> Mr. President, this is an exhibition of magnanimity and patriotism that could hardly be expected of any one. After what he has said against your administration, which has undoubtedly been reported to you, it was hardly to be expected that you would bestow the most important office within your gift on such a man.[266]

(Of course, if this is what your friends say about you, it is clear you have a problem.) Lincoln's succinct response puts the issue of Chase's character in what I think is the precisely right light: "To have done otherwise," he said, "I should have been recreant to my convictions of duty to the Republican party and to the country."[267] And, "[a]s to his talk about me, I do not mind that. Chase is, on the whole, a pretty good fellow and a very able man. His only trouble is that he has 'the White House fever' a little too bad, but I hope this may cure him and that he will be satisfied."[268] As Lincoln told others who criticized his choice of Chase, "[n]ow, I know meaner things about Governor Chase than any of those men can tell me," but "we have stood together in the time of trial, and I should despise myself if I allowed personal differences to affect my judgment of his fitness for the office."[269]

So, when you drive down the street, and you see the name "Chase" illuminated every few blocks, think of all that the man being honored by those signs accomplished and of how Lincoln characterized him: a pretty good fellow and a very able man. Oh, and one of the persons most responsible for ending slavery in the United States. Were it not for Chase, the Republican Party might not have adopted the constitutional stance it did. It was that stance that provoked the South to secede, that led to the Civil War, and that led to slavery's demise.

Upon his death, the *New York Tribune* eulogized: "To Mr. Chase more than any other one man belongs the credit of making the antislavery feeling, what it had never been before, a power in politics. It had been the sentiment of philanthropists; he made it the inspiration of a great political party."[270] Or, as Eric Foner put it, Salmon P. Chase

---

266 Goodwin, supra note 6, at 680.
267 Id.
268 Id.
269 Id. at 679–80.
270 Foner, supra note 87, at 74.

"lived to see his political approach to the slavery issue spread from a handful of abolitionists to become the rallying-cry of a victorious political party."[271] Each of us should envy that accomplishment. All of us should remember it.

---

[271] Id. at 102.

The Writings of Salmon P. Chase: From Antislavery Lawyer to Chief Justice

EDITED BY RANDY E. BARNETT

TABLE OF CONTENTS

PART I: CHASE, THE ANTISLAVERY LAWYER

IN RE MATILDA, 1837
SPEECH OF SALMON P. CHASE IN THE CASE OF THE COLORED WOMAN, MATILDA. WHO WAS BROUGHT BEFORE THE COURT OF COMMON PLEAS OF HAMILTON COUNTY, OHIO BY WRIT OF HABEAS CORPUS MARCH 11, 1837. CINCINNATI

THE ARGUMENT

The case, as presented by the Sheriff's return, was argued to the Court by Mr. S. P. Chase, and Mr. S. Eells, in behalf of the petitioner, and by Mr. M. N. McLean, Gen. R. T. Lytle, and Mr. N.C. Read, in behalf of the claimant. Mr. Chase addressed the Court as follows:

It is very manifest that the questions, involved in this case, are regarded with deep interest by the community. Many seem to feel something of a personal interest in its event: some, as if their own liberty were at stake: others, as if their own rights of property were in peril. There is a topic, also, with which the discussion of this case is thought by many to be closely connected, though in fact no such connection exists: a topic on which an intense and still increasing interest and excitement prevails — interest and excitement not unfelt within these walls. I feel the responsibility which is upon me as an advocate: I perceive the responsibility which rests upon the Court; — responsibility, not to the community alone — not alone to the humble individual who sues for protection here; — but to conscience and to God. It is an awful and affecting responsibility. But how vast the disparity between the opposite consequences of erroneous decision! If there be error on the one hand, it may consign to hopeless bondage, a human being, rightfully free: on the other, it would but deprive a master of the services of a single individual, legally a slave.

In discussing the questions which present themselves in this case, I seek no aid from feeling. I invoke no sympathy for condition or for sex. True, a fellow being sues to this honorable Court for that protection against slavery, which she can look for, nowhere else upon earth. True, it is a helpless and almost friendless woman who sues for this protection: but I know, that, however much individuals of the Court may feel for her, she can expect no aid from such feelings. This Court will administer the law; not that law, sublimely described as receiving the homage of all creatures, both in heaven and in earth, — of the very least as feeling her care, and of the very greatest as not exempt from her power: but that other and far less perfect law, which is written in the books and statutes of fallible men. A poetical imagination may indulge the contemplation of the golden scales of immortal, passionless justice, held forth, evenly poised, on high: but the poet will be sadly disappointed if he expects that his cause will be weighed, in those balances, by a human tribunal. I shall confine myself, therefore, to the legal and constitutional aspects of the case before the Court. I shall enter in to no discussion of the merits or demerits of slavery. I shall not touch the exciting topic of abolition. I shall enquire, only, whether the petitioner, Matilda, is, or is not now unlawfully restrained of her liberty. If she is, it is the duty of this Court to discharge her from that restraint: if not, she must be recommitted to the custody of the Sheriff.

One preliminary observation, however, or two, I will make. Slavery is admitted, on all hands, to be contrary to natural right. Wherever it exists at all, it exists only in virtue of positive law.[1] The right to hold a man as a slave is a naked legal right. It is a right which, in its own nature, can have no existence beyond the territorial limits of the state which sanctions it, except in other states whose positive law recognises and protects it. It vanishes when the master and the slave meet together in a state where positive law interdicts slavery. The moment the slave comes within such a state, he acquires a legal right to freedom. The petitioner, Matilda, is now within the limits of Ohio, by whose fundamental law slavery is positively and forever interdicted. Admitting then, that she was once a slave, and is now claimed as such: admitting that if she is a slave, the present detention is lawful, still, it by no means follows that she is now a slave, or now legally restrained. On the contrary, she is now legally free: legally restored to her natural right; unless some exception to the great interdict can be clearly shown. And is there a man of all who hear me, who would rejoice that this poor woman, if legally free, should nevertheless be given up because once a slave? Is there a citizen of Ohio within these walls, who regards this woman as a mere article of property, the title to which is founded in natural right, and is recognised by the law of nations, and is protected by the positive laws of all states, and as bound to her owner by the same permanent ties which connect him with his horse or his ox? — If there be, let me tell

[1] Lunsford vs. Coquillon, 14 Martin's (Louisiana) Reports: Rankin vs. Lydia, 3 Marshall's (Ky.) Reports, 470: Sommersett's case, 20 Howell's State Trials, 1.

that individual, that the constitution of Ohio frowns upon him, and that the soil of Ohio is dishonored by his tread....

I now approach another and more important aspect of this case. I have hitherto discussed the effect of the act of congress: I now propose to examine the constitutionality of that act.... I maintain . . . that the act of congress which authorizes justices of the peace, without a jury, to try and decide the most important questions of personal liberty, which makes the certificate of a justice a sufficient warrant for the transportation out of the state, of any person, whom he may adjudge to be an escaping servant, — is not warranted by the constitution of the United States, is repugnant to the ordinance of 1787 for the government of the Northwestern territory, and is therefore, null and void.

It is not warranted by the constitution of the United States. The leading object of the framers of our federal constitution was to create a national government, and confer upon it adequate powers. A secondary object was to adjust and settle certain matters of right and duty, between the states and between the citizens of different states, by permanent stipulations having the force and effect of a treaty. Both objects were happily accomplished.

The constitution establishes a form of government, declares its principles, defines its sphere, and confers its powers. It creates the artificial being, denominated "the government," and breathes into it the breath of life, and imparts to each branch and member, the necessary energies and faculties. It also establishes certain articles of compact or agreement between the states. It prescribes certain duties to be performed by each state and its citizens, towards every other state and its citizens: and it confers certain rights upon each state and its citizens, and binds all the states to the recognition and enforcement of these rights.

These different ends of the constitution — the creation of a government and the establishment of a compact, are entirely distinct in their nature. Either might be attained independently of the other. If all the clauses of compact in the constitution were stricken out, the government created by it would still exist. If the articles and sections, establishing a form of government, were blotted from the constitution, the clauses of compact might still remain in full force, as articles of agreement among the states. The clauses of compact confer no powers on the government: and the powers of government cannot be exerted, except in virtue of express provisions, to enforce the matters of compact.

In this view of the national constitution, I am fully sustained by the high authority of chief justice Shaw of Massachusetts. In his recent opinion in the case of the slave child, Med, that eminent justice says, "The constitution of the United States partakes both of the nature of a treaty and of a form of government. It regards the states, to a certain extent, as sovereign and independent communities, with full power to make their own laws and regulate their domestic policy, *and fixes the terms upon which their intercourse shall be conducted*. In respect to foreign relations, it regards the people of the United States as one community, *and constitutes a form of government for them*."

Now what is the clause in the constitution in regard to fugitives from labor, but an article of agreement between the states? It is expressed in these words, "No person held to service or labor in one state, under the laws thereof, escaping into another, shall, in consequence of any law or regulation thereof, be discharged from such service or labor; but shall be delivered up on claim of the party to whom such service or labor may be due." Does this clause confer any power on government, or on any officer or department of government? — Clearly not. It says nothing about the government, or its officers, or its departments. It declares that the citizens of no state in the Union, legally entitled to the service of any person, shall be deprived of that right to service, by the operation of the laws of any state into which the servant may escape; and it requires such state to deliver him up, on the claim of the lawful master.

The clause, then, restrains the operation of state constitutions and state laws in a particular class of cases; and it obliges, so far as a compact can oblige, each state to the performance of certain duties towards the citizens of other states. The clause has nothing to do with the creation of a form of government. It is, in the strictest sense, a clause of compact. The parties to the agreement are the states. The general government is not a party to it, nor affected by it. If the clause stood alone in the constitution, it would mean precisely what it does now, and would be just as obligatory as it is now. Nothing can be plainer, then, than that this clause cannot be construed as vesting any power in the government, or in any of its departments, or in any of its officers; and this is the only provision in the constitution which at all relates to fugitives from labor.

Now the whole legislative power of congress is derived, either from the general grant of power, "to make all laws, necessary and proper for carrying into execution all the powers vested by the constitution in the government of the United States, or in any department or officer thereof;" or from special provisions in relation to particular subjects. If congress has any power to legislate upon the subject of fugitives from labor, it must be derived from one of these sources, — from the general grant, or from some special provision. It cannot be derived from the general grant, because the clause in regard to fugitives from labor, vests no power in the national government, or in any of its departments or officers; and the general grant of legislative power is expressly confined to the enactment of laws, necessary and proper to carry into execution the powers so vested. Nor can it be derived from any special provision: for none is attached to the clause relating to fugitives from service. The conclusion seems inevitable, that the constitution confers on congress no power to legislate in regard to escaping servants.

Where then is this power? Undoubtedly it is reserved to the states; for "all powers not delegated to the United States, nor prohibited to the states, are re-served to the states or to the people." The constitution restrains the operation of the state constitutions and the state laws, which would enfranchise the fugitive. It also binds the states to deliver him up on the claim of the master, and by necessary inference, it obliges them to provide a tribunal before which such claim may be asserted and tried, and by which such claims may be decided upon, and, if valid, enforced: but it confers no jot of legislative power on congress.

This construction of this clause in the constitution is strengthened by reference to another provision. The first clause of the first section of the same article, in which the provision in regard to escaping servants is found, is in these words: "full faith and credit shall be given, in each state, to the public acts, records, and judicial proceedings of every other state." This clause, so far, is of the same nature with the clause in regard to fugitives from labor. It is a clause of compact, and it pledges the faith of each state to the faithful observance of it. But it confers no power on government, or any of its departments or officers. Congress, therefore, could not legislate in reference to the subject of it in virtue of the general grant of legislative power.

Aware of this, the framers of the constitution annexed to this first clause, a second, specially providing that congress might "prescribe, by general laws, the manner in which such acts, records, and proceedings shall be proved, and the effect thereof." Am I not right in saying that the framers of the constitution were aware, that without this special provision, congress would have no power to legislate upon the subject of the section? If the first clause, *proprio vigore*, confers on Congress legislative power, why add the second? Why add it, if legislative power is conferred by the general grant, or by any other provision in the constitution?

I think the counsel for the claimant will find some difficulty in answering these questions. The framers of the constitution were men of large experience, comprehensive knowledge, sound judgment, and great ability. Among them were Hamilton, and Madison, and Washington. Such men, in framing such an instrument would avoid all needless repetition. They would not incorporate into the constitution a special provision upon any subject unnecessarily. To them, therefore, the second clause of the section under consideration, must have appeared not only fit, but necessary.

But if a special provision was necessary to enable congress to legislate in regard to the authentication and effect of records, why is not a special provision necessary to enable congress to legislate in regard to fugitive servants? Can the counsel explain? Both clauses of the constitution are of the same nature. Neither has anything to do with creating, organizing, or energizing a form of the government. Both are articles of compact.

If then, the framers of the constitution had intended that congress might legislate in reference to the subjects of both, would not special provisions, conferring such legislative power, have been annexed to both? Is not the annexation of such a special provision to one clause, and not to the other, decisive evidence that the convention intended to confer legislative power in regard to the subject of one clause, and to withhold legislative power in reference to the subject of the other? This conclusion seems to me inevitable. I see not how the counsel for the claimant, with all their ability and ingenuity, can frame an argument which will conduct to any other.

Nor is it difficult to assign valid and substantial reasons why the convention should not entrust to congress any legislative power upon this subject. Let us suppose that, when this clause about escaping servants was under discussion, a member had proposed to annex another clause in these words, "And congress shall have power to appoint officers in each state to try and determine the validity of such claims; and to provide by law for the apprehension and re-delivery of persons so escaping." Would not the answer have been, "What! give congress power to appoint officers to try questions of personal liberty, and to provide for the arrest and redelivery of all persons who may be claimed as escaping servants? Who would be safe under such a constitution? What personal right, conferred by God and guarantied by the state constitutions, might not be prostrated under it? Who might not be claimed as a fugitive from labor? Who would be secure against condemnation to servitude? To little purpose has liberty been achieved, if only to be placed in jeopardy like this."

And if this answer had failed to satisfy the convention, and the clause had been incorporated into the constitution, can any one believe that it would have received the assent of the states? Let it be remembered that the states existed before the federal constitution, and that the fundamental law of each asserted and guarantied the absolute, inherent, and unalienable rights of every citizen. Among these were reckoned "life, liberty, and the pursuit of happiness:" and can it be supposed that any state, especially any nonslaveholding state, would have assented to a constitution which would withdraw from either of these rights, the ample shield of the fundamental law, and leave it exposed to the almost unlimited discretion of congress, and of officers appointed by congress? I think not.

But a power vested in congress by a special provision as just stated, would not be half so objectionable as the power actually exercised. Under such a provision, congress would have appointed officers by name: and the officers so appointed would have been known and responsible. Process would have been provided for bringing the persons claimed as fugitives before the proper authority, and the benefit of a regular trial would have been secured to those whose personal liberty might thus be called in question.

But how is it in point of fact? Has congress selected individuals fitted by nature and by education for this important trust? Persons of sufficient knowledge, sound judgment and undoubted integrity? Not at all. By one sweeping enactment, it has appointed all the magistrates of all the counties, cities and towns corporate throughout the Union, judges of these grave questions; judges, too, in the last resort; judges from whose decision lies no appeal; judges with whose proceedings, so long as they strictly pursue the act, no state court and no court of the United States can interfere.

And as if this were not enough, the magistrates, in the exercise of this special jurisdiction, are effectually shielded from all responsibility from malconduct. As state magistrates they are not liable to federal impeachment, and as federal officers they are not liable to state impeachment. And if criminally prosecuted, they may protect themselves under their judicial character. Congress cannot remove them from office, for they exercise their powers under the act of congress in virtue of their offices as magistrates, and they derive their appointment as magistrates, not from congress, but from the states.

Some of them are elected by the people, some are appointed by the executive authority — some are appointed by town or city councils: — some hold their offices for a term of years — some are elected annually — some hold during good behavior: — some are compensated by salaries — others by fees — but none by the United States. For their services under the act of congress, they must make the best bargain they can with the claimants who seek their aid. — To complete the picture, the act omits to require them to hear the proofs of claim in public, or to pronounce a public judgment, or to keep any record of their proceedings. And before these magistrates, thus generally unqualified, thus always and completely irresponsible, and thus exposed to temptation, this act of congress provides that any person may be dragged, by any other person who chooses to set up a claim to him as a fugitive servant, to undergo trial for his personal liberty.

And can it be that the framers of the constitution intended to confer on congress power to enact such a law as this? To suppose it would be to rob their names of that reverence with which they have ever been pronounced. Can it be that the states adopted this constitution, knowing and understanding that it authorized the enactment of this or any similar law? If they did, the great principles which had hallowed their recent struggle, were strangely forgotten. We have little cause to boast of the security with which our institutions surround personal rights, so long as this act is held to be sanctioned by the constitution of the United States.

But this act is not only unauthorized by the federal constitution, but is directly repugnant to some of its plainest provisions. By the second section of the second article, it is made the duty of the President of the United States, with the advice and consent of the Senate, to appoint all judicial officers. — Congress, it is true, may vest the appointment of inferior officers in the President alone, in the courts of law, or in the heads of departments; but there is no clause in the constitution which authorizes congress to retain the appointment of a single officer in its own hands: and yet, here we have congress appointing thousands of federal officers at once.

The act on which I am commenting, appointed all who then were, and all who might afterwards become magistrates of counties, cities, and towns corporate throughout the Union, judges of the United States, with a special jurisdiction. What law can be repugnant, to the constitution if this be not? What law may not congress enact, if they can enact this law? Can the learned counsel for the claimant inform us? . . .

The act relating to fugitives from service, is also repugnant to the fourth and fifth amendments of the constitution, proposed by congress, at the instance of Virginia,[2] to the states, and by the states adopted and ratified as parts of that instrument. The first clause of the fourth amendment, is in these words: "The right of the people to be secure in their persons, houses, papers, and effects, against unreasonable searches and seizures, shall not be violated." Now how could the people be more completely exposed to "unreasonable seizures," than by this act of congress?

Under its sanction, any man who claims another as his servant, may seize and confine him. It is idle to say that none but escaping servants can be seized. The first step is to seize: the next is to take the person seized before a magistrate: and then the validity of the claim is to be tried. It may turn out to be invalid: and in that case, personal rights have been grossly violated. Very frequently instances occur, in which personal rights are thus violated.

And when we reflect, that the questions on which the validity of the claim depends, are often nice and intricate; that it may be the interest of the magistrate to resolve every question as the claimant may desire; that the claimant is permitted to make out his case by affidavits; that these affidavits, there being no cross-examination, will always be strongly in his favor, and may often be false; can we wonder that these outrages against personal rights do not always terminate at the thresh-hold of the magistrate? Can we wonder that, "upon pretence of seizing fugitives from labor, under the provisions of this act, unprincipled persons have kidnapped free persons, transported them out of the state, and sold them into slavery?[3] Is not "this inhuman and infamous practice,"[4] the natural and inevitable consequence of this act? And can such an act consist with that security from unreasonable seizure, which the constitution solemnly guaranties to the people"? I think not.

The third clause in the fourth amendment, of the constitution's in these words: "No man shall be deprived of life, liberty, or property, without due process of law." But the act of congress provides, that persons may be deprived of their liberty without any process of law. It provides no process for the apprehension; none for the detention; none for the final delivery of the escaping servant.

Everything is to be done by the claimant. He is to arrest the fugitive, or the person whom he may take to be the fugitive; he is to bring him before the magistrate: he is to keep him in custody while the magistrate examines the evidences of the claim; he is to remove him when the certificate is granted. From beginning to end of the

---

[2] 4 Elliott's Debates, 216, 217.

[3] Chase's Statutes of Ohio, 1052.

[4] Ib.

proceeding, there is nothing like legal process. And yet, the whole proceeding is recognized by the act of congress. The act then, is palpably and utterly repugnant to the very letter, as well as the whole spirit of the constitution.

And not only so, but it is subversive of the fundamental principles on which all civil society rests. Let such acts be passed in reference to other civil rights. Let each man be authorized to reclaim property, and enforce rights, in this summary way. If one claims a horse found in the possession of another, instead of resorting to his old fashioned action of replevin, and to "due process of law," let him "seize or arrest" him and take him before the nearest magistrate, and there prove his claim. If a man claims services of another, which he will not perform, instead of going to law about the matter, let him drag his recusant neighbor before a justice, prove his claim to service, and then remove him to his task. How long would society hold together, if this principle were carried into general application?

I might here rest this case, but I feel bound to present it under another aspect. . . . [The ordinance of 1787] declared that there should be "neither slavery nor involuntary servitude within the territory, otherwise than in the punishment of crimes." And in order to ensure the permanent inviolability of these great first principles, it declared that the articles of the ordinance by which they were established, should "be considered as articles of compact between the original states and the people and states in the territory, AND FOREVER REMAIN UNALTERABLE, unless by common consent."

This remarkable instrument . . . pronounced, for the first time in the history of the world, a solemn national censure upon slavery, by interdicting forever, its existence in the only district, subject, in this respect, to the control of congress. So long as the ordinance endures, the people of the states, formed within this district, cannot introduce slavery, nor can it be introduced by the people of the other states. "The ordinance," as one of our own great statesmen has most truly said, "impressed on the soil itself, an incapacity to bear up any other than freemen. It laid the interdict against personal servitude in original compact, not only deeper than all local law, but deeper also than all local constitutions."

Every settler within the territory, by the very act of settlement, became a party to this compact, and bound by its perpetual covenants, and forever entitled to the benefit of its provisions, for himself and his posterity. No subsequent act of the original states could affect it, without his consent. It could not be affected, therefore, by the adoption of the federal constitution, for that was the act of the people of the original states, to which the people of the territory were not parties. The constitution of the United States neither did, nor could repeal, impair, abridge, or alter the terms of this compact. It left them as it found them, in the full force of their original obligation.

Faithful to the letter and spirit of the compact, the framers of our state constitution, incorporated its leading provisions into that instrument, thereby claiming for the people of Ohio the benefit of those provisions, recognizing their perpetual obligation, and imparting to them an additional sanction. . . .

I arrive then at the conclusion, that the return of the Sheriff shows no sufficient cause for the caption and detention of the petitioner, and that she must be discharged from custody: . . .

Because the act of congress, which alone purports to confer on the magistrate jurisdiction in cases of escaping servants, not being necessary or proper to carry into execution any power vested in the government of the United States, or in any department, or officer thereof, is not warranted by the constitution of the United States:

Because this act of congress, being an exercise by congress of the power of appointment, or a transfer of federal judicial [sic] power to state tribunals, is in one or both these respects, repugnant to the constitution of the United States:

Because this act of congress, authorizing, as it does, the arrest confinement, trial and removal of escaping servants, "without due process of law," is, in this respect, also repugnant to the constitution of the United States:

Because this act of congress, authorizing, as it does, a course of proceedings, unknown to the common law, and the recaption of fugitives from labor, in a class of cases not within the exceptive provision of the ordinance of 1787, violates the fundamental compact contained in that ordinance:

Because this act of congress, exposing as it does, every citizen to trial for his dearest rights, without a jury, violates, in this respect, also, that fundamental compact:

Because this act of congress derives no validity from any act of the state legislature; nor is in any sense incorporated into our state legislation: nor could, even if it were so incorporated, acquire, thereby, any obligatory quality, inasmuch as it would then be repugnant, not only to the provision in the ordinance, but also to the provision in the state constitution, securing, inviolably, the right of trial by jury:

Because this act of congress, exposing as it does, every member of the community to arrest, confinement and forcible transportation, without process of law, by every other man who may claim him as a fugitive from service, is repugnant to the first principles of civil liberty and subversive of the very ends of civil society.

I have now done with this case. I have presented, feebly perhaps and unsuccessfully, but honestly and fearlessly, the great principles, legal and constitutional, which, in my judgment, ought to govern it. I have not asked — I do not now ask, in behalf of my humble client, deliverance from imprisonment, because that imprisonment is against natural right, but because it is against the constitution and against the law. I claim, however in her behalf, that it be borne in mind that there is such a thing as natural right, derived, not from any civil constitution or civil code, but from the constitution of human nature and the code of heaven.

This court, I am sure, need not to be reminded of the original, paramount truth, written upon the hearts of all men by the finger of God, the same in all ages and in all climes, and destined to no change, proclaimed by our fathers, in the declaration of independence, to be selfevident [sic], and reiterated in our state constitution as its fundamental axiom, that all men are born "equally free." And if the petitioner at the bar cannot expect, here, the full benefit of this fundamental truth; if her right to freedom must, here, be vindicated upon narrower grounds, let her have, at least this advantage from it.

Let her be regarded as free, until it be shown by the fullest and clearest evidence, that her case falls within some exception to the universal law of human liberty. Let the proceedings by which she is now, without the accusation of crime, and without the suspicion of guilt, deprived of freedom and driven a suppliant to this bar, be narrowly scrutinized.

Let every provision, unfavorable to liberty, whether legal or constitutional, receive a strict and rigorous interpretation. And if, when thus scrutinized, these proceedings shall be found insufficient, and especially if they shall be found to be warranted by no law and repugnant to the most vital principles of our social system; if, when thus interpreted, those provisions, which exclude a certain class of persons from the benefit of these vital principles, shall be found not broad enough to reach the case of this petitioner; I demand her discharge in the name of justice, of liberty, and of our common humanity. . . .

JAMES G. BIRNEY V. THE STATE OF OHIO, 1837
8 OHIO 230 (1837)
SUPREME COURT OF OHIO, IN BANK

An indictment for harboring and secreting a mulatto slave is bad, unless it aver that the accused knew the person harbored was a slave....

S. P. CHASE, for the plaintiff in error:

The count, in the indictment of which the defendant was found guilty charged that he 'unlawfully harbored and secreted a certain mulatto girl by the name of Matilda, then *being a slave and the property* of one Larkin Lawrence.' The act, under which the prosecution was instituted, makes it a penal offense to 'harbor or secrete any black or mulatto person, *being the property* of any person whatever.'

I maintain that it is impossible, in Ohio, to commit the offense of harboring, or secreting a person *being the property* of another person. I maintain that the relation of owner and property, as existing between person and person, has, or can have, no existence in this state; and I maintain these propositions as the inevitable results of a sound interpretation of the constitution of Ohio; and as in full harmony with every provision of the constitution of the United States, and of the ordinance of 1787. If I can establish these propositions as I maintain them, it must follow that so much of this act of 1804, as inflicts a penalty for violating a relation which cannot constitutionally exist, must be repugnant to the constitution, and therefore void.

And, certainly, no argument is needed to prove that the relation of owner and property, as between man and man, cannot exist under the constitution of Ohio. This instrument declares 'that all men are born *equally free* and independent, and have certain natural, inherent, and unalienable rights, among which are the enjoying and defending life and liberty; acquiring, possessing and protecting property, and pursuing and obtaining happiness and safety.' It also declares as a direct consequence of these fundamental truths, 'that there shall be neither slavery nor involuntary servitude in this state, otherwise than for the punishment of crimes;' and that 'no alteration of the constitution shall ever take place, so as to introduce slavery or involuntary servitude into this state.'

From these extracts, it appears, that the one principle which the framers were especially anxious to make prominently conspicuous, and to surround with safeguards the most impregnable, was the *equal freedom of all men;* and the one thing which they sought to brand with deepest reprobation, and to exclude forever from the institution of the state, was the *slavery of man to man.* It cannot be doubted, then, that were Ohio a distinct and independent nation, no such relation as owner and property could exist, as between man and man; nor could any law, recognizing and protecting such a relation, be of the least validity.

But Ohio is not a separate and independent nation. We regard the federal constitution and the ordinance of 1787, as of higher authority than our state constitution. If these recognize this relation and sanction it, state legislation may constitutionally recognize and protect it. We must examine, then, and endeavor to ascertain the import of the provisions in the ordinance, and in the constitution of the United States.

The provision in the ordinance is in these words – "any person escaping into the same" (*i. e.* the Northwest Territory) "from whom labor or service is lawfully claimed in any one of the original states, may be lawfully reclaimed and conveyed to the person claiming his or her labor or service, as aforesaid." The provision in the federal constitution was obviously taken from that in the ordinance, and is as follows: "No person, held to service or labor in one state, under the laws thereof, escaping into another, shall, in consequence of any law or regulation therein, be discharged from such service or labor; but shall be delivered up on claim of the party to whom such labor or service may be due."

In order to arrive at the true import of these provisions, it is proper to refer to the history of the country at the time when they were incorporated, first into the fundamental compact of the territory and people northwest of the Ohio with the states and people of the Union; and soon after, into that of all the states with each other.

It was then acknowledged that, in some of the states, institutions existed so incompatible with slavery, they the slave who might escape into them would become a free man the moment he should enter their territory, while in other states, slavery was recognized and protected by fundamental law and legislative enactments. This state of things is implied in the constitutional provision just cited.

Institutions must have existed in some states, by the operation of which, the servant escaping into them, was discharged from his involuntary service, for otherwise this claim would have been nugatory. And Mr. Madison, in the course of the debates in the convention of Virginia, speaking of the condition of things then existing, says: "At present, if any slave elopes to any of those states where slaves are free, he becomes emancipated by their laws."

The slaveholding states were apprehensive of the losses they might sustain in consequence of this state of things, and all dreaded its consequences to the Union. To obviate the apprehended evil, the clause, which has just been cited, was introduced into the constitution as a clause of compact between the states, similar to the clause which had been just before inserted in the ordinance, and expressly declared to be a clause of compact between the original states and the people and states of the northwest territory.

It was cautiously framed, so as to avoid all recognition of the condition of slavery, or the relation of ownership between man and man.

It left the several states free to create, or continue, or abolish such relations between individuals within their several territories as they pleased, just as they had been under the articles of confederation.

It required each state to deliver up servants escaping into its territory from other states, to their lawful masters — to deliver them up as servants, not as slaves — far less as property.

It bound each state to recognize and protect, in a particular class of cases, the relation of master and servant, as established by the laws of sister states, but no other additional relation.

It left the whole responsibility of all other relations upon the states which might establish or continue them.

I am very confident that this construction exhibits the true import of this constitutional provision, and the more confident, because the very terms of the provision seem to exclude every other interpretation. For who is to be delivered up? Any person held to service and escaping. Are slaves and human chattels alone held to service? Surely not. To say nothing of servants for hire, there is the great class of apprentices who are 'held to service' in the strictest sense of the terms, and are yet neither slaves nor property.

It cannot be denied that the provision embraces the case of an escaping apprentice, and if so, all argument, whether or not it recognizes property as a relation of one human being to another, must be at an end. It recognizes no such relation. On the contrary, the exact reverse of such recognition is strongly implied. . . .

If I am correct in this construction of the constitution and the ordinance, it follows that there is nothing in either which requires or authorizes the legislature of any state to pass laws for the protection of the right of property in human beings. Every purpose intended to be answered by the provisions in either instrument, may be effectually accomplished without any such degradation of the non-slaveholding states. And if so, the provision of the act under which this indictment was found, abhorrent as it is to the whole spirit of our institutions, and to the express provisions of our constitution, must be void. . . .

Admitting, for argument's sake, the prosecution to be constitutional, was the offense, charged in the indictment, actually committed? Now, it is certain that slavery, wherever it exists, is a creature of positive institutions. It has no support in natural right; on the contrary, it is in direct derogation of natural right.

Before slavery can be, natural right must be overborne by force, custom, or legislation. In the language of the highest court in Louisiana, Lunsford *v.* Coquillon, 14 Martin, 401, "the relation of owner and slave is, in the states of this Union, in which it has a legal existence, a creature of the municipal law." In the still more emphatic language of the Supreme Court of Mississippi, Harvey et al. *v.* Decker and Hopkins, Walk. 36, "Slavery is condemned by reason and the laws of nature. It exists, and can only exist, through municipal regulations; and in matters of doubt, is it not an unquestioned rule, that courts must lean *in favorem vitoe et libertatis?*" It is also certain that the municipal regulations of no state have *proprio vigore*, any extra territorial force. . . . It is also certain that "no nation is under any obligation to give effect to the laws of another nation, which are prejudicial to itself or its citizens; that in all cases each nation must judge for itself what foreign laws are so prejudicial or not; and it is only in cases not so prejudicial that a spirit of comity and a sense of mutual utility ought to induce every nation to allow full force and effect to the laws of every other nation." Story on Confl. of Laws, 75.

It is also undeniably true that in all enlightened nations, which do not tolerate slavery, the laws of other states in which it is tolerated, are held to be so prejudicial to the non-slaveholding states and their citizens, and so repugnant to the spirit of their institutions, that slaves held under such laws, cease to be slaves the moment they come within their territories. "It has been decided that the law of England abhors and will not endure the existence of slavery within the nation; and consequently, as soon as a slave lands in England he becomes, *ipso facto*, a free man, and discharged from the state of servitude." Ib. 92. So that the fervid exclamation of Cowper is, in truth, an undisputed exiom of English law:

"Slaves can not breathe in England; if their lungs Receive our air, that moment they are free: — They touch our country, and their shackles fall. That's noble!". . .

There is an excepted class of cases, it is true — excepted in the ordinance and excepted in the constitution of the United States, which is paramount to the state constitution. But upon every slave brought within the limits of Ohio, and not embraced within the strict terms of the exception, this great interdict operates with unbroken force. . . . What then is that exception? What persons compose that unfortunate class, whose fetters cannot be broken by the spirit of our state institutions?

The clause creating the exception has been already cited. It provides that no persons held to service in one state, under the laws thereof, escaping into another, shall by any law or regulation therein, be discharged from such service. Persons held to service in one state, and escaping into another, then, compose the class which are not to be enfranchised by the operation of the ordinance and our state constitution.

Was the woman Matilda a person of this class? Was she held to service in one state, and did she escape into another? Plainly not. At the time she left the individual who claimed to be her master, she was within the territorial limits of Ohio, by the consent of that individual. If she had ever been a slave, she had ceased to be such that moment when she was brought by Lawrence within these limits, and she had power to go whithersover she chose. Her act in leaving Lawrence, under these circumstances, was in no just sense of the term, an escape. It was the first exercise of that freedom, which the constitution of Ohio had conferred upon her. . . .

If follows, then, that at the time the woman Matilda was received into the service of the defendant she was not a slave, or the property of any person, and of course that the offense charged has not been, in fact, committed.

No argument was submitted for the state.

Opinion

JUDGE WOOD delivered the opinion of the court:

The statute upon which the indictment is predicated enacts, "that if any person shall harbor or secrete any black or mulatto person, the property of another, the person so offending shall, on conviction thereof, be fined any sum not less than ten nor more than fifty dollars." We are first called to consider whether, under this enactment, the indictment is sufficient?

It is required that every indictment shall have a precise and sufficient certainty. The omission of a word of substance is fatal. Here the plaintiff in error is charged with harboring and secreting a certain mulatto girl, by the name of Matilda, the *property of L. Larkin*. There is no averment that the plaintiff in error *knew the facts alleged*, that Matilda was a slave, and the property of L. Larkin, or of any other person; and such is not the legal inference in a state whose constitution declares that all are born free and equal, and that there shall be neither slavery nor involuntary servitude within its limits, except as a punishment for the commission of crimes.

On the contrary, the presumption is in favor of freedom. The *scienter*, or knowledge of the plaintiff in error, of this material fact, was an ingredient necessary to constitute his guilt. This knowledge should have been averred in the indictment, and proved on the trial, for, without such knowledge, the act charged as a crime was innocent in its character. We know of no case where positive action is held criminal, unless the intention accompanies the act, either expressly or necessarily inferred from the act itself. . . .

This judgment must be reversed for this cause, and it thus becomes unnecessary to decide upon the other points, so laboriously argued for the plaintiff in error, and of a character too important in their bearing upon the whole country to be adjudicated upon without necessity.

PRIGG V. PENNSYLVANIA, 1842
41 U.S. (16 PET.) 539 (1842)

[With the apparent acquiescence of her owner, Margaret Morgan left Maryland to marry a free black man in Pennsylvania where at least one of their children were born. Five years later, after her owner's death, his daughter sent Edward Prigg and others to recaptured Margaret. They captured her, her husband, and their children in York County, Pennsylvania. After the York County justice of the peace refused to consider the case, Prigg took Margaret and her children (but not her husband) to Maryland, in violation of Pennsylvania's "personal liberty law," which required that certificates of removal be obtained from a state judge, justice of the peace, or alderman. The York County prosecutor obtained indictments against Prigg and his helpers for kidnapping and violating the Pensylvania statute. After a public outcry and extensive negotiations between state officials, Maryland sent Prigg to Pennsylvania where he was convicted of kidnapping. Margaret and her children were "sold down the river" and shipped south where they remained in bondage. After the Pennsylvania Supreme Court affirmed his conviction, Prigg challenged its constitutionality in the U.S. Supreme Court.]

MR. JUSTICE STORY delivered the opinion of the court....

Few questions which have ever come before this Court involve more delicate and important considerations; and few upon which the public at large may be presumed to feel a more profound and pervading interest....

Before, however, we proceed to the points more immediately

before us, it may be well—in order to clear the case of difficulty—to say, that in the exposition of this part of the Constitution, we shall limit ourselves to those considerations which appropriately and exclusively belong to it, without laying down any rules of interpretation of a more general nature. It will, indeed, probably, be found, when we look to the character of the Constitution itself, the objects which it seeks to attain, the powers which it confers, the duties which it enjoins, and the rights which it secures, as well as the known historical fact that many of its provisions were matters of compromise of opposing interests and opinions; that no uniform rule of interpretation can be applied to it which may not allow, even if it does not positively demand, many modifications in its actual application to particular clauses. And, perhaps, the safest rule of interpretation after all will be found to be to look to the nature and objects of the particular powers, duties, and rights, with all the lights and aids of contemporary history; and to give to the words of each just such operation and force, consistent with their legitimate meaning, as may fairly secure and attain the ends proposed.

There are two clauses in the Constitution upon the subject of fugitives, which stand in juxtaposition with each other, and have been thought mutually to illustrate each other. They are both contained in the second section of the fourth article, and are in the following words:

> A person charged in any state with treason, felony or other crime, who shall flee from justice, and be found in another state, shall, on demand of the executive authority of the state from which he fled, be delivered up, to be removed to the state having jurisdiction of the crime.
>
> No person held to service or labor in one state under the laws thereof, escaping into another, shall in consequence of any law or regulation therein, be discharged from such service or labor; but shall be delivered up, on claim of the party to whom such service or labor may be due.

The . . . true interpretation [of the last clause] is directly in judgment before us. Historically, it is well known, that the object of this clause was to secure to the citizens of the slaveholding states the complete right and title of ownership in their slaves, as property, in every state in the Union into which they might escape from the state where they were held in servitude. The full recognition of this right and title was indispensable to the security of this species of property in all the slaveholding states; and, indeed, was so vital to the preservation of their domestic interests and institutions, that it cannot be doubted that it constituted a fundamental article, without the adoption of which the Union could not have been formed. Its true design was, to guard against the doctrines and principles prevalent in the non-slaveholding states, by preventing them from intermeddling with, or obstructing, or abolishing the rights of the owners of slaves.

By the general law of nations, no nation is bound to recognise the state of slavery, as to foreign slaves found within its territorial dominions, when it is in opposition to its own policy and institutions, in favour of the subjects of other nations where slavery is recognised. If it does it, it is as a matter of comity, and not as a matter of international right. . . .

It is manifest from this consideration, that if the Constitution had not contained this clause, every non-slaveholding state in the Union would have been at liberty to have declared free all runaway slaves coming within its limits, and to have given them entire immunity and protection against the claims of their masters; a course which would have created the most bitter animosities, and engendered perpetual strife between the different states. The clause was, therefore, of the last importance to the safety and security of the southern states; and could not have been surrendered by them without endangering their whole property in slaves. The clause was accordingly adopted into the Constitution, by the unanimous consent of the framers of it; a proof at once of its intrinsic and practical necessity.

How, then, are we to interpret the language of the clause? The true answer is, in such a manner, as, consistently with the words, shall fully and completely effectuate the whole objects of it. If by one mode of interpretation, the right must become shadowy and unsubstantial, and without any remedial power adequate to the end; and by another mode it will attain its just end and secure its manifest purpose; it would seem, upon principles of reasoning, absolutely irresistible, that the latter ought to prevail. No Court of justice can be authorized so to construe any clause of the Constitution as to defeat its obvious ends, when another construction, equally accordant with the words and sense thereof, will enforce and protect them.

The clause manifestly contemplates the existence of a positive, unqualified right on the part of the owner of the slave, which no state law or regulation can in any way qualify, regulate, control, or restrain. The slave is not to be discharged from service or labor, in consequence of any state law or regulation. Now, certainly, without indulging in any nicety of criticism upon words, it may fairly and reasonably be said, that any state law or state regulation, which interrupts, limits, delays, or postpones the right of the owner to the immediate possession of the slave, and the immediate command of his service and labour, operates, *pro tanto*, a discharge of the slave therefrom. The question can never be, how much the slave is discharged from; but whether he is discharged from any, by the natural or necessary operation of state laws or state regulations. The question is not one of quantity or degree, but of withholding, or controlling the incidents of a positive and absolute right.

We have said, that the clause contains a positive and unqualified recognition of the right of the owner in the slave, unaffected by any state law or legislation whatsoever, because there is no qualification or restriction of it to be found therein; and we have no right to insert any which is not expressed, and cannot be fairly implied; especially are we estopped from so doing, when the clause puts the right to the service or labour upon the same ground, and to the same extent in every other state as in the state from which the slave escaped, and in which he was held to the service or labour.

If this be so, then all the incidents to that right attach also; the owner must, therefore, have the right to seize and repossess the slave, which the local laws of his own state confer upon him as property; and we all know that this right of seizure and recaption is universally acknowledged in all the slaveholding states. . . .

Upon this ground we have not the slightest hesitation in holding, that, under and in virtue of the Constitution, the owner of a slave is clothed with entire authority, in every state in the Union, to seize and recapture his slave, whenever he can do it, without any breach of the peace, or any illegal violence. In this sense, and to this extent this clause of the Constitution may properly be said to execute itself; and to require no aid from legislation, state or national.

But the clause of the Constitution does not stop here; nor indeed, consistently with its professed objects, could it do so. Many cases must arise in which, if the remedy of the owner were confined to the mere right of seizure and recaption, he would be utterly without any adequate redress. He may not be able to lay his hands upon the slave. He may not be able to enforce his rights against persons who either secrete or conceal, or withhold the slave. He may be restricted by local legislation, as to the mode of proofs of his ownership; as to the Courts in which he shall sue, and as to the actions which he may bring; or the process he may use to compel the delivery of the slave. Nay, the local legislation may be utterly inadequate to furnish the appropriate redress....; and this may be innocently as well as designedly done, since every state is perfectly competent, and has the exclusive right, to prescribe the remedies in its own judicial tribunals, to limit the time as well as the mode of redress, and to deny jurisdiction over cases, which its own policy and its own institutions either prohibit or discountenance.

If, therefore, the clause of the Constitution had stopped at the mere recognition of the right, without providing or contemplating any means by which it might be established and enforced, in cases where it did not execute itself, it is plain, that it would have been, in a great variety of cases, a delusive and empty annunciation. . . .

And this leads us to the consideration of the other part of the clause, which implies at once a guarantee and duty. It says, "But he (the slave) shall be delivered up, on claim of the party to whom such service or labor may be due." Now, we think it exceedingly difficult, if not impracticable, to read this language and not to feel that it contemplated some further remedial redress than that which might be administered at the hands of the owner himself. . . .

If, indeed, the Constitution guaranties the right, and if it requires the delivery upon the claim of the owner, (as cannot well be doubted), the natural inference certainly is, that the national government is clothed with the appropriate authority and functions to enforce it. The fundamental principle applicable to all cases of this sort, would seem to be, that where the end is required, the means are given; and where the duty is enjoined, the ability to perform it is contemplated to exist on the part of the functionaries to whom it is intrusted.

The clause is found in the national Constitution, and not in that of any state. It does not point out any state functionaries, or any state action to carry its provisions into effect. The states cannot, therefore, be compelled to enforce them; and it might well be deemed an unconstitutional exercise of the power of interpretation, to insist that the states are bound to provide means to carry into effect the duties of the national government, nowhere delegated or intrusted to them by the Constitution.

On the contrary, the natural, if not the necessary conclusion is, that the national government, in the absence of all positive provisions to the contrary, is bound, through its own proper departments, legislative, judicial, or executive, as the case may require, to carry into effect all the rights and duties imposed upon it by the Constitution. . . .

Congress has taken this very view of the power and duty of the national government. As early as the year 1791, the attention of Congress was drawn to it, (as we shall hereafter more fully see), in consequence of some practical difficulties arising under the other clause, respecting fugitives from justice escaping into other states. The result of their deliberations was the passage of the act of the 12th of February 1793. . . .

In a general sense, this act may be truly said to cover the whole ground of the Constitution . . . not because it exhausts the remedies which may be applied by Congress to enforce the rights, if the provisions of the act shall in practice be found not to attain the object of the Constitution; but because it points out fully all the modes of attaining those objects, which Congress, in their discretion, have as yet deemed expedient or proper to meet the exigencies of the Constitution.

If this be so, then it would seem, upon just principles of construction, that the legislation of Congress, if constitutional, must supersede all state legislation upon the same subject; and by necessary implication prohibit it. For if Congress have a constitutional power to regulate a particular subject, and they do actually regulate it in a given manner, and in a certain form, it cannot be that the state legislatures have a right to interfere, and as it were, by way of compliment to the legislation of Congress, to prescribe additional regulations, and what they may deem auxiliary provisions for the same purpose.

In such a case, the legislation of Congress, in what it does prescribe, manifestly indicates that it does not intend that there shall be any further legislation to act upon the subject-matter. Its silence as to what it does not do, is as expressive of what its intention is as the direct provisions made by it. . . .

[W]here Congress have exercised a power over a particular subject given them by the Constitution, it is not competent for state legislation to add to the provisions of Congress upon that subject; for that the will of Congress upon the whole subject is as clearly established by what it has not declared, as by what it has expressed.

But it has been argued, that the act of Congress is unconstitutional, because it does not fall within the scope of any of the enumerated powers of legislation confided to that body; and therefore it is void. Stripped of its artificial and technical structure, the argument comes to this, that although rights are exclusively secured by, or duties are exclusively imposed upon the national government, yet, unless the power to enforce these rights, or to execute these duties can be found among the express powers of legislation enumerated in the Constitution, they remain without any means of giving them effect by any act of Congress; and they must operate solely *proprio vigore*, however defective may be their operation; nay, even although, in a practical sense, they may become a nullity from the want of a proper remedy to enforce them, or to provide against their violation.

If this be the true interpretation of the Constitution, it must, in a great measure, fail to attain many of its avowed and positive objects as a security of rights, and a recognition of duties. Such a limited construction of the Constitution has never yet been adopted as correct, either in theory or practice. No one has ever supposed that Congress could, constitutionally, by its legislation, exercise powers, or enact laws beyond the powers delegated to it by the Constitution; but it has, on various occasions, exercised powers which were necessary and proper as means to carry into effect rights expressly given, and duties expressly enjoined thereby. The end being required, it has been deemed a just and necessary implication, that the means to accomplish it are given also; or, in other words, that the power flows as a necessary means to accomplish the end. . . .

The remaining question is, whether the power of legislation upon this subject is exclusive in the national government, or concurrent in the states, until it is exercised by Congress. In our opinion it is exclusive; and we shall now proceed briefly to state our reasons for that opinion. . . .

[T]he nature of the provision and the objects to be attained by it, require that it should be controlled by one and the same will, and act uniformly by the same system of regulations throughout the Union. If, then, the states have a right, in the absence of legislation by Congress, to act upon the subject, each state is at liberty to prescribe just such regulations as suit its own policy, local convenience, and local feelings. . . . The right, therefore, would never, in a practical sense be the same in all the states. It would have no unity of purpose, or uniformity of operation. The duty might be enforced in some states; retarded, or limited in others; and denied, as compulsory in many, if not in all. Consequences like these must have been foreseen as very likely to occur in the non-slaveholding states; where legislation, if not silent on the subject, and purely voluntary, could scarcely be presumed to be favorable to the exercise of the rights of the owner.

It is scarcely conceivable that the slaveholding states would have been satisfied with leaving to the legislation of the non-slaveholding states, a power of regulation, in the absence of that of Congress, which would or might practically amount to a power to destroy the rights of the owner. If the argument, therefore, of a concurrent power in the states to act upon the subject-matter, in the absence of legislation by Congress, be well founded; then, if Congress had never acted at all; or if the act of Congress should be repealed without providing a substitute, there would be a resulting authority in each of the states to regulate the whole subject at its pleasure; and to dole out its own remedial justice, or withhold it at its pleasure and according to its own views of policy and expediency. Surely such a state of things never could have been intended, under such a solemn guarantee of right and duty.

On the other hand, construe the right of legislation as exclusive in Congress, and every evil, and every danger vanishes. The right and the duty are then co-extensive and uniform in remedy and operation throughout the whole Union. The owner has the same security, and the same remedial justice, and the same exemption from state regulation and control, through however many states he may pass with his fugitive slave in his possession, *in transitu* to his own domicile. But, upon the other supposition, the moment he passes the state line, he becomes amenable to the laws of another sovereignty, whose regulations may greatly embarrass or delay the exercise of his rights; and even be repugnant to those of the state where he first arrested the fugitive. Consequences like these show that the nature and objects of the provisions imperiously require, that, to make it effectual, it should be construed to be exclusive of state authority. . . .

These are some of the reasons, but by no means all, upon which we hold the power of legislation on this subject to be exclusive in Congress. To guard, however, against any possible misconstruction of our views, it is proper to state, that we are by no means to be understood, in any manner whatsoever to doubt or to interfere with the police power belonging to the states in virtue of their general sovereignty. That police power extends over all subjects within territorial limits of the states; and has never been conceded to the United States. It is wholly distinguishable from the right and duty secured by the provision now under consideration; which is exclusively derived from and secured by the Constitution of the United States, and owes its whole efficacy thereto.

We entertain no doubt whatsoever, that the states, in virtue of their general police power, possesses full jurisdiction to arrest and restrain runaway slaves, and remove them from their borders, and otherwise to secure themselves against their depredations and evil example, as they certainly may do in cases of idlers, vagabonds, and paupers. The rights of the owners of fugitive slaves are in no just sense interfered with, or regulated by such a course; and in many cases, the operations of this police power, although designed generally for other purposes, for protection, safety, and peace of the state, may essentially promote and aid the interests of the owners. But such regulations can never be permitted to interfere with or to obstruct the just rights of the owner to reclaim his slave, derived from the Constitution of the United States, or with the remedies prescribed by Congress to aid and enforce the same.

Upon these grounds, we are of opinion that the act of Pennsylvania upon which this indictment is founded, is unconstitutional and void. It purports to punish as a public offence against that state, the very act of seizing and removing a slave, by his master, which the Constitution of the United States was designed to justify and uphold. . . .

MR. CHIEF JUSTICE TANEY, concurring. . . .

I concur in the opinion pronounced by the court, that the law of Pennsylvania, under which the plaintiff in error was indicted, is unconstitutional and void; and that the judgment against him must be reversed. But as the questions before us arise upon the construction of the Constitution of the United States, and as I do not assent to all the principles contained in the opinion just delivered, it is proper to state the points on which I differ. . . .

The opinion of the Court maintains that the power over this subject is so exclusively vested in Congress, that no state, since the adoption of the Constitution, can pass any law in relation to it. In other words, according to the opinion just delivered, the state authorities are prohibited from interfering for the purpose of protecting the right of the master and aiding him in the recovery of his property. I think the states are not prohibited; and that, on the contrary, it is enjoined upon them as a duty to protect and support the owner when he is endeavoring to obtain possession of his property found within their respective territories.

The language used in the Constitution does not, in my judgment, justify this construction given to it by the Court. It contains no words prohibiting the several states from passing laws to enforce this right. They are in express terms forbidden to make any regulation that shall impair it. But there the prohibition stops. And according to the settled rules of construction for all written instruments, the prohibition being confined to laws injurious to the right, the power to pass laws to support and enforce it, is necessarily implied. And the words of the article which direct that the fugitive "shall be delivered up," seem evidently designed to impose it as a duty upon the people of the several states to pass laws to carry into execution, in good faith, the compact into which they thus solemnly entered with each other.

The Constitution of the United States, and every article and clause in it, is a part of the law of every state in the Union; and is the paramount law. The right of the master, therefore, to seize his fugitive slave, is the law of each state; and no state has the power to abrogate or alter it. And why may not a state protect a right of property, acknowledged by its own paramount law? Besides, the laws of the different states, in all other cases, constantly protect the citizens of other states in their rights of property, when it is found within their respective territories; and no one doubts their power to do so. And in the absence of any express prohibition, I perceive no reason for establishing, by implication, a different rule in this instance; where, by the national compact, this right of property is recognised as an existing right in every state of the Union. . . .

The Constitution of the United States declares that the citizens of each state shall be entitled to all the privileges and immunities of citizens in the several states. And although the privileges and immunities, for greater safety, are placed under the guardianship of the general government; still the states may by their laws and in their tribunals protect and enforce them. They have not only the power, but it is a duty enjoined upon them by this provision in the constitution.

The individual right now in question, stands on the same grounds, and is given by similar words, and ought to be governed by the same principles. The obligation to protect rights of this description is imposed upon the several states as a duty which they are bound to perform; and the prohibition extends to those laws only which violate the right intended to be secured.

I cannot understand the rule of construction by which a positive and express stipulation for the security of certain individual rights of property in the several states, is held to imply a prohibition to the states to pass any laws to guard and protect them. . . .

JONES V. VAN ZANDT, 1846
AN ARGUMENT FOR THE DEFENDANT SUBMITTED TO THE SUPREME COURT OF THE UNITED STATES AT THE DECEMBER TERM, 1846, IN THE CASE OF WHARTON

JONES V. JOHN VAN ZANDT BY S. P. CHASE

ARGUMENT

Mr. Chief Justice and Judges:

I beg leave to submit to your consideration an argument in behalf of an old man, who is charged, under the act of Congress, of February 12, 1793, with having concealed and harbored a fugitive slave.

Oppressed, and well nigh borne down by the painful consciousness, that the principles and positions, which it will be my duty to maintain, can derive no credit what-ever from the reputation of the advocate, I have spared no pains in gathering around them whatever of authority and argument the most careful research, and the most deliberate reflection could supply. I have sought instruction wherever I could find it; I have looked into the reported decisions of almost all the state courts, and of this court; I have examined and compared state legislation and federal; above all, I have consulted the constitution of the Union, and the history of its formation and adoption.

I have done this, because I am well assured, that the issues, now presented to this court for solemn adjudication, reach to whatever is dear in constitutional liberty, and whatever is precious in political union. Not John Vanzaridt alone — not numerous individuals only — but the States also, and the Nation itself must be deeply affected by the decision to be pronounced in this case. I ask, therefore — and the character of this venerable court strongly assures me I shall not ask in vain, — for a deliberate, unprejudiced, and thorough examination of the several positions I shall assume, and of the reasonings and arguments by which they are defended. . . .

The defendant, John Vanzandt, is an old man, of limited education and slender means, but distinguished by unquestioned integrity and benevolence of heart. He is a farmer, occupying a small property in the neighborhood of Cincinnati, and maintaining himself and family by the sale of its products in the markets of the city.

On Saturday, the 23rd day of April, 1842, after attending the market as usual, he went out of the city to Walnut Hills, where he passed the night with a friend. The next morning, when he rose very early to go home, he found in the road a company of negroes, consisting of a middle aged man, his wife, their children, the wife's mother, and two or three other persons, — nine in all. These persons, it appears, had escaped from slavery in Kentucky, and had been conducted, some twelve miles or more, from where they crossed the Ohio, to Walnut Hills.

Vanzandt saw them for the first time in the road where he found them. He had nothing to do with their escape. But, upon their solicitation, or that of the person who had conducted them to Walnut Hills, he undertook to convey them in his wagon to Lebanon or Springborongh, thirty or thirty-five miles northward from Cincinnati.

There was no evidence that he had any positive knowledge that they were fugitives from slavery, or any information whatever on the subject, except what he derived from the statements of the negroes themselves. He believed doubtless, that they were fugitive slaves, but he had no notice whatever, — unless such intelligence as this be notice, — that the negroes had been held to service, or labor in Kentucky under the laws thereof, and had escaped from that state into Ohio.

Under these circumstances he received them into his wagon, which was a covered vehicle of the kind commonly used by farmers attending the markets, and proceeded towards Springborough. One of them, a man named Andrew, took his seat in front, in open view, as the driver of the wagon.

They had travelled about fifteen miles in four hours, when their farther progress was arrested by two bold villains, who, without any legal process, without any authority or request from any claimant or any other person, in broad day, in open breach of the laws of Ohio, undertook to seize the blacks and carry them out of the state by force, on suspicion that they were fugitive slaves. In this daring; and criminal attempt they were successful, except as to Andrew, the driver, who leaped from his seat, and escaped.

All the negroes had been the slaves of Wharton Jones, the plaintiff, and all of them, except Andrew, were recovered. He never returned.

Under these circumstances the plaintiff prosecuted two suits against Vanzandt: one in case, to recover the damages he had sustained by reason of the loss of Andrew, and the expenses of recapturing the others, and another in debt to recover the penalty of five hundred dollars given by the Act of 1793. The first of these actions is still pending in the Circuit Court: the second, which was grounded upon alleged acts of the defendant in relation to Andrew only, has been brought into this Court upon a certificate of division upon various questions, which arose during the progress of the trial, and, after verdict, upon a motion in arrest of judgment.

. . .

I now reach the gravest and most momentous question in this important controversy: — Is the act of 1793 repugnant to the Constitution of the United States?

I am met at the threshold, by the objection, that this question has already received the full consideration and final decision of this court, and is no longer an open question. But, with the greatest deference, I submit that no single decision of any tribunal, however exalted, upon a question of such high consequence as this, should be regarded as absolutely final and conclusive.

I need not, I am sure, remind your honors, that the most thorough investigation, the clearest apprehension, and the largest learning, are not absolute safeguards against error. Even this court has found occasion, heretofore, to revise, qualify, and sometimes, overrule its former decisions: and I feel well assured that the enlightened judges, who now sit here, will not refuse to hear with patience, and consider with candor, an argument, urged, respectfully and in good faith, by the humblest member of the profession, to induce them to recall any decision, however well weighed and unanimous, if pronounced after a single hearing.

Especially will this Court listen to such an argument, when the opinion sought to be changed, was not unanimous; not necessary to the determination of the precise question before the court at the time; and, sustained by those who concurred in it, upon different, if not repugnant, reasons.

The precise question before this Court, in the memorable case of *Prigg v. Pennsylvania*, was this: — Are the statutes of the states, — which denounce as a crime, the abduction from their respective jurisdictions, of persons residing or being within them, — unconstitutional, in their application to the masters and the agents and attorneys of masters, who remove fugitive servants by force, and without any sanction from the laws of the state or from the acts of Congress? In other words, — Does the Constitution of the United States, of itself and without legislation by Congress or the States, confer on the masters of fugitive servants, the right, in person or by their agents, to retake them by force, in any state to which they may have escaped, and convey them out of such state to that from which they fled, without process or judicial sanction; and are all laws of the states to prevent kidnapping or abduction by private force, unconstitutional and void in their application to such cases?

The court held that the master of a fugitive slave may pursue and recapture him, and convey him out of the state in which the seizure is made, without complying with the provisions of the act of Congress or of the state laws on the subject, and that all state legislation making such seizure and abduction penal, is unconstitutional and void.

It may be doubted, indeed, whether this decision can be quite consistent with the affirmation of the constitutionality of the act of 1793. It would rather seem, if it was the intention of the framers of the constitution that the clause respecting fugitive servants should have the effect attributed to it, that they meant to dispense with legislation by Congress and the states altogether; and this conclusion is greatly strengthened by the fact that no power to legislate on the subject is conferred, unless by very remote implication, upon Congress, by the constitution. . . . But, be this matter as it may, it is, at all events, quite certain that it was not at all necessary, in order to reach the decision to which the court came, to affirm the constitutionality of the act of 1793.

No question, therefore, as to the constitutionality of that act was necessarily before the court in the *Prigg* case. Its constitutionality was indeed, affirmed; by some of the judges, as the exercise of a power vested exclusively in Congress; by others, as the exercise of power concurrent in Congress and in the state Legislatures. . . .

In no former case, I think, has so great a diversity of views marked the reasonings by which the several judges of this Court have reached their respective conclusions. Perhaps, also, it is not too much to say, that the decision of the majority, both as to the right of recaption under the constitution, and as to the constitutionality of the act of Congress, has failed to command the assent of the profession, especially in the nonslaveholding states. The decision has been submitted to, as the judgment of the highest constitutional tribunal of the country; but submitted to, generally, in the hope and with the expectation, sometimes expressed and sometimes silently entertained, of its ultimate reversal here.

It is quite certain, also, as I think, that the right of reclamation, converted by the decision into a right of recaption, has not been fortified, but, on the contrary, seriously impaired by it. The right is placed, by the opinion of the court, upon a ground, so repugnant to the feelings of all classes of men in the north and north-west, and so subversive of the sovereignty and independence of the states, that it encounters, at this moment, a degree of jealousy and hostility beyond all former precedent.

The presence of the slave hunter, ranging, at will, through the free states, and clothed with a power, above the control of state laws, and state constitutions, and state authorities, to seize and drag beyond state limits, without legal process, and without any judicial sanction, state or federal, persons, who, for aught that appears beyond his bare assertion, are as much entitled to the protection of the law as he is himself, is a portentous anomaly, not to be contemplated without alarm and irritation. Every attempt to put this power into actual exercise, leads, and must necessarily lead, to commotion and violence; and every scene of commotion and violence tends to gather around the right of reclamation an indignant public sentiment, which must, at length, deprive it of all practical value.

It has been said, that, to the extent of giving the right of recaption, the constitution executes itself. It may be said, 1 think, with entire truth, that, upon the construction given, it not only *executes* itself, but the right of recaption also. If there can be a suicidal power, it is that of seizing, in a free state, persons claimed as fugitives from service, and taking them beyond its limits, by private force, and without judicial sanction.

I proceed, without further delay, to state the proposition which I shall endeavor to maintain. It is this:

The act of Congress of February, 1793, so far as re-lates to fugitives from service, is unconstitutional and void:

1. Because the provisions of the act are repugnant to several positive provisions of the Constitution.
2. Because the Constitution confers on Congress no power to legislate at all upon the subject.

I insist, first, that the provisions of the act of 1793 are repugnant to several positive provisions of the Constitution. In order to obtain a clear understanding of this matter, it will be necessary to advert to the circumstances of the country, and the state of public opinion, at the time of the adoption of the Constitution; and it will also be proper to consider what slavery, as a legal condition, really is.

It is thought, by some, that a leading object in the formation of the Federal Constitution was to secure to the citizens of the slaveholding states their rights of property in slaves. But what is there in the history of the country, or of the Constitution, to warrant such an opinion? On the contrary, does not that history prove that it was the clear understanding of all parties concerned in the establishment of the National Government, that the practice of slaveholding was inconsistent with the principles on which that government was to be founded? And that it was their settled purpose, — however that practice might be tolerated or legalized in certain states, with whose legislation the General Government could not interfere, — that it should receive no national sanction whatever?

It seems to me that no unprejudiced student of our history can come to any other conclusion than this.

The very first act of the first Congress of the Confederation— the memorable non-importation, non-consumption and non-exportation agreement of that illustrious body — contained a clause, by which the delegates pledged themselves and their constituents to discontinue, wholly, the traffic in slaves. This clause has been often quoted, but is of sufficient interest to justify its introduction here:

> We will neither import nor purchase any slave imported, after the first day of December next, (1774,) after which time we will wholly discontinue the slave trade, and neither be concerned in it ourselves, nor will we hire our vessels or sell our commodities or manufactures to those

who may be concerned in it."

Two years afterwards the Declaration of Independence was promulgated. No one will be willing to say that its language was not carefully considered, or that the patriot statesmen, who put their names to it, were hypocrites who sought to delude the world by empty flourishes of rhetoric. It will be admitted that they were earnest men, who meant what they said. Well, these men at that solemn moment, and in that solemn appeal to God and Mankind, chose to put their cause upon the solid foundation of equality of rights among men. "We hold" they said, "these truths to be self-evident; that all men are created equal; that they are endowed by their CREATOR with certain inalienable rights; that among these are life, liberty, and the pursuit of happiness."

This declaration was put forth to the world as an expression of the deliberate judgment of the American People. It was adopted and recognized as its own act by every Colony which acceded to the Confederation. It is not going too far, in my poor judgment, to hold this declaration to be an authentic promulgation of the common law of the Union in respect to the inviolability and inalienability of personal liberty, and inconsistent with the longer continuance of slavery in any of the States. It is not impossible that such was the effect expected from it, by some, at least, of those who put it forth.

Be this as it may, however, it seems to me quite certain that the language of the declaration is wholly inconsistent with the idea that the American States, as *One Nation*, were expected, in any national act, or by any national document, to acknowledge or endure slavery, as an institution fit to be fostered or sustained by national authority.

When the war of the revolution terminated in the recognized independence of the republic, the Congress issued an address to the states, the leading object of which, was to persuade to the provision of a fund for the discharge of the public engagements. In the conclusion of this address, I find this passage, which I deem worthy to be considered in this connection: "Let it be remembered, finally, that it has ever been the pride and boast of America, that the rights for which she contended, were the rights of human nature." Whatever else may be said of this, it cannot be denied that it proves, beyond controversy, that the Declaration was intended to assert the right to liberty, not as vested in a part of mankind only, but as inseparable from human nature itself.

Is it asked, Why did not the Congress of the Confederation, if it intended to assert the rights of all men to liberty, take measures for the abolition of slavery through-out the states? The answer is easy: The Congress possessed no powers adequate to that object. The confederation was a league, rather than an union. The delegates of the states in Congress had no powers, except those conferred upon them in terms by the Articles of Confederation, and those which resulted necessarily from the fact, that the Congress was the sole public representative of the states, in their confederate capacity.

The Congress, therefore, could not intermeddle with the domestic concerns of the states. It could announce principles of justice and right, but it could give practical efficiency to them, as rules of law, only within territory subject to its exclusive jurisdiction. . . .

If any man be disposed to reproach the fathers of the republic with inconsistency and hypocrisy, in not giving practical effect to their declarations in favor of liberty and the rights of human nature, let him turn to the Ordinance of 1787, and be silent. By that great instrument the Congress of the Confederation dedicated that immense national domain to liberty forever, and thus, by one illustrious act, manifested its own sincerity, and furnished a precedent for national action, in all future cases of like nature.

By a single provision, the slavery, then existing in the territory, was abolished, and its future introduction was forever prohibited. And thus the Congress directly asserted, what it had before often indirectly declared, that slavery was incompatible with "the fundamental principles of civil and religious liberty," which constitute the basis of American Government.

These several national acts, it seems to me, supply conclusive proof that it was never intended that the American Nation, should be, in any sense, or in any degree, implicated in the support of slavery: but, on the contrary, that it was the original policy of the government of the United States, to prohibit slavery, in all territory subject to its exclusive jurisdiction, and to discountenance it by the moral influence of its example and declarations, in the states and districts over which it had no legislative control.

Nor is there, as it seems to me, any room for doubt that it was the general expectation, at that time, that slavery, under the influence thus exerted, would disappear from the legislation and the polity of every state, at no very distant period. Evidences of this anticipation, and of the satisfaction with which the prospect was contemplated, abound in the writings of Washington, of Jefferson, of Martin, and other distinguished men of that era: and I am not aware of any single instance of the utterance of a different expectation in any quarter.

Already, at the time of the promulgation of the ordinance, had seven states abolished slavery, or taken decisive measures for abolishing it: and the admission of Maine and Vermont, as nonslaveholding states, was looked upon as certain. On the other hand, there were only seven states in which no measures had been taken for the removal of slavery; and, although the admission of Kentucky and Tennessee was anticipated, I am not aware that history furnishes any warrant whatever, for saying that they were to come in as slaveholding states. On the contrary, the powerful public sentiment in favor of emancipation in Maryland, Virginia, and North Carolina, shared, — especially in Virginia and Maryland, by nearly all the most illustrious public men of the time, — would justly authorize a different expectation.

But, waving this, and conceding, against the weight of evidence, that emancipation was not anticipated in any state south of Pennsylvania, and that every state south of the Ohio was expected to come in as a slaveholding state, it is still certain that the number of slaveholding states, within the limits of the United States, as they existed up to the close of the last century, could, in no event, exceed eleven.

Under these circumstances, the promulgation of the ordinance, by which deliberate provision was made, by the unanimous assent of all the states, for the admission of five new nonslaveholding states, and, consequently, for the permanent ascendancy of the nonslaveholding interest in the councils of the confederacy, proves to me, beyond the possibility of doubt, that it was not expected, at that time, that slavery would be a permanent institution of any state.

Such was the state of opinion at the time the constitution was framed; and the pages of Mr. Madison's report of the Debates in the Constitutional Convention are full of proofs of its influence upon the proceedings of that body. Everywhere we see the clearest evidence of deliberate purpose, to exclude all recognition of the rightfulness of slaveholding, and all national sanction to the practice, from every provision of the constitution.

Mr. Madison, himself, declared that it was "wrong to admit in the constitution the idea, that there can be property in men." Neither the word "slave," nor the word "slavery," nor any term equivalent to either, is to be found in the instrument; and the exclusion of these words, is a most emphatic censure of the practice represented by them. Even the word "servitude," as we have seen, was stricken out on the motion of Governor Randolph of Virginia, and the word "service" inserted in the clause relating to fugitives from service, upon the express ground that the "former was thought to express the condition of slaves, and the latter the obligation of free persons."

It is quite true that the constitution contains several clauses which were designed to refer to slaves; but not one of them refers to slavery as a national institution, to be upheld by national law. On the contrary, every clause, which ever has been, or can be construed as referring to slavery, treats it as the creature of state law, and dependent, wholly, upon state law, for its existence and continuance. Under the constitution, as under the confederation, the national government was intended to be kept free from all connection with it; without power to establish or continue it anywhere; but pledged by every public act of the nation, from the date of the assembling of the first Congress, in 1774, to exert its legitimate authority to exclude it from all national territories, and to discourage it elsewhere, by the powerful influence of example and recommendation.

A different doctrine has sprung up and found favorers since; but that doctrine is not the constitution. It is a pernicious parasite, rather, which, planted by the side of the constitutional oak, by other hands than those of the Founders of the Republic, and nurtured with malignant care, has twined itself around the venerable tree, and now displays its poisonous fruits and foliage from every branch. . . .

I call upon this honorable court to restore the true construction of the charter of our union, by stamping with its decisive disapprobation, every attempt to introduce into it, what its framers studiously excluded from it, a sanction to "the idea that there can be property in men."

The government of the United States, has nothing whatever to do, directly, with slavery. It may, indeed, and does recognize legal and political rights, growing out of the condition of certain persons, under the laws of the states, but it cannot, consistently with the letter or spirit of the constitution, regard these persons as slaves. Under the constitution, all the inhabitants of the United States are, without exception, persons, — persons, it may be, not free, — persons, held to service, — persons, who may migrate, or be imported, — but still, persons, clothed, so far as the constitution is concerned, with those highest attributes of personality, which belong, of right and equally, unless the Declaration of Independence be a fable, to all men. The constitution takes notice indeed, of persons, held, under the laws of the states, in peculiar relations; but it takes notice of such persons, by its own descriptions, and not by those which state laws furnish, it knows no slaves.

What is a slave? I know no definition, shorter or more complete, than this: A slave is a person held, as property, by legalized force, against natural right. Slavery is the condition in which men are thus held. The law, which enables one man to hold his fellow man as a slave, making the private force of the individual efficient for that purpose by aid of the public force of the community, must necessarily, be local and municipal in its character.

It cannot, speaking with strict accuracy, make men property, for man is not, by nature, the subject of ownership. It can only determine that within the sphere of its operation, certain of the people may be held and treated as property of others. It can punish resistance to the authority of the master, and compel submission to his disposal. But, if I may be allowed to introduce here the homely, but most forcible expression of the greatpoet of Scotland: — "A man's a man, for a' that."

The law of the Creator, which invests every human being

with an inalienable title to freedom, cannot be repealed by any inferior law, which asserts that man is property. Such a law may be enforced by power; but the exercise of the power must be confined within the jurisdiction of the state, which establishes the law. It cannot be enforced, — it can have no operation whatever, — in any other jurisdiction.

The very moment a slave passes beyond the jurisdiction of the state, in which he is held as such, he ceases to be a slave; not because any law or regulation of the state which he enters confers freedom upon him, but because he continues to be a man and bares behind him the law of force, which made him a slave. Even if the slave passes from one slave state into another, he is not held as a slave in the state to which he comes, by the law of the state which he has left. So far as that law is concerned, he is free; for he is beyond its reach. He may remain enslaved, or, more properly speaking, he may be re-enslaved under the law of the state he enters: or, that law may refuse to recognize the relation imposed on him by the foreign law, and then he will be absolutely free. There are familiar examples of this, in many slave states. The law of Virginia does not permit the enslavement of native American Indians brought into that state since 1691. Such a person, therefore, though a slave in another state, becomes free, on being brought into Virginia, for the law which enslaved him cannot follow him there.[5] So, also, in other slave states, slaves brought into them, under certain circumstances or for certain purposes, become free. The law of the state, into which they are brought, refuses to lend its aid to their enslavement, and the law of the state, whence they came, cannot reach them, having no force in another jurisdiction.

If I am correct, then, in the position that the Government of the United States, cannot, under the constitution, create, continue, or enforce any such relation as that of owner and property, or, — what is, under the slave codes, the same thing, — of master and slave, between man and man, it must follow that no claim to

---

[5] *Butt v. Rachel*, 4 *Mun*. 211. *Hudgins v. Wright*, 1 *Hen. & Mun*. 133. The first of these cases was argued by those eminent lawyers, Messrs. Wickham and Wirt: the latter of whom the writer is happy to acknowledge as his instructor in the law. They both agreed that slavery is an institution of positive law alone. . . .

persons as property can be maintained, under any clause of the constitution, or any law of the United States.

The clause in relation to fugitives from service is no exception to this remark.

Indeed, it may well be doubted, whether the majority of the convention regarded the clause as applicable, at all, to escaping slaves. The delegates from no state, except South Carolina, appear to have been anxious for any provision of the kind. And after it was introduced, various amendments were made, as we have seen, with the express purpose, of excluding any implication that slavery was "legal in a moral point of view," and of adapting the language of the clause to "the obligations of free persons," and not to "the condition of slaves." It requires no great boldness, with the support of these facts, to affirm that the clause should be construed as providing only for the enforcement of the "obligations of free persons," and not for reconsigning men to the "condition of slaves."

Not insisting on this, however, nor waiving it, it seems to me quite certain, that this clause takes up and deals with no other relation than that of master and servant. It contains no recognition whatever, of any right of property in man. It establishes no rule in relation to negro or mulatto servants, which does not apply equally to white servants held by law.

If, under the clause, a fugitive slave may be reclaimed, it is, not because he is a slave, but because he is a person held to labor. In that character, and only in that character, can he be reclaimed. After he has been brought back to the state where he was held to service, he resumes the condition, whether of servant, apprentice, involuntary servant, or slave, in which he was held prior to his escape: but while out of the state he is as free as any other person until reclaimed.

It follows from this, that any provisions which would be unconstitutional, in their application to other persons, are equally unconstitutional, in their application to escaping servants. Any immunities secured by the constitution to "persons" without distinction, belong, of right, to "persons" escaped from service.

So far as the act of 1793 authorizes the reclamation of servants, escaped into the territories of the United States, it is clearly unconstitutional. If a citizen of a territory cannot sue or be sued in the courts of the union, as a citizen of a state, — surely a person, escaped into a territory, cannot be reclaimed, under a clause, which authorizes, only, the reclamation of persons escaped into a state. It seems highly probable that no provision for the reclamation of servants escaping into a national territory was made, because the ordinance had already provided for such reclamation as to servants escaping from the original states. And this is made almost certain by the fact, that the constitution and the ordinance are almost contemporaneous documents, and the provision as to reclamation in the former, was taken, substantially, from the latter. . . .

I submit, further, that the act is unconstitutional, in all its leading provisions.

It authorizes seizure and confinement, by private force, without legal process. But the third clause of the fifth amendment of the constitution is in these words, "No person shall be deprived of life, liberty, or property, without due process of law." It is vain to say that the fugitive is not a person: for the claim to him can be maintained only on the ground that he is a person.

It is vain to say that the amendment did not regard fugitives from service as persons within its intendment. Not only is there no authority for any such assertion, but it is directly contradicted by historical documents. The recommendation for this amendment came from Virginia, and, as proposed by her legislature, it provided that "no free man shall be deprived of life, liberty or property, but by the law of the land."[6] Congress altered this phraseology, by substituting, for the words quoted, these: "No person shall be deprived of life, liberty, or property, without due process of law."

Now, unless it can be shewn that no process of law at all, is the same thing as due process of law, it must be admitted that the act which authorizes seizure without process, is repugnant to a constitution which expressly forbids it. And this right to seize, and hold, and take before a magistrate constitutes the very essence of the act. Without this right, the act is of no avail whatever. If it fails

---

[6] Consult 2 *Elliott's Debates*, 483, for the amendment as proposed by Virginia: also, 4 *Elliot's Debates*, 216, for the same amendment, as proposed by *New York*, nearly in the terms in which it was finally adopted. (2) 16, Peters 613.

in this, it fails altogether. . . .

But the amendment, prohibiting imprisonment or other privation of liberty, without process, is not the only clause of the constitution infringed by this act. It is equally repugnant to that provision, which declares that "the right of the people to be secure in their persons * * against unreasonable searches and seizures shall not be violated." I ask, how can the people be subjected to seizures more unreasonable, than under this act of Congress?

Even upon the unwarrantable assumption that the escaping servant has no rights, the act still violates this provision of the constitution. The claimant must necessarily select the object of seizure. He is not confined, by the act, to negroes, nor to slaves. He may seize any one, whom he chooses to claim as an escaping servant, and take him before a judge, or a magistrate, without authority except as the claimant's agent. He may be mistaken. He may intend to kidnap. No matter, he may seize, confine, transport; being responsible only in an action for a wrongful taking, if his victim shall ever be fortunate enough to find an opportunity to bring one. Surely, an act which authorizes seizure by private force, upon mere claim, violates that security from unreasonable seizure, which the constitution guaranties to the people.

The constitution, also, declares that, "In suits at common law, where the value of the matter in controversy, shall exceed twenty dollars, the right of trial by jury shall be preserved." Of what value is this provision, if Congress may, by legislation, provide a mode, in which every man, may, at the option of a slave claimant, be put upon trial of his liberty without a jury. . . .

I insist, therefore, that Congress has no power to authorize the seizure and trial of any person without a jury. If Congress has such power in this case, then, in every other, where the constitution confers or guaranties a right. Congress may, without regard to constitutional restriction or limitation, adopt its own mode of enforcing that right, and the people must submit. If this be so, the constitution is waste paper, and we live under a despotism.

The provisions of the constitution, contained in the amendments, like the provisions of the ordinance, contained in the articles of the compact, were mainly designed to establish as written law, certain great principles of natural right and justice, which exist independently of all such sanction. They rather announce restrictions upon legislative power, imposed by the very nature of society and of government,[7] than create restrictions, which, were they erased from the constitution, the Legislature would be at liberty to disregard.

No Legislature is omnipotent. No Legislature can make right wrong; or wrong, right. No Legislature can make light, darkness; or darkness, light. No Legislature can make men, things; or things, men. Nor is any Legislature at liberty to disregard the fundamental principles of rectitude and justice. Whether restrained or not by constitutional provisions, there are acts beyond any legitimate or binding legislative authority.

There are certain vital principles, in our national government, which will ascertain and overrule an apparent and flagrant abuse of legislative power. The Legislature cannot authorize injustice by law; cannot nullify private contracts; cannot abrogate the securities of life, liberty and property, which, it is the very object of society, as well as of our constitution of government, to provide; cannot make a man judge in his own case; cannot repeal the laws of nature; cannot create any obligation to do wrong, or neglect duty.

No court is bound to enforce unjust law; but, on the contrary, every court is bound, by prior and superior obligations, to abstain from enforcing such law. It must be a clear case, doubtless, which will warrant a court in pronouncing a law so unjust that it ought not to be enforced; but, in a clear case, the path of duty is plain. I rejoice that I have the sanction of this Court to all these positions. I rejoice that I am able to add, that much of the language, in which I have stated them, is taken from one of its

---

[7] *Per Marshall, C. J. in Fletcher v. Peck*, 2 *Cond. Rep*. 421.

judgments.[8]

I see not how the judicial enforcement of the claim to property in man can be at all reconciled with these principles; for that claim is admitted by all jurists, and by none more emphatically, than by those distinguished lawyers, whose opinions I have cited from the reports of slaveholding states, to be, not only unsupported by, but directly against natural right.[9]

However this may be, I cannot doubt that the act of 1793, and much more the law of recaption, which has been thought to be contained in the constitutional provision relating to fugitives from service, fall within the very terms of one of the descriptions of unauthorized legislation given by this court, in *Calder v. Bull*; for they make a man the judge in his own cause, and, even more, the executioner of his own sentence. The act of 1793 authorizes the claimant to seize the defendant, without process; to take him, by force, before any magistrate he may select; to hold him, by force, while the magistrate examines the evidences of claim; to remove him, by force, when the certificate is granted.

---

[8] *Colder v. Bull*, 1 *Cond. Rep*. 173. See also, *Dwarris on Statutes*, 11. All writers agree that there is a rule of right, which is of superior obligation to every human law. It is called by Aristotle, 'Ο χcίνος υομος; and I submit two translated extracts from his writings, as descriptive of it. "The law of nature" he says, "is inflexible and has always the same force; as fire burns alike here, and among the Persians." *Rhet. B*. 5, *c*. 10. "For what all men divine is true," he says in another place, "that, by nature, there is a common rule of right and wrong, which has its origin in no common consent, or compact among men." *Rhet. B*. l, *c*. 13, 15.

Cicero speaks frequently of this law: "Est vera ratio, naturae congruens, diffusa in onmes, constans, sempiterna."—"Est recta ratio, numine deorum tracta, impe-rans honesta, et prohibens contraria." — "Lex vera atque princeps, apta ad jubendum et ad vetandum, ratio est recta summi Jovis."

An eminent christian moralist and divine, thus states the same truth: "The law of nature is the only rule and measure of all laws." *Jeremy Taylor's Works*, *Vol*. 3. *pp*. 197 *and* 212.

And an Apostle sums up the whole matter in these words: "We ought to obey God rather than men." *Acts* 5, 29.

[9] It will be observed that I do not rely on the authority of doctors of theology for an account of the nature of slavery. I prefer that of jurisprudents, accustomed to consider questions of right and justice. It will, in future times, be regarded, doubtless, as a melancholy proof of the corruption of religion in our day, that it ministers were so often found among the justifiers and advocates of slavery; and it will be looked upon, probably, as "evidencing, (I use the words of Judge Read, of the Supreme Court of Ohio,) a sort of moral insanity, a breaking up as it were, of the faculties to perceive or distinguish moral truth." See 2 *West. Law Jour*. 286.

The defendant, thus seized and held by force, has no rights, under the law. The act affords him no opportunity to adduce evidence, and imposes no duty on the magistrate to hear it, if adduced. On the other hand, the claimant is allowed to make out his claim by affidavits, which, taken by himself and without cross examination, will always be partial, and, often, false. And, upon such evidence, while the defendant is under such duress and without any right to be heard, the magistrate is to decide.

To complete the atrocious business, and leave no semblance of justice whatever to the transaction, the magistrate is entitled to no compensation for his services, under any law, state or federal; but is left to make such bargain with the claimant as he may. What is this, but to make the claimant, judge, jury and sheriff in his own cause, and to establish his will as law? What is it but to legalize assault and battery, and private imprisonment?

I say fearlessly, that such acts of legislation as this, are subversive of the fundamental principles, on which all civil society rests. Let such acts be passed in relation to other claims. Let every man be authorized to enforce his demands in this summary manner. If he finds a horse, which he thinks his, in the possession of another, instead of resorting to due process of law, and the old fashioned replevin, let him seize the animal, take him before *his own hired magistrate*, and prove his claim by affidavits. If he claims the services of another, which that other will not perform, instead of suing him for breach of contract, let him drag his reluctant neighbor before his magistrate, establish his claim, and then remove him to his task. How long would society hold together, if this principle were carried into general application?

But I am not obliged to resort to any general principle of the natural law, however firmly established. I find firm footing in the constitution, and I take my stand upon its express provisions. The American People, speaking through the constitution, have forbidden Congress to enact, and this Court to enforce any law which authorizes unreasonable seizures, or privation of liberty without due process of law. This prohibition, in my humble judgment, nullifies the act of 1793.

A single proposition remains to be considered. I shall maintain that the act of 1793 is void, because Congress had no power at all to legislate in relation to escaping servants.... What, then, is the true construction of the constitutional provision in relation to escaping servants?

I insist, most respectfully, but most earnestly, that the whole clause shall be interpreted by the ordinary rules of construction, applicable to all provisions of the constitution. It seems to me indefensible, "in order to clear the case of difficulty,"[10] to adopt a special rule of interpretation for this particular clause.

It seems to me, impossible, after a deliberate consideration of the facts of history, and of the most authentic account of the circumstances which attended the incorporation of the clause into the constitution, to maintain that the object of the provision was "to secure, to the citizens of the slaveholding states, the complete right and title of ownership in their slaves, as property, in every state of the union into which they might escape from the state where they were held in servitude." Nor have I been able to discover any historical warrant, or any warrant of any kind, for the statement, that the clause in question "constituted a fundamental article, without the adoption of which, the union could not have been formed."

The provision is, undoubtedly, in restraint of liberty, and it is to be construed strictly. One of the leading objects of the constitution itself was to secure personal freedom: and every particular clause, in derogation of this general object, should be restrained within the plain and necessary import of its terms. In order to ascertain the true sense of any clause, the whole of it should be taken together. No rule of interpretation should be applied, which will not be regarded as valid, when occasion may require, in the construction of every other.

I submit that these are the true principles upon which the provision concerning fugitives from service should be construed, and shall endeavor to ascertain its true import, as to the mode of reclamation, by their aid.

Taking the whole clause together, and examining it in the light of history, I cannot doubt that the intention was, to impose the duty of giving effect to the right of reclamation, upon the states. I would willingly think otherwise. All, or nearly all, the citizens of the free states would, I doubt not, gladly leave the whole responsibility of legislation, upon this subject, to Congress.

---

[10] 16 *Peters* 610 [quoting Justice Story's opinion in *Prigg*].

But, looking at the terms of the provision, and comparing it with similar provisions then in existence, it seems to me clear, that Congress cannot, constitutionally, legislate upon it.

The great purpose of the framers of the constitution was to create a national government, and confer upon it adequate powers. A secondary purpose was to adjust and settle certain matters of right and duty between the states, and between the citizens of different states, by permanent stipulations, having the force and effect of treaty obligations. Both objects were accomplished.

The constitution establishes a government, declares its principles, defines its sphere, prescribes its duties, and confers its powers. It also establishes certain articles of compact or agreement between the states. It prescribes certain duties, to be performed by each state and its citizens, towards every other state and its citizens: and it confers certain rights upon each state and its citizens, and binds all the states to the recognition and enforcement of these rights. These different ends of the constitution, — the creation of a government and the establishment of a compact, — are entirely distinct in their nature.

If all the clauses of compact in the constitution were stricken out, the government created by it would still exist; and, if the articles and sections establishing a form of government were abrogated, the clauses of compact might still remain in force, as articles of agreement among the states. The clauses of compact confer no powers on the government; and the powers of government cannot be executed, except in virtue of express provisions, to enforce the matters of compact.

The clause, in relation to fugitives from service, is nothing else than a covenant or compact, between the states. It has nothing, whatever, to do with the creation of a government, and it confers no powers, whatever, upon the government created by other provisions. It declares that no person, held to service in any state under its laws, escaping into another, shall be discharged from the service, to which he was thus held in the state from which he lied, but shall be delivered up, on claim of the party to whom the service may be due. It restrains the operation of state laws in a particular class of cases, and it obliges each state to the performance of certain duties to the citizens of other states. It is, in the strictest sense, a clause of compact; and the natural, if not necessary, inference from its terms, seems to be that its execution, like that of other compacts, is to be left to the parties to it.

Four similar clauses stand, in juxtaposition, in one article of the constitution. The first stipulates that full faith shall be given in each state, to the public records and judicial proceedings of every other state: the second, that the citizens of each state shall enjoy the immunities of citizens, in the several states: the third, that persons, charged with crime in any state and fugitive from justice, shall, if found in any other state, be delivered up, on demand of the executive authorities of the state from which they fled: the fourth, is the clause under consideration.

There are clauses in other articles which prohibit the exercise of powers by the states; but there are no others, I believe, in the constitution, as originally adopted, intended to secure positive rights to the citizens of each state in all the states. This circumstance is entitled to weight in determining the character of these provisions; and, it certainly points to the conclusion, that they are in the nature of treaty covenants, provision for the execution of which is to be made by the legislation of the parties.

This conclusion is, indeed, excluded as to the first of them, by an express provision that Congress may legislate: but the omission of a similar provision in connection with the others mightily confirms my position as to them. Why make the provision as to the first clause, and omit it as to the other three? It must have been done deliberately and of purpose. Why do it, unless the convention *designed* that Congress might legislate in reference to records, but not in reference to the rights stipulated for in the other clauses?

And is not the reason for the distinction plain? Would not the convention naturally give power to prescribe the proof and effect of records, which could not affect the personal liberty of the citizens? — while they would scrupulously abstain from giving any such power in regard to the subjects of the other clauses, because its exercise would necessarily interfere with the great first right and duty of the State Governments to protect the rightful claims, to personal liberty and security, of all persons within their several jurisdictions.

Another circumstance deserves to be seriously considered. All the provisions I have just enumerated, were taken, with modifications, from instruments in which they stood, without question, as clauses of compact, and nothing else. The provisions in relation to records, to immunities, and to fugitives from justice, were taken from the Articles of Confederation. The provision in relation to fugitives from service, was taken from the Ordinance of 1787. What evidence is there that the Convention, when it transferred these clauses from the Articles and the Ordinance into the Constitution, had any intention to change their nature. Standing where they did, they conferred no power on the general government; what reason is there for holding that they confer such power, standing where they now do?

The clause in relation to records, as it stood in the articles, included no provision authorizing legislation by Congress The Convention, on transferring the clause to the constitution, appended a provision authorizing such legislation; but they appended no such provision to the other clauses. *Expressio unius, exclusio est alterius.* I see not how the inference can be resisted, that it was not the intention of the Convention to authorize legislation by Congress oh the subjects of the other clauses.

There is another, and wholly independent reason for denying the constitutional competency of Congress to legislate in regard to fugitives from service. The whole legislative power of Congress is derived either from the general grant in the eighth section of the first article of the constitution, or from special provisions in relation to particular subjects. We have already seen that there is no special provision authorizing the legislation in question; we must look for such authority, then, in the general grant.

That grant is in these words: "Congress shall have power * * * to make all laws, necessary and proper for carrying into execution all the powers vested by the constitution, in the government of the United States, or any department, or officer thereof." — It is quite certain that the clause, relating to fugitives from service, vests no power in the national government or any of its departments, or officers. How then can the conclusion be avoided, that Congress has no power to legislatc on this subject?

It is urged in the opinion delivered by Mr. Justice Story, that this is too narrow a view of the power of Congress; and various examples are given of legislation by that body, in cases where no legislative power has been directly conferred upon it. But it will be found, I think, that every example fails to sustain the view of the constitution, in support of which it is adduced. — Acts of apportionment, acts to carry treaties into effect, and acts to secure the privileges of members of Congress, acts to suspend the writ of habeas corpus, — all come under the head of laws, necessary and proper for carrying into execution, powers vested in the government, or its departments, or officers. Nor is it going too far to say, that where a duty is enjoined upon the government, or its departments, or its officers. Congress may, by legislation, provide for its performance. Where the constitution enjoins a duty, it is a necessary inference that it gives power to perform it. But the difficulty is, that the fugitive servant clause does not purport to confer a power, or enjoin a duty, on the general government, or any of its departments, or officers. . . .

But the powers of Congress have not hitherto been supposed to be so extensive. — If they are, they certainly warrant the legislation in question, and much more. Congress may, in the exercise of these powers, nullify any state legislation which the constitution forbids. It may, and should, under the clause which secures to the citizens of such state the immunities of citizens of all the states, enforce, in South Carolina and Louisiana, the rights of the negro citizens of Massachusetts, and the quadroon citizens of Ohio.

It may, also, and should, under the clause which forbids privation of liberty, without due process of law, provide for the abolition of slavery throughout the United States. If the premises, furnished by the opinion of Mr. Justice Story, are valid, these, certainly, are legitimate inferences. The doctrine, that, in all cases, where the constitution secures rights to states or individuals. Congress has power to legislate for the protection and enforcement of those rights is original, I think, in that opinion. In view of the consequences which must spring from it, it seems hardly possible that it can be sustained. . . .

It is said, finally, that the nature of the provision furnishes solid reasons for the conclusion, that it could not have been the intention of its framers to entrust its execution to state authorities. This is dangerous ground on which to build a construction of the constitution, in disregard of the plain import of its terms. It may be well met by a direct negative, and by the assertion that the nature of the provision proves, that, neither the Convention, which formed, nor the People, who adopted the Constitution, could have intended to entrust to Congress any legislative power on the subject.

Let it be supposed that when the clause was under discussion, it had been proposed to annex a provision in these words; "and Congress shall have power to appoint officers, and pro-vide by law, for the arresting and delivering up of persons escaping, and to provide, also, for the punishment of all interference with the right herein secured, by harboring, or otherwise:" Can any man believe that such a clause would have received the assent of the Convention? or, that, a constitution with such a clause in it, could have obtained the ratification of the States?

It must be remembered that the States existed before the Constitution, and that the fundamental law of each asserted and guarantied the absolute, inherent and inalienable rights of all the inhabitants or citizens: and it can hardly be supposed that any state, especially any non-slaveholding state, would have agreed to a constitution which would withdraw, from any of these rights, the ample shield of the fundamental law, and leave them exposed to the almost unlimited discretion of Congress, and of officers appointed by Congress? If they could, they must have strangely forgotten the great principles which hallowed their recent struggle.

Am I mistaken, then, in thinking that the whole argument establishes the proposition, that the power to legislate, in reference to escaping servants, is "a power not delegated to the United States by the Constitution, nor prohibited by it to the states, and is, therefore, reserved to the states respectively, or, to the people?"

Much yet presses for utterance: but I have already trespassed too far on the patience of the court.

I have presented, defectively, doubtless, and, perhaps, unsuccessfully, but honestly, and with the best effort of my humble ability, the great principles, legal and constitutional, which, in my judgment, govern this case: and now, with a perfect assurance that all I have urged will receive from your honors a full, patient, and indulgent consideration, I leave the controversy in your hands.

It is the chief glory of Courts of Justice, that they are regarded as the safest sanctuaries of Human Freedom. May such ever be the honorable distinction of this court!

It is a maxim of the common law that he who will not favor liberty, shall be held accursed. "*Execrandus, qui non favct libertali*!" The courts of England, ever presuming, in obedience to this maxim, in favor of freedom, extinguished villeinage, and established an impregnable barrier against the introduction of a new slavery. May I not trust that the favor, shown to Liberty by the courts of the Chief Monarchy of Europe, will not be allowed to surpass that which Liberty will receive, from the courts of the Chief Republic of America?

I am aware that this court will administer the law as it is written in the Constitution: but may I not confidently expect that you will not, willingly, allow any construction of that honored instrument, which will bring its provisions into conflict with that other CONSTITUTION which, rising, in sublime majesty, over all human enactments. — antedating them all, surviving them all, — finds its "seat in the bosom of God," and utters its "voice," as "the harmony of the world?"

Upon questions. — such as are some of those involved in this case, — which partake largely of a moral and political nature, the judgment, even of this Court, cannot be regarded as altogether final. The decision, to be made here, must, necessarily, be rejudged at the tribunal of public opinion — the opinion, not of the American People only, but of the Civilized World. At home, as is well known, a growing disaffection to the Constitution prevails, founded upon its supposed allowance and support of Human Slavery: abroad, the national character suffers under the same reproach.

I most earnestly hope, and, — I trust it may not be deemed too serious to add, — I most earnestly pray, that the judgment of your honors in this case, may commend itself to the reason and conscience of Mankind; that it may rescue the Constitution from the undeserved opprobrium of lending its sanction to the idea that there may be property in men; that it may gather around that venerable charter of Republican Government the renewed affection and confidence of a generous People: and that it may win for American Institutions the warm admiration and profound homage of all, who, everywhere, love Liberty and revere Justice.

PART II: CHASE, THE ANTISLAVERY POLITICAL ORGANIZER

PLATFORM OF THE LIBERTY PARTY—1840

Resolved, That, in our judgment, every consideration of duty and expediency which ought to control the action of Christian freemen requires of the Abolitionists of the United States to organize a distinct and independent political party, embracing all the necessary means for nominating candidates for office and sustaining them by public suffrage.

PLATFORM OF THE LIBERTY PARTY—1843

1. *Resolved*, That human brotherhood is a cardinal principle of true democracy, as well as of pure Christianity, which spurns all inconsistent limitations; and neither the political party which repudiates it, nor the political system which is not based upon it, can be truly democratic or permanent.

2. *Resolved*, That the liberty party, placing itself upon this broad principle, will demand the absolute and unqualified divorce of the general government from slavery, and also the restoration of equality of rights among men, in every state where the party exists, or may exist.

3. *Resolved*, That the liberty party has not been organized for any temporary purpose by interested politicians, but has arisen from among the people, in consequence of a conviction, hourly gaining ground, that no other party in the country represents the true principles of American liberty, or the true spirit of the constitution of the United States.

4. *Resolved*, That the liberty party has not been organized merely for the overthrow of slavery; its first decided effort must, indeed, be directed against slaveholding as the grossest and most revolting

manifestation of despotism, but it will also carry out the principle of equal rights into all its practical consequences and applications, and support every just measure conducive to individual and social freedom.

5. *Resolved*, That the liberty party is not a sectional party, but a national party; was not originated in a desire to accomplish a single object, but in a comprehensive regard to the great interests of the whole country; is not a new party, nor a third party, but it is the party of 1776, reviving the principles of that memorable era, and striving to carry them into practical application.

6. *Resolved*, That it was understood in the times of the declaration and the constitution, that the existence of slavery in some of the states was in derogation of the principles of American liberty, and a deep stain upon the character of the country, and the implied faith of the states and the nation was pledged that slavery should never be extended beyond its then existing limits, but should be gradually, and yet, at no distant day, wholly abolished by state authority.

7. *Resolved*, That the faith of the states and the nation thus pledged, was most nobly redeemed by the voluntary abolition of slavery in several of the states, and by the adoption of the ordinance of 1787, for the government of the territory northwest of the river Ohio, then the only territory in the United States, and, consequently, the only territory subject, in this respect, to the control of Congress, by which ordinance slavery was forever excluded from the vast regions which now compose the states of Ohio, Indiana, Illinois, Michigan, and the territory of Wisconsin, and an incapacity to bear up any other than freemen was impressed on the soil itself.

8. *Resolved*, That the faith of the states and nation thus pledged, has been shamefully violated by the omission, on the part of many of the states, to take any measures whatever for the abolition of slavery within their respective limits; by the continuance of slavery in the District of Columbia, and in the territories of Louisiana and Florida; by the legislation of Congress; by the

protection afforded by national legislation and negotiation to slaveholding in American vessels, on the high seas, employed in the coastwise slave traffic; and by the extension of slavery far beyond its original limits, by acts of Congress admitting new slave states into the Union.

9. *Resolved*, That the fundamental truths of the declaration of independence, that all men are endowed by their Creator with certain inalienable rights, among which are life, liberty, and the pursuit of happiness, was made the fundamental law of our national government, by that amendment of the constitution which declares that no person shall be deprived of life, liberty, or property, without due process of law.

10. *Resolved*, That we recognize as sound the doctrine maintained by slaveholding jurists, that slavery is against natural rights, and strictly local, and that its existence and continuance rests on no other support than state legislation, and not on any authority of Congress.

11. *Resolved*, That the general government has, under the constitution, no power to establish or continue slavery anywhere, and therefore that all treaties and acts of Congress establishing, continuing or favoring slavery in the District of Columbia, in the territory of Florida, or on the high seas, are unconstitutional, and all attempts to hold men as property within the limits of exclusive national jurisdiction ought to be prohibited by law.

12. *Resolved*, That the provision of the constitution of the United States which confers extraordinary political powers on the owners of slaves, and thereby constituting the two hundred and fifty thousand slaveholders in the slave states a privileged aristocracy; and the provision for the reclamation of fugitive slaves from service, are anti-republican in their character, dangerous to the liberties of the people, and ought to be abrogated.

13. *Resolved*, That the practical operation of the second of these provisions, is seen in the enactment of the act of Congress respecting persons escaping from their masters, which act, if the

construction given to it by the Supreme Court of the United States in the case of *Prigg v. Pennsylvania* be correct, nullifies the habeas corpus acts of all the states, takes away the whole legal security of personal freedom, and ought, therefore, to be immediately repealed.

14. *Resolved*, That the peculiar patronage and support hitherto extended to slavery and slaveholding, by the general government, ought to be immediately withdrawn, and the example and influence of national authority ought to be arrayed on the side of liberty and free labor.

15. *Resolved*, That the practice of the general government, which prevails in the slave states, of employing slaves upon the public works, instead of free laborers, and paying aristocratic masters, with a view to secure or reward political services, is utterly indefensible and ought to be abandoned.

16. *Resolved*, That freedom of speech and of the press, and the right of petition, and the right of trial by jury, are sacred and inviolable; and that all rules, regulations and laws, in derogation of either, are oppressive, unconstitutional, and not to be endured by a free people.

17. *Resolved*, That we regard voting, in an eminent degree, as a moral and religious duty, which, when exercised, should be by voting for those who will do all in their power for immediate emancipation.

18. *Resolved*, That this convention recommend to the friends of liberty in all those free states where any inequality of rights and privileges exists on account of color, to employ their utmost energies to remove all such remnants and effects of the slave system.

Whereas, The constitution of these United States is a series of agreements, covenants or contracts between the people of the United States, each with all, and all with each; and, Whereas, It is a principle of universal morality, that the moral laws of the Creator are paramount to all human laws; or, in the language of an

Apostle, that "we ought to obey God rather than men;" and,

Whereas, The principle of common law — that any contract, covenant, or agreement, to do an act derogatory to natural right, is vitiated and annul led by its inherent immorality — has been recognized by one of the justices of the Supreme Court of the United States, who in a recent case expressly holds that "any contract that rests upon such a basis is void;" and,

Whereas, The third clause of the second section of the fourth article of the constitution of the United States, when construed as providing for the surrender of a fugitive slave, does “rest upon such a basis,” in that it is a contract to rob a man of a natural right— namely, his natural right to his own liberty — and is therefore absolutely void. Therefore,

19. *Resolved*, That we hereby give it to be distinctly understood by this nation and the world, that, as abolitionists, considering that the strength of our cause lies in its righteousness, and our hope for it in our conformity to the laws of God, and our respect for the rights of man, we owe it to the Sovereign Ruler of the universe, as a proof of our allegiance to him, in all our civil relations and offices, whether as private citizens, or public functionaries, sworn to support the constitution of the United States, to regard and to treat the third clause of the fourth article of that instrument, whenever applied to the case of a fugitive slave, as utterly null and void, and, consequently, as forming no part of the constitution of the United States, whenever we are called upon or sworn to support it.

20. *Resolved*, That the power given to Congress by the constitution, to provide for calling out the militia to suppress insurrection, does not make it the duty of the government to maintain slavery by military force, much force; when freemen unsheathe the sword it should be to strike for liberty, not for despotism.

21. *Resolved*, That to preserve the peace of the citizens, and secure the blessings of freedom, the legislature of each of the free states ought to keep in force suitable statutes, rendering it penal for any of its inhabitants to transport, or aid in transporting from such

state, any person sought to be thus transported, merely because subject to the slave laws of any other state; this remnant of independence being accorded to the free states by the decision of the supreme court, in the case of *Prigg v. The State of Pennsylvania.*

THE ADDRESS OF THE SOUTHERN AND WESTERN LIBERTY CONVENTION HELD AT CINCINNATI, JUNE 11 & 12, 1845[11] TO THE

---

[11][From the published version of the Address:] The Southern and Western Liberty Convention, held at Cincinnati, on the 11th and 12th June, 1845, was the most remarkable Anti-Slavery body yet assembled in the United States. The call embraced all those who were resolved to act against Slavery, by speech, by the pen, by the press, and by the ballot. It was not therefore exclusively a Convention of the Liberty party; and accordingly not a few were in attendance, who had not acted with that party. The whole number present as Delegates, was about two thousand — from the States of Ohio, Indiana, Illinois and Michigan; from the Territories of Wisconsin and Iowa; from Western Pennsylvania, and Western Virginia, and from Kentucky. Deputations were also present from Massachusetts, New York and Rhode Island; and the whole assembly, including spectators, varied during the sittings from two thousand five hundred, to four thousand persons. Letters were received from *Samuel Fessenden* and *Samuel H. Pond*, Me., *Titus Hutchinson*, Vt., *Elihu Burritt* and *H. B. Stanton*, and *Phineas Crandell*, Mass.; *Wm, Jay*, *Wm. H. Seward*, *Gerrit Smith*, *Horace Greeley*, *Wm. Goodell*, *Lewis Tappan*, New York; *C. D. Cleveland*, *F. Julius Lemoyne*, *Thomas Earle*, Pennsylvania; *F. D. Parish*, Ohio; *Cassius M. Clay*, Lexington, Ky., and *John Gilmore*, Virginia.

It is proper to say, that the Chairman of the Committee which reported this very able address, and by whom the same was written, was *S. P. Chase*, Esq., of Cincinnati.

PEOPLE OF THE UNITED STATES

Having assembled in Convention as friends of Constitutional Liberty, who believe the practice of slaveholding to be inconsistent with the fundamental principles of Republicanism, of Religion, and of Humanity, we think it our duty to declare, frankly, to you, our fellow-citizens, the views which we hold, the principles by which we are governed, and the objects which we desire, by your co-operation, to accomplish. We ask and expect from you a candid and respectful hearing.

We are not a band of fanatics, as some foolishly imagine, and others slanderously assert, bent on the overthrow of all Government and all Religion. We are citizens of the United States, having our homes in the West and the Southwest, some in the Slave States, and some in the Free, bound to our country by the most endearing ties and the most solemn obligations, filled with the most ardent desires for her prosperity and glory, and resolved, so far as in us lies, to carry forward and perfect the great work of individual, social, and civil elevation which our fathers nobly began.

THE REVOLUTION

The American Revolution was not a mere political accident. It was an inevitable result of a long train of causes, all conspiring to make men impatient of oppression. It was a necessary battle in the progress of the great conflict between Despotism and Freedom, between the Aristocratic and the democratic principle. Our fathers so regarded it. They claimed for themselves no new or peculiar rights: they only demanded security in the enjoyment of those rights to which, as descendants of Englishmen, they were entitled under the Great Charter: to which, as men, they were entitled under the grant of their Creator. They asserted the equal right of all men to the immunities which they claimed for themselves. It was impossible that they should not see and feel the gross inconsistency of the practice of slaveholding with their avowed political faith.

The writings of the Revolutionary period afford the amplest evidence that they did perceive and feel it. But slavery was already in the country, interwoven with domestic habits, pecuniary interests and legal rights. It existed under the sanction of the laws of the several colonies, beyond the reach of the direct legislation of Congress. The consequences of an immediate affranchisement of the enslaved were, also, generally dreaded.

Our fathers, therefore, confined themselves to general declarations of the great doctrine of equal rights, which lies at the basis of all just government; and without directly interfering with the legislation of any particular member of the confederacy, endeavoured to establish the National Government and Policy upon such principles as would bring about, at length, the desired result of Universal Freedom.

We solicit your particular attention, fellow citizens, to this statement. It has been the practice of many to represent the American government as the patron and guardian of slavery. Some have even dared to say that it was the purpose of the founders of the government that it should fulfil this office. We join issue with all such persons. We denounce all such representations as libels upon the great men who won and bequeathed to us the precious heritage of Free Institutions. We insist that from the assembling of the First Congress in 1774, until its final organization under the existing constitution in 1789, the American Government was anti-slavery in its character and policy. . . .

First Congress

We, therefore, invite your attention to a memorable act of the First Congress, which assembled in 1774.

The Non-Importation, Non-Consumption, and Non-Exportation Agreement of that illustrious body, signed in their individual and representative capacities, by the delegates of all the represented colonies, and promulgated to the world as the solemn act of United America, contained this remarkable clause: — "We will neither import nor purchase any slave imported after the first day of December next: after which time we will wholly discontinue the slave trade, and neither be concerned in it ourselves, nor will we hire our vessels or sell our commodities or manufactures to those who may be concerned in it.". . . It was, in fact, a deliberate national vow and covenant against all traffic in human beings, and was so understood by the people at large. Virginia proceeded, soon after, to abolish the slave trade by a solemn act of legislation, and her example was followed by all or nearly all the States.

DECLARATION OF INDEPENDENCE

Two years afterwards, the Declaration of Independence was promulgated to the world. In a single sentence of this great Act, our fathers imbodied the fundamental principles on which they proposed to establish the free government of the United States. "We hold these truths to be self-evident; that all men are created equal; that they are endowed by their Creator with certain inalienable rights; that among these are life, liberty, and the pursuit of happiness."

In these words, for the first time in the history of the world, was the doctrine of the inalienable right of every man to life, liberty, and the pursuit of happiness, solemnly proclaimed AS THE BASIS OF NATIONAL POLITICAL FAITH. This declaration pledged its authors, and the nation which made it its own, by adoption, to eternal hostility to every form of despotism and oppression. With this declaration inscribed upon their banners, they went into the war of the Revolution, invoking the attestation of "the Supreme Judge of the world" to the rectitude of their purposes.

After a protracted and dubious struggle the independence of the American Republic was at length achieved, and the attention of Congress was turned to the establishment and extension of free institutions. Beyond the Alleghany Mountains, then the western limit of civilization, stretched a vast territory, untrodden except by the savage, but destined in the hope and faith of the patriots of the Revolution to be the seat of mighty states.

To this territory, during the war just terminated, various States had set up conflicting claims: while the Congress had urged upon ail, the cession of their several pretensions for the common good. The recommendations of Congress prevailed. Among the States which signalized their patriotism by the cession of claims to Western Territory, Virginia was pre-eminently distinguished, both by the magnitude of her grant and the spirit in which it was made.

The claim of Virginia comprehended almost all that is now Ohio, Indiana, and Illinois. She yielded it all, almost with no other condition than that the territory should be disposed of for the common benefit, and finally erected into Republican States. The absence of all stipulations in behalf of slavery in these cessions, and especially in that of Virginia, furnishes strong evidence of the prevalence of anti-slavery sentiment at that day. But the action of Congress, in relation to the territory thus acquired, supplies decisive proof.

ORDINANCE OF 1787

It was in 1787, that Congress promulgated the celebrated Ordinance for the Government of the Territory northwest of the river Ohio. In this ordinance, for the purpose of "extending the fundamental principles of civil and religious liberty; * * to fix and establish those principles as the basis of all laws, constitutions, and governments, which forever thereafter should be formed in said territory," Congress established "certain articles of compact between the original States and the people and States in the territory to remain forever unalterable, unless by common consent."

One of these articles of compact declared that there should be "neither slavery nor involuntary servitude in the territory, otherwise than in the punishment of crimes;" providing, however, that the right of retaking fugitives from service should be preserved to the citizens of the original States. This ordinance was adopted by the unanimous vote of all the States, there being but a single individual negative, which was given by a member from New York. Upon the question of excluding slavery, we may fairly assume that there was entire unanimity.

It seems to us impossible to conceive of a more significant indication of National Policy. The Congress was about to fix forever the relation of five future States to the question of slavery. Under the influence of the liberal opinions of 1776, Massachusetts, New Hampshire, Connecticut, Rhode Island, Vermont and Pennsylvania, had already abolished or had taken measures for abolishing slavery within their limits. It was expected that other Atlantic States would follow their example.

The creation of five non-slaveholding States in the West would evidently secure a permanent majority on the side of Freedom against Slavery. There was, at that time, no other national territory out of which slaveholding States could be carved: nor was there any thought of acquiring territory with such an object. And yet the votes of Delaware, Maryland, Virginia, North Carolina, South Carolina and Georgia were given, and unanimously given, for the positive exclusion of slavery from all the vast region now possessed by Ohio, Indiana, Illinois, Michigan and Wisconsin, and for the virtual restriction of the right of reclaiming fugitive servants to cases of escape from the original States.

There was very little compromise here. There was clear, unqualified, decisive action in the fulfilment and in renewal of the solemn pledge given in 1774, reiterated in 1776, and in pursuance of the settled national policy of restricting slavery to the original States, and of excluding it from all national territory and from all new States. . . .

[N]either in this ordinance, nor in the national acts which preceded it, did the Congress undertake to legislate upon the actual personal relations of the inhabitants of the original States. They sought to impress upon the national character and the national policy the stamp of Liberty; but they did not, so far as we can see, attempt to interfere with the internal arrangements of any State, however inconsistent those arrangements might be with that character and policy.

They expected, however, and they had reason to expect, that slavery would be excluded from all places of national jurisdiction, and that whatever in the arrangements of particular States savoured of despotism and oppression, and especially that the system of slavery, which concentrates in itself the whole essence and all the attributes of despotism and oppression, would give way before the steady action of the national faith and the national policy.

Such was the state of opinion, when the Convention for framing the Constitution of the United States assembled. The ordinance of 1787, which was the most significant and decisive expression of this opinion, was promulgated while the Constitution-Convention was in session. The Constitution, therefore, is to be examined with reference to the public acts which preceded it, and the prevalent popular sentiment.

THE CONSTITUTION

And the first thing which arrests the attention of the inquirer, is the remarkable preamble which is prefixed to the operative clauses of the instrument, in which the objects to be attained by it are particularly enumerated. — These are "to form a more perfect union, establish justice, ensure domestic tranquillity, provide for the common defence, promote the general welfare, and secure the blessings of liberty."

It would be singular, indeed, if a constitution adopted for such objects, and under such circumstances, should be found to contain guaranties of slavery. We should expect, on the contrary, that, although the national government created by it, might not be directly authorized to act upon the slavery already existing in the States, all power to create or continue the system by national sanction, would be carefully withheld, and some safeguards would be provided against its further extension. And such, in our judgment, was the true effect of the Constitution.

We are not prepared to deny, on the one hand, that several clauses of the instrument were intended to refer to slaves; nor to admit, on the other, all the consequences which the friends of slavery would deduce from these clauses. We abstain from these questions.

It is enough for our purpose, that it seems clear, that neither the framers of the Constitution, nor the people who adopted it, intended to violate the pledges given in the covenant of 1774, in the declaration of 1776, in the ordinance of 1787; that they did not purpose to confer on Congress or the General Government any power to establish, or continue, or sanction slavery anywhere; that, if they did not intend to authorize direct national legislation for the removal of the slavery existing in particular States under their local laws, they did intend to keep the action of the national government free from all connection with the system; to discountenance and discourage it in the States; and to favour the abolition of it by State authority — a result, then, generally expected; and, finally, to provide against its further extension by confining the power to acquire new territory, and admit new States to the General Government, the line of whose policy was clearly marked out by the ordinance and preceding public acts.

We cannot think that any unprejudiced student of the Constitution, examining it in the light of precedent action, and contemporary opinion, can arrive at any other conclusion than this. No amendment of the Constitution would be needed to adapt it to the new condition of things, were every State in the Union to abolish slavery forthwith. There is not a line of the instrument which refers to slavery as a national institution, to be upheld by national law.

On the contrary, every clause which ever has been or can be construed as referring to slavery, treats it as the creature of State law, and dependent wholly upon State law for its existence and continuance. So careful were the framers of the Constitution to negative all implied sanction of slaveholding, that not only were the terms "slave," "slavery," and "slaveholding," excluded, but even the word "servitude," which was at first inserted to express the condition, under the local law, of the persons who were to be delivered up, should they escape from one State into another, was, on motion of Mr. Randolph of Virginia, stricken out, and "service" unanimously inserted, "the former being thought to express the condition of slaves, and the latter the obligation of free persons."

That such was the general understanding of the people will be the more manifest if we extend our examination beyond the Constitution as originally adopted, to the amendments subsequently incorporated into it. One of these amendments, as originally proposed by Virginia, provided that "no freeman should be deprived of life, liberty or property but by the law of the land," and was copied, substantially, from the English Magna Charta. Congress altered the phraseology by inserting, in lieu of the words quoted, "no person shall be deprived of life, liberty, or property, without due process of LAW. . . ." and, thus altered, the proposed amendment became part of the Constitution.

We are aware that it has been held by distinguished authority, that the section of the amended Constitution, which contains this provision, operates as a limitation only on national and not upon State legislation. Without controverting this opinion here, it is enough to say that, at the least, the clause prohibits the

General Government from sanctioning slaveholding, and renders the continuance of slavery, as a legal relation, in any place of exclusive national jurisdiction impossible.

For, what is slavery? It is the complete and absolute subjection of one person to the control and disposal of another person, by legalized force. We need not argue that no person can be, rightfully, compelled to submit to such control and disposal. All such subjection must originate in force; and, private force not being strong enough to accomplish the purpose, public force, in the form of law, must lend its aid.

The Government comes to the help of the individual slaveholder, and punishes resistance to his will and compels submission. The Government, therefore, in the case of every individual slave is THE REAL ENSLAVER, depriving each person enslaved of all liberty and all property, and all that makes life dear, without imputation of crime or any legal process whatsoever.

This is precisely what the Government of the United States is forbidden to do by the Constitution. The Government of the United States, therefore, cannot create or continue the relation of master and slave. Nor can that relation be created or continued in any place, district or territory, over which the jurisdiction of the National Government is exclusive; for slavery cannot subsist a moment after the support of the public force has been withdrawn. . . .

We need not go further to prove that slaveholding in the States can have no rightful sanction or support from national authority, but must depend wholly upon State law for existence and continuance.

We have thus proved, from the Public Acts of the Nation, that, up to the time of the adoption of the Constitution, the people of the United States were an anti-slavery people; that the sanction of the national approbation was never given, and never intended to be given, to slaveholding; that, on the contrary, the Government of the United States was expressly forbidden to deprive any person of liberty, without due legal process; and that the policy of excluding slavery from all national territory, and restricting it within the limits of the original States, was early adopted and practically applied.

Sentiments of Distinguished Men of the Revolutionary Period.

Permit us now, fellow citizens, to call your attention to the recorded opinions of the Patriots and Sages of the Revolutionary Era; from which you will learn that many of them, so far from desiring that the General Government should sanction slavery or extend its limits, were displeased that it was not, in terms, empowered to take action for its final extinction in the States, and that almost all looked forward to its final removal by State authority with expectation and hope. . . .

The sentiments of Mr. Jefferson are too well known to justify large quotations from his writings. We invite, however, your attention to two sentences; and will observe, in passing, that his opinions were shared by almost every Virginian of distinguished patriotism or ability.

In his Notes on Virginia, he said: — "I think a change already perceptible since the origin of the present revolution. The spirit of the master is abating, that of the slave is rising from the dust, his condition mollifying, the way, I hope, preparing, under the auspices of Heaven, for a total emancipation; and that is disposed, in the order of events, to be with the consent of the masters, rather than by their extirpation."

On another occasion he said, "Nobody wishes more ardently than I to see an abolition not only of the trade, but of the condition of slavery; and certainly nobody will be more willing to encounter every sacrifice for that object."

In a letter to John F. Mercer, George Washington said, "I never mean, unless some particular circumstances should compel me to it, to possess another slave by purchase; it being among my first wishes to see some plan adopted by which slavery in this country may be abolished by law."

In a letter to Sir John Sinclair, assigning reasons for the depreciation of Southern lands, he said, "There are in Pennsylvania laws for the gradual abolition of slavery, which neither Virginia nor Maryland have at present, but which nothing is more certain than that they must have, and at a period not remote."

General Lee of Virginia, in his "Memoirs on the

Revolutionary War," remarked, "The Constitution of the United States, adopted lately with so much difficulty, has effectually provided against this evil, (the slave trade,) after a few years. It is much to be lamented, that having done so much in this way, a provision had not been made for the gradual abolition of slavery."

Judge Tucker of Virginia, in a letter to the General Assembly of that State, in 1796, recommending the abolition of slavery, and speaking of the slaves in Virginia, said, "Should we not at the time of the Revolution have loosed their chains and broken their fetters or, if the difficulties and dangers of such an experiment prohibited the attempt during the convulsions of a revolution, is it not our duty to embrace the first moment of constitutional health and vigour to effectuate so desirable an object, and to remove from us a stigma with which our enemies will never fail to upbraid us, nor our consciences to reproach us?"

Luther Martin, of Maryland, left the Convention before the Constitution was finally completed. He opposed its adoption, and assigned, in his report to the Maryland legislature, as a leading reason for his opposition, the absence from the instrument of express provisions against slavery. He said that it was urged in the Convention, "that by the proposed system we were giving the General Government full and absolute power to regulate commerce, under which general power it would have a right to restrain or totally prohibit the slave-trade; it must, therefore, appear to the world absurd and disgraceful to the last degree, that we should except from the exercise of that power the only branch of commerce which is unjustifiable in its nature, and contrary to the rights of mankind: — that, on the contrary, we ought rather to prohibit expressly in our Constitution the further importation of slaves, and to authorize the General Government, from time to time, to make such regulations as should be thought most advantageous for the gradual abolition of slavery, and the emancipation of the slaves which are already in the States."

James Wilson, of Pennsylvania, signed the Constitution, taking a very different view of its provisions, bearing upon slavery, from that of Mr. Martin, but agreeing with him entirely as to slavery itself. In the Ratification Convention of Pennsylvania, speaking of the clause relating to the power of Congress over the slave-trade after twenty years, he said: "I consider this clause as laying the foundation for banishing slavery out of this country. It will produce the same kind of gradual change which was produced in Pennsylvania: the new States, which are to be formed, will be under the control of Congress in this particular, and SLAVERY WILL NEVER BE INTRODUCED AMONG THEM. It presents us with the pleasing prospect that the rights of mankind will be acknowledged and established through-out the Union."

In the Ratification Convention of Massachusetts, Gen. Heath declared that "Slavery was CONFINED TO THE STATES NOW EXISTING: *it could not be extended.* By their ordinance Congress had declared that THE NEW STATES should be republican, and have no slavery."

In the Ratification Convention of North Carolina, Mr. Iredell, afterwards a Justice of the Supreme Court of the United States, observed, "When the entire abolition of slavery takes place, it will be an event which must be pleasing to every generous mind and every friend of human nature."

In the Ratification Convention of Virginia, Mr. Johnson said, "The principle of emancipation has begun since the revolution. Let us do what we will, it will come round."

In the course of the debate in the Congress of 1789, the first under the Constitution, on a petition against the slave-trade, Mr. Parker, of Virginia, remarked, that "he hoped Congress would do all that lay in their power to restore human nature to its inherent privileges, and, if possible, wipe off the stigma which America laboured under. The inconsistency in our principles, with which we are justly charged, should be done away, that we may show by our actions the pure beneficence of the doctrine which we held out to the world in our Declaration of Independence." In the same debate Mr. Brown, of North Carolina, observed, "The emancipation of the slaves will be effected in time: it ought to be a gradual business; but he hoped *Congress would not precipitate it* to the great injury of the Southern States." And Mr. Jackson, of Georgia, complained, "THAT IT WAS THE FASHION OF THE DAY to favour the liberty of the slaves." . . .

These citations might be indefinitely multiplied, but we forbear. Well might Mr. Leigh, of Virginia, remark, in 1832, "I thought, till very lately, that it WAS KNOWN TO EVERYBODY, that during the revolution, and for many years after, *the abolition of slavery was a favourite topic with many of our ablest statesmen*, who entertained, with respect, all the schemes which wisdom or ingenuity could suggest for accomplishing the object."

THE CONSEQUENCES EXPECTED TO FOLLOW SUCH ACTS AND OPINIONS

Fellow-Citizens: The public acts, and the recorded opinions of the fathers of the revolution are before you. Let us pause here. Let us reflect what would have been the condition of the country had the original policy of the nation been steadily pursued, and contrast what would have been with what is.

At the time of the adoption of the Constitution, Massachusetts, Rhode Island, Connecticut, New Hampshire, and Pennsylvania, had become non-slaveholding States. By the ordinance of 1787, provision had been made for the erection of five other non-slaveholding States. The admission of Vermont and the District of Maine, as separate States, without slavery, was also anticipated. There was no doubt that New York and New Jersey would follow the example of Pennsylvania. Thus it was supposed to be certain that the Union would ultimately embrace at least fourteen free states, and that slavery would be excluded from all territory thereafter acquired by the nation, and from all States created out of such territory.

This was the true understanding upon which the Constitution was adopted. It was never imagined that new slave States were to be admitted; unless, perhaps, which seems probable, it was contemplated to admit the western districts of Virginia and North Carolina, now known as Kentucky and Tennessee, as States, without any reference to the slavery already established in them.

In no event, to which our fathers looked forward, could the number of slave States exceed eight, while it was almost certain that the number of free States would be at least fourteen. It was never supposed that slavery was to be a cherished interest of the country, or even a permanent institution of any State. It was expected that all the States, stimulated by the examples before them, and urged by their own avowed principles recorded in the Declaration, would, at no distant day, put an end to slavery within their respective limits.

So strong was this expectation, that James Campbell, in an address at Philadelphia, before the Society of the Cincinnati, in 1787, which was attended by the Constitution Convention, then in session, declared "the time is not far distant when our sister States, in imitation of our example, shall turn their vassals into freemen." And Jonathan Edwards predicted in 1791, that, "in fifty years from this time, it will be as disgraceful for a man to hold a negro slave, as to be guilty of common robbery or theft." . . .

It cannot be doubted that, had the original policy and original principles of the Government been adhered to, this expectation would have been realized. The example and influence of the General Government would have been on the side of freedom. Slavery would have ceased in the District of Columbia immediately upon the establishment of the Government within its limits. Slavery would have disappeared from Louisiana and Florida upon the acquisition of those territories by the United States. No laws would have been enacted, no treaties made, no measures taken for the extension or maintenance of slavery.

Amid the rejoicings of all the free, and the congratulations of all friends of freedom, the last fetter would, ere now, have been stricken from the last slave, and the principles and institutions of liberty would have pervaded the entire land.

ACTUAL RESULTS.

How different — how sadly different are the facts of history! LUTHER MARTIN complained, at the time of the adoption of the Constitution, "that when our own liberties were at stake, we warmly felt for the common rights of men: the danger being thought to be passed which threatened ourselves, we are daily growing more and more insensible to those rights."

This insensibility continued to increase, and prepared the way for the encroachments of the political slave power, which originated in the three-fifths rule of the Constitution. This rule, designed, perhaps, as a censure upon slavery, by denying to the slave States the full representation to which their population would entitle them, has had a very different practical effect. It has virtually established in the country an aristocracy of slaveholders.

It has conferred on masters the right of representation for three-fifths of their slaves.

The representation from the slave States in Congress has always been from one-fifth to one-fourth greater than it would have been, were freemen only represented.[12] Under the first apportionment, according to this rate, a district in a free State containing thirty thousand free inhabitants would have one representative.

A district in a slave State, containing three thousand free persons and forty-five thousand slaves, would also have one. In the first district a representative could be elected only by the majority of five thousand votes: in the other, he would need only the majority of five hundred. Of course, the representation from slave States, elected by a much smaller constituency, and bound together by a common tie, would generally act in concert, and always with special regard to the interests of masters whose representatives in fact they were.

Every aristocracy in the world has sustained itself by encroachment, and the aristocracy of slaveholders in this country has not been an exception to the general truth. The nation has always been divided into parties, and the slaveholders, by making the protection and advancement of their peculiar interests the price of their political support, have generally succeeded in controlling all.

This influence has greatly increased the insensibility to human rights, of which MARTIN indignantly complained. It has upheld slavery in the District of Columbia and in the Territories in spite of the Constitution: it has added to the Union six slave States created out of national Territories:[13] it has usurped the

---

[12] The whole number of representatives in the House, is 333. Of these the free States have 135, the slave, 88; and of these 88, but 68 are the representatives of freemen, the remaining 30 being representatives of slave property. . . .

[13] Louisiana, Mississippi, Alabama, Missouri, Arkansas, and Florida.

control of our foreign negotiation,[14] and domestic legislation:[15] it has dictated the choice of the high officers of our Government at home,[16] and of our national representatives abroad: it has filled every department of executive and judicial administration with its friends and satellites:[17] it has detained in slavery multitudes who are constitutionally entitled to their freedom: it has waged unrelenting war with the most sacred rights of the free, stifling the freedom of speeches and of debate, setting at naught the right of petition, and denying in the slave States those immunities to the citizens of the free, which the Constitution guaranties: and, finally, it has dictated the acquisition of an immense foreign territory, not

---

[14] It is well known that by far the greater number of our foreign ministers have been from the Slave States, and that they have ever been most vigilant to promote the interests of those States, while the far more important interests of the Free States have been, comparatively, neglected. In 1841, out of seven persons nominated, in succession, for diplomatic stations, six were from the Slave States, which were all immediately confirmed, while the nomination of the seventh, Edward Everett of Massachusetts, was laid on the table, till the slaveholders could satisfy themselves that he had no views adverse to their "peculiar institutions." What untold benefit would it have been to our Free States, if foreign nations had been induced, as they doubtless might have been, to favour our agricultural and manufacturing products, as they have been induced, by slave-holding ministers, to favour cotton, tobacco, and rice!

[15] No one man has so much influence over our "domestic legislation," as the Speaker of the House of Representatives. He it is that appoints all the committees, which committees bring before the House such subjects, and present them in such aspects, as best suit their views. Since the organization of our government, in 1789, out of the 56 years, the Slave States have had the speaker 38 years, the Free, 18 years. With the exception of John W. Taylor, of New York, who served three years, the Free States did not give a speaker to the House from 1809 to 1845.

[16] Of the TEN Presidents, since 1789, the Slave States have had six. . Next in importance to the President, is the office of Secretary of Slate. . . . Of the 15 who have filled this office, up to 1845, the Slave States have had 10, who have served 37 years; the Free States 5, who have served 19 years.

[17] The Judiciary is the balance-wheel of our government. It takes cognizance of questions of the highest earthly moment— questions of constitutional law — questions of chartered rights and privileges— questions involving millions of property— and, above all, questions that decide the liberty and slavery of man. If there be any spot, therefore, that should be free from sectional bias, it is the Supreme Court of the United States, the judges of which should be appointed, not only for their high legal attainments and integrity, but with reference to the number of inhabitants, and, consequently, to the legal interests of the different parts of the country. But how entirely opposite has been the practice. Of the 30 Judges of that Court, the Slave States have had 17; the Free States 13; and that, too, while the free inhabitants of the Slave States are but about four and a half millions ; the inhabitants of the Free States nine and a half millions— more than double. . . .

for the laudable purpose of extending the blessings of freedom, but with the bad design of diffusing the curse of slavery, and thereby consolidating and perpetuating its own ascendency.

WHAT WE MEANT TO DO.

Against this influence, against these infractions of the Constitution, against these departures from the national policy originally adopted, against these violations of the national faith originally pledged, we solemnly protest. Nor do we propose only to protest.

We recognize the obligations which rest upon us as descendants of the men of the revolution, as inheritors of the institutions which they established, as partakers of the blessings which they so dearly purchased, to carry forward and perfect their work. We mean to do it, wisely and prudently, but with energy and decision.

We have the example of our fathers on our side. We have the Constitution of their adoption on our side. It is our duty, and our purpose, to rescue the Government from the control of the slaveholders; to harmonize its practical administration with the provisions of the Constitution, and to secure to all, without exception, and without partiality, the rights which the Constitution guaranties.

We believe that slaveholding, in the United States, is the source of numberless evils, moral, social and political; that it hinders social progress; that it embitters public and private intercourse; that it degrades us as individuals, as States, and as a nation; that it holds back our country from a splendid career of greatness and glory.

We are, therefore, resolutely, inflexibly, at all times, and under all circumstances, hostile to its longer continuance in our land. We believe that its removal can be effected peacefully, constitutionally, without real injury to any, with the greatest benefit to all.

HOW WE MEAN TO DO IT

We propose to effect this by repealing all legislation, and

discontinuing all action, in favour of slavery, at home and abroad; by prohibiting the practice of slaveholding in all places of exclusive national jurisdiction, in the District of Columbia, in American vessels upon the seas, in forts, arsenals, navy yards; by forbidding the employment of slaves upon any public work; by adopting resolutions in Congress, declaring that slaveholding, in all States created out of national territories, is unconstitutional, and recommending to the others the immediate adoption of measures for its extinction within their respective limits; and by electing and appointing to public station such men, and only such men as openly avow our principles, and will honestly carry out our measures.

The constitutionality of this line of action cannot be successfully impeached. That it will terminate, if steadily pursued, in the utter overthrow of slavery at no very distant day, none will doubt. We adopt it, because we desire, through and by the Constitution, to attain the great ends which the Constitution itself proposes, the establishment of justice, and the security of liberty.

We insist not, here, upon the opinions of some, that no slaveholding, in any State of the Union, is compatible with a true and just construction of the Constitution; nor upon the opinions of others, that the Declaration of Independence, setting forth the creed of the nation, that all men are created equal, and endowed by their Creator with an inalienable right of liberty, must be regarded as the common law of America, antecedent to, and unimpaired by, the Constitution; nor need we appeal to the doctrine that slaveholding is contrary to the supreme law of the Supreme Ruler, preceding and controlling all human law, and binding upon all legislatures in the enactment of laws, and upon all courts in the administration of justice.

We are willing to take our stand upon propositions generally conceded: — that slaveholding is contrary to natural right and justice; that it can subsist nowhere without the sanction and aid of positive legislation; that the Constitution expressly prohibits Congress from depriving any person of liberty without due process of law. From these propositions we deduce, by logical inference, the doctrines upon which we insist.

We deprecate all discord among the States; but do not dread discord so much as we do the subjugation of the States and the people to the yoke of the slaveholding oligarchy. We deprecate the dissolution of the Union, as a dreadful political calamity; but if any of the States shall prefer dissolution to submission to the Constitutional action of the people on the subject of slavery, we cannot purchase their alliance by the sacrifice of inestimable rights, and the abandonment of sacred duties.

Such, fellow citizens, are our views, principles, and objects. We invite your co-operation in the great work of delivering our beloved country from the evils of slavery. . . .

THE DIFFERENT PARTIES

1. *The Democratic Party*

What, then, is the position of the political parties of the country in relation to this subject? One of these parties professes to be guided by the most liberal principles. "Equal and exact justice to all men;" "equal rights for all men;" "inflexible opposition to oppression," are its favourite mottoes. It claims to be the true friend of popular government, and assumes the name of Democratic. Among its members are, doubtless, many who cherish its professions as sacred principles, and believe that great cause of Freedom and Progress is to be served by promoting its ascendency.

But when we compare the maxims of the so-called Democratic party with its acts, its hypocrisy is plainly revealed. Among its leading members we find the principal slaveholders, the chiefs of the oligarchy. It has never scrupled to sacrifice the rights of the Free States, or of the people, to the demands of the slave power. . . .

[I] ts northern leaders . . . declaim loudly against all monopolies, all special privileges, all encroachments on personal rights, all distinctions founded upon birth, and compensate themselves for these efforts of virtue, by practising the vilest oppression upon all their countrymen, in whose complexions the slightest trace of African derivation can be detected.

Profoundly do we revere the maxims of true Democracy; they are identical with those of true Christianity, in relation to the rights and duties of men as citizens. And our reverence for

Democratic principles is the precise measure of our detestation of the policy of those who are permitted to shape the action of the Democratic party. Political concert with that party, under its present leadership, is, therefore, plainly impossible.

Nor do we entertain the hope, which many, no doubt, honestly cherish, that the professed principles of the party will, at length, bring it right upon the question of slavery. Its professed principles have been the same for nearly half a century, and yet the subjection of the party to the slave power is, at this moment, as complete as ever. There is no prospect of any change for the better, until those democrats whose hearts are really possessed by a generous love of liberty for all, and by an honest hatred of oppression, shall manfully assert their individual independence, and refuse their support to the panders of slavery.

2. The Whig Party.

There is another party which boasts that it is conservative in its character. Its watchwords are "a tariff," "a banking system," "the Union as it is." Among its members, also, are many sincere opponents of slavery; and the party itself, seeking aid in the attainment of power, and anxious to carry its favourite measures, and bound together by no such professed principles as secure the unity of the Democratic party, often concedes much to their anti-slavery views. It is not unwilling, in those States and parts of States where anti-slavery sentiment prevails, to assume an anti-slavery attitude, and claim to be an anti-slavery party.

Like the Democratic party, however, the Whig party maintains alliances with the slaveholders. It proposes, in its national conventions, no action against slavery. It has no anti-slavery article in its national creed. Among its leaders and champions in Congress, and out of Congress, none are so honoured and trusted as slaveholders, in practice and in principle. Whatever the Whig party, therefore, concedes to anti-slavery, must be reluctantly conceded. Its natural position is conservative. Its natural line of action is to maintain things as they are. Its natural bond of union is regard for interests rather than for rights. . . .

With what party, then, shall we act? Or shall we act with none? Act, in some way, we must: for the possession of the right of suffrage, the right of electing our own law-makers and rulers, imposes upon us the corresponding duty of voting for men who will carry out the views which we deem of paramount importance and obligation. Act together we must; for upon the questions which we regard as the most vital we are fully agreed.

We must act then; act together; and act against slavery and oppression. Acting thus, we necessarily act as a party; for what is a party, but a body of citizens, acting together politically, in good faith, upon common principles, for a common object? And if there be a party already in existence, animated by the same motives, and aiming at the same results, as ourselves, we must act with and in that party.

The Liberty Party

That there is such a party, is well known. It is the Liberty Party of the United States. Its principles, measures, and objects we cordially approve. It founds itself upon the great cardinal principle of true Democracy and of true Christianity, the brotherhood of the Human Family. It avows its purpose to wage implacable war against slaveholding as the direst form of oppression, and then against every other species of tyranny and injustice.

Its views on the subject of slavery in this country are, in the main, the same as those which we have set forth in this address. Its members agree to regard the extinction of slavery as the most important end which can, at this time, be proposed to political action; and they agree to differ as to other questions of minor importance, such as those of trade and currency, believing that these can be satisfactorily disposed of, when the question of slavery shall be settled, and that, until then, they cannot be satisfactorily disposed of at all. . . .

[T]he Liberty party must exist[,] not as a mere Abolition party, but as a truly Democratic party, which aims at the extinction of slavery, because slaveholding is inconsistent with Democratic principles; aims at it, not as an ultimate end, but as the most important present object; as a great and necessary step in the work of reform; as an illustrious era in the advancement of society, to be wrought out by its action and instrumentality. The Liberty party of 1845 is, in truth, the Liberty party of 1776 revived. It is more:

It is the party of Advancement and Freedom, which has, in every age, and with varying success, fought the battles of Human Liberty, against the party of False Conservatism and Slavery.

WILL YOU NOT JOIN IT?

And now, fellow citizens, permit us to ask, whether you will not give to this party the aid of your votes, and of your counsels? Its aims are lofty, and noble, and pacific; its means are simple and unobjectionable. Why should it not have your co-operation?

ANTI-SLAVERY MEN!

Are you already anti-slavery men? Let us ask, is it not far better to act with those with whom you agree on the fundamental point of slavery, and swell the vote and augment the moral force of antislavery, rather than to act with those with whom you agree only on minor points; and thus, for the time, swell a vole and augment an influence which must be counted against the Liberty movement, in the vain hope that those with whom you thus act now, will, at some indefinite future period, act with you for the overthrow of slavery?

There are, perhaps, nearly equal numbers of you in each of the pro-slavery parties, honestly opposed to each other on questions of trade, currency, and extension of territory, but of one mind on the great question of slavery; and yet you suffer yourselves to be played off against each other by parties which agree in no-thing except hostility to the great measure of positive action against slavery, which seems to you, and is, of paramount importance.

What can you gain by this course? What may you not gain by laying your minor difference on the altar of duty, and uniting as one man, in one party, against slavery? Then every vote would tell for freedom, and would encourage the friends of liberty to fresh efforts. Now every vote, whether you intend it so or not, fells for slavery, and operates as a discouragement and hindrance to those who are contending for equal rights.

Let us entreat you not to persevere in your suicidal, fratricidal course; but to renounce at once all proslavery alliances, and join the friends of liberty. It is not the question now whether a Liberty party shall be organized; it is organized and in the field. The real question, and the only real question, is: Will you, so far as your votes and influence go, hasten or retard the day of its triumph?

ALL MEN OF THE FREE STATES!

Are you men of the Free States? And have you not suffered enough of wrong, of insult, and of contumely, from the slaveholding oligarchy? Have you not been taxed enough for the support of slavery?[18] Is it not enough that all the powers of the government are exerted for its maintenance, and that all the Departments of the Government are in the hands of the Slave power?

How long will you consent by your votes to maintain slavery at the seat of the National Government, in violation of the Constitution of your country, and thus, give your direct sanction to the whole dreadful system? How long will you consent to be represented in the National Councils by men who will not dare to assert their own rights or yours in the presence of an arrogant aristocracy; and, in your State Legislatures, by men whose utmost height of courage and manly daring, when your citizens are imprisoned, without allegation of crime, in slave States, and your agents, sent for their relief, are driven out, as you would scourge from your premises an intrusive cur, is to PROTEST and submit.

Rouse up, men of the free States, for shame, if not for duty! Awake to a sense of your degraded position. Behold your President, a slaveholder; his cabinet composed of slaveholders or their abject instruments; the two Houses of Congress submissive and servile; your representatives with foreign nations, most of them slaveholders; your supreme administrators of justice, most of them slaveholders; your officers of the army and navy, most of them slaveholders. Observe the results. What numerous appointments of pro-slavery citizens of slave States to national

---

[18] According to the Constitution, direct taxes must be apportioned among the several States in the ratio of their representation; and as the slave representatives would increase this number, it would also increase the amount of the tax in the same ratio. . . .

employments! What careful exclusion of every man who holds the faith of Jefferson and Washington in respect to slavery, and believes with Madison "that it is wrong to admit in the Constitution the idea of property in man," from national offices of honour and trust.[19] What assiduity in negotiations for the reclamation of slaves, cast, in the Providence of God, on foreign shores, and for the extension of the markets of cotton, and rice, and tobacco, ay, and of men! What zeal on the judicial bench in wresting the Constitution and the law to the purposes of slaveholders, by shielding kidnappers from merited punishment, and paralyzing State legislation for the security of personal liberty! What readiness in legislation to serve the interests of the oligarchy by unconstitutional provisions for the recovery of fugitive slaves and by laying heavy duties on slave-labour products thereby compelling non-slaveholding labourers to support slaveholders in idleness and luxury!

When shall these things have an end? How long shall servile endurance be protracted? It is for you, fellow citizens, to determine. The shameful partiality to slaveholders and slavery which has so long prevailed, and now prevails, in the administration or the government, will cease when you determine that it shall cease, and act accordingly.

ALL NON-SLAVEHOLDERS OF THE SLAVE STATES!

Are you non-slaveholders of the slave States? Let us ask you to consider what interest you have in the system of slavery. What benefits does it confer on you? What blessings does it promise to your children? You constitute the vast majority of the population of the slave States. The aggregate votes of all the slaveholders do not exceed one hundred and fifty thousand, while the votes of the non-slaveholders are at least six hundred thousand, supposing each adult male to possess a vote. It is clear, therefore, that the continuance of slavery depends upon your suffrages. We repeat,

---

[19] Never was this policy of the slaveholders more conspicuous than in filling the vacancy on the bench of the Supreme Court, occasioned by the death of Judge Thompson, in December, 1843. Two or three most able and upright men were rejected by the Senate, because it was feared that they had sentiments adverse to slavery. And how tame, on all such occasions, have been the Senators from the Free States! But such instances might be multiplied indefinitely.

what interest have you in supporting the system?

THE FRUITS OF SLAVERY.

Slavery diminishes your population and hinders your prosperity. Compare New York with Virginia, Ohio with Kentucky, Arkansas with Michigan, Florida with Iowa. Need we say more?

It prevents general education. It is not the interest of slaveholders that poor non-slaveholders should be educated. The census of 1840 reveals the astounding facts that more than one-seventeenth of the white population in the slave States are unable to read or write, while not a hundred and fiftieth part of the same class in the free are in the same condition, and that there are more than twelve times as many scholars at public charge in the free States as in the slave States.

It paralyzes your industry and enterprise. . . . It degrades and dishonours labour. In what country did an aristocracy ever care for the poor? When did slaveholders ever attempt to improve the condition of the free labourer? . . . Of course the slaveholders are the noble, and you, the non-slaveholders, are the ignoble, of this social system.

Slavery corrupts the religion and destroys the morals of a community. . . . Slavery is a source of most deplorable weakness. What a panic is spread by the bare suggestion of a servile insurrection! And how completely are the slaveholding States at the mercy of any invading foe who will raise the standard of emancipation! In the revolutionary war, according to the secret journals of Congress, South Carolina was "unable to make any effectual efforts with militia, by reason of the great proportion of citizens necessary to remain at home to prevent insurrection among the negroes, and to prevent the desertion of them to the enemy." We need not say that if the danger of insurrection was then great, it would be, circumstances being similar, tenfold greater now. . . .

TO NON-SLAVEHOLDERS.

These, non-slaveholders of the Slave States, are the fruits of slavery. You surely can have no reason to love a system which entails such consequences. Yet it lives by your sufferance. You have only to speak the word at the ballot-box, and the system falls. Will you be restrained from speaking that word by the consideration that the enslaved will be benefited as well as yourselves or by the selfish expectation that you may yourselves become slaveholders hereafter, and so be admitted into the ranks of the aristocracy? If such considerations withhold you, we bid you beware lest you prepare a bitter retribution for yourselves, and find, to your mortification and shame, that a patent of nobility, written in the tears and blood of the pressed, is a sorry passport to the approbation of mankind.

To Slaveholders

We would appeal, also, to slaveholders themselves. We would enter at once within the lines of selfish ideas and mercenary motives, and appeal to your consciences and your hearts. You know that the system of slaveholding is wrong. Whatever theologians may teach and cite scripture for, you know — all of you who claim freedom for yourselves and your children as a birthright precious beyond all price, and inalienable as life — that no person can rightfully hold another as a slave.

Your courts, in their judicial decisions, and your books of common law in their elementary lessons, rise far above precepts of most of your religious teachers, and declare all slaveholding to be against natural right. You feel it to be so. God has so made the human heart, that, in spite of all theological sophistry and pretended scripture proofs, you cannot help feeling it to be so. There is a law of sublimer origin and more awful sanction than any human code, written in ineffaceable characters, upon every heart of man, which binds all to do unto others as they would than others should do unto them.

And where is there one of all your number who would exchange conditions with the happiest of all your slaves? Produce the man! And until he is produced, let theological apologists for slaveholding keep silence. Most earnestly would we entreat you to listen to the voice of conscience and obey the prompting of humanity.

We are not your enemies. We do not pretend to any superior virtue; or that we, being in your circumstances, would be likely to act differently from you. But we are all fellow citizens of this same great republic. We feel slaveholding to be a dreadful incubus upon us, dishonouring us in the eyes of foreign nations; nullifying the force of our example of free institutions; holding us back from a glorious career of prosperity and renown; sowing broadcast the seeds of discord, division, disunion: and we are anxious for its extinction. . . .

We would not invade the Constitution; but we would have the Constitution rightly construed and administered according to its true sense and spirit. We would not dictate the mode in which slavery shall be attacked in particular States; but we would have it removed at once from all places under the exclusive jurisdiction of the national government, and also, have immediate measures taken, in accordance with constitutional rights and the principles of justice, for its removal from each State by State authority. In this work we ask your cooperation. . . .

TO ALL FRIENDS OF LIBERTY, AND OF OUR COUNTRY'S BEST INTERESTS

Finally, we ask all true friends of liberty, of impartial, universal liberty, to be firm and steadfast.

The little handful of voters, who, in 1840, wearied of compromising expediency, and despairing of anti-slavery action by pro-slavery parties, raised anew the standard of the Declaration, and manfully resolved to vote right then and vote for freedom, has already swelled to a GREAT PARTY, strong enough, numerically, to decide the issue of any national contest, and stronger far in the power of its pure and elevating principles. . . .

Let it not be said that we are factious or impracticable. We adhere to our views because we believe them to be sound, practicable and vitally important. We have already said that we are ready to prove our devotion to our principles by co-operation with either of the other two great American Parties, which will openly and honestly, in State and National Conventions, avow our doctrines and adopt our measures, until slavery shall be overthrown.

We do not, indeed, expect any such adoption and avowal by either of those parties, because we are well aware that they fear more, at present, from the loss of slaveholding support than from the loss of anti-slavery co-operation. But we can be satisfied with nothing less, for we will compromise no longer; and, therefore, must of necessity maintain our separate organization as the true Democratic Party of the country, and trust our cause to the patronage, of the people and the blessing of God!

Carry then, friends of freedom and free labour, your principles to the ballot-box. Let no difficulties discourage, no dangers daunt, no delays dishearten you. Your solemn vow that slavery must perish is registered in heaven. Renew that vow! Think of the martyrs of truth and freedom; think of the millions of the enslaved; think of the other millions of the oppressed and degraded free; and renew that vow!

Be not tempted from the path of political duty. Vote for no man, act with no party politically connected with the supporters of slavery. Vote for no man, act with no party unwilling to adopt and carry out the principles which we have set forth in this address. To compromise for any partial or temporary advantage is ruin to our cause. To act with any party, or to vote for the candidates of any party, which recognises the friends and supporters of slavery as members in full standing, because in particular places or under particular circumstances, it may make large professions of anti-slavery zeal, is to commit political suicide.

Unswerving fidelity to our principles; unalterable determination to carry those principles to the ballot-box at every election; inflexible and unanimous support of those, and only those, who are true to those principles, are the conditions of our ultimate triumph. Let these conditions be fulfilled, and our triumph is certain. The indications of its coming multiply on every hand.

The clarion trump of freedom breaks already the gloomy silence of slavery in Kentucky, and its echoes are heard throughout the land. A spirit of inquiry and of action is awakened everywhere. The assemblage of the convention, whose voice we utter, is itself an auspicious omen. Gathered from the North and the South, and the East and West, we here unite our counsels, and consolidate our action. We are resolved to go forward, knowing that our cause is just, trusting in God.

We ask you to go forward with us, invoking His blessing who sent his Son to redeem mankind. With Him are the issues of all events. He can and He will disappoint all the devices of oppression. He can, and we trust He will, make our instrumentality efficient for the redemption of our land from slavery, and for the fulfilment of our fathers' pledge in behalf of freedom, before Him and before the world.

PLATFORM OF THE FREE SOIL PARTY—1848

We have assembled in convention as a union of free men, for the sake of freedom, forgetting all past political differences, in a common resolve to maintain the rights of free labor against the aggression of the slave power, and to secure free soil to a free people; and

Whereas, The political conventions recently assembled at Baltimore and Philadelphia—the one stifling the voice of a great constituency entitled to be heard in its deliberations, and the other abandoning its distinctive principles for mere availability—have dissolved the national party organization heretofore existing, by nominating for the chief magistracy of the United States, under the slaveholding dictation, candidates neither of whom can be supported by the opponents of slavery extension without a sacrifice of consistency, duty and self-respect; and

Whereas, These nominations so made furnish the occasion and demonstrate the necessity of the union of the people under the banner of free democracy, in a solely and formal declaration of their independence of the slave power, and of their fixed determination to rescue the federal government from its control;

1. *Resolved*, Therefore, that we, the people here assembled, remembering the example of our fathers in the days of the first Declaration of Independence, putting our trust in God for the triumph of our cause, and invoking his guidance in our endeavors to advance it, do now plant ourselves upon the national platform of freedom, in opposition to the sectional platform of slavery.

2. *Resolved*, That slavery in the several states of this Union which recognize its existence depends upon the state law, alone, which cannot be repealed or modified by the federal government, and for which laws that government is not responsible. We therefore propose no interference by Congress with slavery within the limits of any state.

3. *Resolved*, That the proviso of Jefferson, to prohibit the existence of slavery after 1800 in all the territories of the United States, southern and northern; the votes of six states and sixteen delegates in the Congress of 1784 for the proviso, to three states and seven delegates against it; the actual exclusion of slavery from the Northwestern Territory, by the Ordinance of 1787, unanimously adopted by the states in Congress, and the entire history of that period,--clearly show that it was the settled policy of the nation not to extend, nationalize, or encourage, but to limit, localize, and discourage slavery; and to this policy, which should never have beef departed from, the government ought to return.

4. *Resolved*, That our fathers ordained the Constitution of the United States in order, among other great national objects, to establish justice, promote the general welfare, secure the blessings of liberty; but expressly denied to the federal government, which they created, a constitutional power to deprive any person of life, liberty, or property, without due legal process.

5. *Resolved*, That in the judgment of this convention Congress has no more power to make a slave than to make a king; no more power to institute or establish slavery than to institute or establish a monarchy. No such power can be found among those specifically conferred by the Constitution, or derived by just implication from them.

6. *Resolved*, That it is the duty of the federal government to relieve itself from all responsibility for the existence or continuance of slavery wherever the government possesses constitutional power to legislate on that subject, and is thus responsible for its existence.

7. *Resolved*, That the true and, in the judgment of this convention,

the only safe means of preventing the extension of slavery into territory now free is to prohibit its extension in all such territory by an act of Congress.

8. *Resolved*, That we accept the issue which the slave power has forced upon us; and to their demand for more slave states and more slave territory, our calm but final answer is: No more slave states and no more slave territory. Lei the soil of our extensive domain be kept free for the hardy pioneers of our own land and the oppressed and banished of other lands seeking homes of comfort and fields of enterprise in the new world.

9. *Resolved*, That the bill lately reported by the committee of eight in the Senate of the United States was no compromise, but an absolute surrender of the rights of the non-slaveholders of the states; and while we rejoice to know that a measure which, while opening the door for the introduction of slavery into the territories now free, would also have opened the door to litigation and strife among the future inhabitants thereof, to the ruin of their peace and prosperity, was defeated in the House of Representatives, its passage in hot haste by a majority, embracing several Senators who voted in open violation of the known will of their constituents, should warn the people to see to it that their representatives be not suffered to betray them. There must be no more compromises with slavery; if made, they must be repealed.

10. *Resolved*, That we demand freedom and established institutions for our brethren in Oregon now exposed to hardships, peril, and massacre, by the reckless hostility of the slave power to the establishment of free government for free territories; and not only for them, but for our brethren in California and New Mexico.

11. *Resolved*, It is due not only to this occasion, but to the whole people of the United States, that we should also declare ourselves on certain other questions of national policy; therefore,

12. *Resolved*, That we demand cheap postage for the people; a retrenchment of the expenses and patronage of the federal government; the abolition of all unnecessary offices and salaries;

and the election by the people of all civil officers in the service of the government so far as the same may be practicable.

13. *Resolved,* That river and harbor improvements, when demanded by the safety and convenience of commerce with foreign nations, or among the several states, are objects of national concern, and that it is the duty of Congress, in the exercise of its constitutional power, to provide therefor.

14. *Resolved,* That the free grant to actual settlers, in consideration of the expenses they incur in making settlements in the wilderness, which are usually fully equal to their actual cost, and of the public benefits resulting therefrom, of reasonable portions of the public lands under suitable limitations, Is a wise and just measure of public policy, which will promote, in various ways, the interest of all the states of this Union; and we therefore recommend it to the favorable consideration of the American people.

15. *Resolved,* That the obligations of honor and patriotism require the earliest practical payment of the national debt, and we are therefore in favor of such a tariff of duties as will raise revenue adequate to defray the expenses of the federal government, and to pay annual instalments of our debt, and the interest thereon.

16. *Resolved,* That we inscribe on our banner, "Free Soil, Free Speech, Free Labor, and Free Men," and under it we will fight on, and fight forever, until a triumphant victory shall reward our exertions.

PLATFORM OF THE FREE SOIL PARTY—1852

Having assembled in national convention as the democracy of the United States, united by a common resolve to maintain right against wrong, and freedom against slavery; confiding in the intelligence, patriotism, and dis criminating justice of the American people; putting our trust in God for the triumph of our cause, and invoking his guidance in our endeavors to advance it, we now submit to the candid judgment of all men, the following declaration of principles and measures:

1. That governments, deriving their just powers from the consent of the governed, are instituted among men to secure to all those inalienable rights of life, liberty, and the pursuit of happiness, with which they are endowed by their creator, and of which none can be deprived by valid legislation, except for crime.

2. That the true mission of American democracy is to maintain the liberties of the people, the sovereignty of the states, and the perpetuity of the Union, by the impartial application to public affairs, without sectional discriminations, of the fundamental principles of human rights, strict justice, and an economical administration.

3. That the federal government is one of limited powers, derived solely from the constitution, and the grants of power therein ought to be strictly construed by all the departments and agents of the government, and it is inexpedient and dangerous to exercise doubtful constitutional powers.

4. That the constitution of the United States, ordained to form a more perfect Union, to establish justice, and secure the blessings of liberty, expressly denies to the general government all power to deprive any person of life, liberty, or property, without due process of law; and, therefore, the government, having no more power to make a slave than to make a king, and no more power to establish slavery than to establish a monarchy, should at once proceed to relieve itself from all responsibility for the existence of slavery, wherever it possesses constitutional power to legislate for its extinction.

5. That, to the persevering and importunate demands of the slave power for more slave states, new slave territories, and the nationalization of slavery, our distinct and final answer is — no more slave states, no slave territory, no nationalized slavery, and no national legislation for the extradition of slaves.

6. That slavery is a sin against God, and a crime against man, which no human enactment nor usage can make right; and that

Christianity, humanity, and patriotism alike demand its abolition.

7. That the fugitive slave act of 1850 is repugnant to the constitution to the principles of the common law, to the spirit of Christianity, and to the sentiments of the civilized world; we, therefore, deny its binding force on the American people, and demand its immediate and total repeal.

8. That the doctrine that any human law is a finality, and not subject to modification or repeal, is not in accordance with the creed of the founders of our government, and is dangerous to the liberties of the people.

9. That the acts of Congress, known as the compromise measures of 1850, by making the admission of a sovereign state contingent upon the adoption of other measures demanded by the special interests of slavery; by their omission to guarantee freedom in the free territories; by their attempt to impose unconstitutional limitations on the powers of Congress and the people to admit new states; by their provisions for the assumption of five millions of the state debt of Texas, and for the payment of five mil lions more, and the cession of large territory to the same state under menace, as an inducement to the relinquishment of a groundless claim; and by their invasion of the sovereignty of the states and the liberties of the people, through the enactment of an unjust, oppressive, and unconstitutional fugitive slave law, are proved to be inconsistent with all the principles and maxims of democracy, and wholly inadequate to the settlement of the questions of which they are claimed to be an adjustment.

10. That no permanent settlement of the slavery question can be looked for except in the practical recognition of the truth that slavery is sectional and freedom national; by the total separation of the general government from slavery, and the exercise of its legitimate and constitutional influence on the side of freedom; and by leaving to the states the whole subject of slavery and the extradition of fugitives from service.

11. That all men have a natural right to a portion of the soil; and

that as the use of the soil is indispensable to life, the right of all men to the soil is as sacred as their right to life itself.

12. That the public lands of the United States belong to the people, and should not be sold to individuals, nor granted to corporations, but should be held as a sacred trust for the benefit of the people, and should be granted in limited quantities, free of cost, to landless settlers.

13. That due regard for the federal constitution, a sound administrative policy, demand that the funds of the general government be kept separate from banking institutions; that inland and ocean postage should be reduced to the lowest possible point; that no more revenue should be raised than is required to defray the strictly necessary expenses of the public service, and to pay off the public debt; and that the power and patronage of the government should be diminished by the abolition of all unnecessary offices, salaries, and privileges, and by the election by the people of all civil officers in the service of the United States, so far as may be consistent with the prompt and efficient transaction of the public business.

14. That river and harbor improvements, when necessary to the safety and convenience of commerce with foreign nations, or among the several states, are objects of national concern; and it is the duty of Congress, in the exercise of its constitutional powers, to provide for the same.

15. That emigrants and exiles from the old world should find a cordial welcome to homes of comfort and fields of enterprise in the new; and every attempt to abridge their privilege of becoming citizens and owners of soil among us ought to be resisted with inflexible determination.

16. That every nation has a clear right to alter or change its own government, and to administer its own concerns in such manner as may best secure the rights and promote the happiness of the people; and foreign interference with that right is a dangerous violation of the law of nations, against which all independent

governments should protest, and endeavor by all proper means to prevent; and especially is it the duty of the American government, representing the chief republic of the world, to protest against, and by all proper means to prevent, the intervention of kings and emperors against nations seeking to establish for themselves republican or constitutional governments.

17. That the independence of Hayti ought to be recognized by our government, and our commercial relations with it placed on the footing of the most favored nations.

18. That as by the constitution, "the citizens of each state shall be entitled to all the privileges and immunities of citizens in the several states," the practice of imprisoning colored seamen of other states, while the vessels to which they belong lie in port, and refusing the exercise of the right to bring such cases before the Supreme Court of the United States, to test the legality of such proceedings, is a flagrant violation of the constitution, and an invasion of the rights of the citizens of other states, utterly inconsistent with the professions made by the slaveholders, that they wish the provisions of the constitution faithfully observed by every state in the Union.

19. That we recommend the introduction into all treaties hereafter to be negotiated between the United States and foreign nations, of some provision for the amicable settlement of difficulties by a resort to decisive arbitrations.

20. That the free democratic party is not organized to aid either the whig or democratic wing of the great slave compromise party of the nation, but to defeat them both; and that repudiating and renouncing both as hopelessly corrupt and utterly unworthy of confidence, the purpose of the free democracy is to take possession of the federal government and administer it for the better protection of the rights and interests of the whole people.

21. That we inscribe on our banner Free Soil, Free Speech, Free Labor, and Free Men, and under it will fight on and fight ever, until a triumph ant victory shall reward our exertions.

22. That upon this platform, the convention presents to the American people, as a candidate for the office of President of the United States, John P. Hale, of New Hampshire, and as a candidate for the office of Vice President of the United States, George W. Julian, of Indiana, and earnestly commend them to the support of all freemen and all parties.

PLATFORM OF THE REPUBLICAN PARTY—1856

This convention of delegates, assembled in pursuance of a call addressed to the people of the United States, without regard to past political differences or divisions, who are opposed to the repeal of the Missouri compromise, to the policy of the present administration, to the extension of slavery into free territory; in favor of admitting Kansas as a free state, of restoring the action of the federal government to the principles of Washington and Jefferson; and who purpose to unite in presenting candidates for the offices of President and Vice-President, do resolve as follows:

Resolved, That the maintenance of the principles promulgated in the Declaration of Independence, and embodied in the federal constitution, is essential to the preservation of our republican institutions, and that the federal constitution, the rights of the states, and the union of the states, shall be preserved.

Resolved, That with our republican fathers we hold it to be a self-evident truth that all men are endowed with the inalienable rights to life, liberty, and the pursuit of happiness, and that the primary object and ulterior design of our federal government were, to secure these rights to all persons within its exclusive jurisdiction; that as our republican fathers, when they had abolished slavery in all our national territory, ordained that no person should be deprived of life, liberty, or property, without due process of law, it becomes our duty to maintain this provision of the constitution against all attempts to violate it for the purpose of establishing slavery in any territory of the United States, by positive legislation, prohibiting its existence or extension therein. That we deny the authority of Congress, of a territorial legislature, of any individual or association of individuals, to give legal existence to slavery in any territory of the United States, while the present constitution shall be maintained.

Resolved, That the constitution confers upon Congress sovereign power over the territories of the United States for their government, and that in the exercise of this power it is both the right and the imperative duty of Congress to prohibit in the territories those twin relics of barbarism — polygamy and slavery.

Resolved, That while the constitution of the United States was ordained and established, in order to form a more perfect union, establish justice, insure domestic tranquility, provide for the common defense, promote the general welfare, and secure the blessings of liberty, and contains ample provisions for the protection of the life, liberty, and property of every citizen, the dearest constitutional rights of the people of Kansas have been fraudulently and violently taken from them; their territory has been invaded by an armed force; spurious and pretended legislative, judicial, and executive officers have been set over them, by whose usurped authority, sustained by the military power of the government, tyrannical and unconstitutional laws have been enacted and enforced; the rights of the people to keep and bear arms have been infringed; test oaths of an extraordinary and entangling nature have been imposed, as a condition of exercising the right of suffrage and holding office; the right of an accused person to a speedy and public trial by an impartial jury has been denied; the right of the people to be secure in their persons, houses, papers, and effects against unreasonable searches and seizures, has been violated; they have been deprived of life, liberty, and property without due process of law; that the freedom of speech and of the press has been abridged; the right to choose their representatives has been made of no effect; murders, robberies, and arsons have been instigated or encouraged, and the offenders have been allowed to go unpunished; that all these things have been done with the knowledge, sanction, and procurement of the present national administration; and that for this high crime against the constitution, the Union, and humanity, we arraign the administration, the President, his advisers, agents, supporters, apologists, and accessories, either before or after the facts, before the country and before the world; and that it is our fixed purpose to bring the actual perpetrators of these atrocious outrages, and their accomplices, to a sure and condign punishment hereafter.

Resolved, That Kansas should be immediately admitted as a state of the Union with her present free constitution, as at once the most effectual way of securing to her citizens the enjoyment of the rights and privileges to which they are entitled, and of ending the civil strife now raging in her territory. Resolved, That the highwayman's plea that " might makes right," embodied in the Ostend circular, was in every respect unworthy of American diplomacy, and would bring shame and dishonor upon any government or people that gave it their sanction.

Resolved, That a railroad to the Pacific ocean, by the most central and practicable route, is imperatively demanded by the interests of the whole country, and that the federal government ought to render immediate and efficient aid in its construction, and, as an auxiliary thereto, the immediate construction of an emigrant route on the line of the railroad.

Resolved, That appropriations of Congress for the improvement of rivers and harbors of a national character, required for the accommodation and security of our existing commerce, are authorized by the constitution, and justified by the obligation of government to protect the lives and property of its citizens.

Resolved, That we invite the affiliation and co-operation of the men of all parties, however differing from us in other respects, in support of the principles herein declared; and believing that the spirit of our institutions, as well as the constitution of our country, guarantees liberty of conscience and equality of rights among citizens, we oppose all prescriptive legislation affecting their security.

PLATFORM OF THE REPUBLICAN PARTY—1860

Resolved, That we, the delegated representatives of the republican electors of the United States, in convention assembled, in discharge of the duty we owe to our constituents and our country, unite in the following declarations:

1. That the history of the nation, during the last four years, has fully established the propriety and necessity of the organization

and perpetuation of the Republican Party, and that the causes which called it into existence are permanent in their nature, and now, more than ever before, demand its peaceful and constitutional triumph.

2. That the maintenance of the principles promulgated in the Declaration of Independence, and embodied in the federal constitution, "That all men are created equal; that they are endowed by their Creator with certain inalienable rights; that among these are life, liberty, and the pursuit of happiness; that to secure these rights, governments are instituted among men, deriving their just powers from the consent of the governed," is essential to the preservation of our republican institutions; and that the federal constitution, the rights of the states, and the union of the states, must and shall be preserved.

3. That to the union of the states this nation owes its unprecedented increase in population, its surprising development of material resources, its rapid augmentation of wealth, its happiness at home and its honor abroad; and we hold in abhorrence all schemes for disunion, come from whatever source they may; and we congratulate the country that no republican member of Congress has uttered or countenanced the threats of disunion so often made by Democratic members, without rebuke and with applause from their political associates; and we denounce those threats of disunion, in case of a popular overthrow of their ascendancy, as denying the vital principles of a free government, and as an avowal of contemplated treason, which it is the imperative duty of an indignant people sternly to rebuke and forever silence.

4. That the maintenance inviolate of the rights of the states, and especially the right of each state to order and control its own domestic institutions according to its own judgment exclusively, is essential to that balance of powers on which the perfection and endurance of our political fabric depends; and we denounce the lawless invasion, by armed force, of the soil of any state or territory, no matter under what pretext, as among the gravest of crimes.

5. That the present Democratic administration has far exceeded our worst apprehensions, in its measureless subserviency to the exactions of a sectional interest, as especially evinced in its desperate exertions to force the infamous Lecompton constitution upon the protesting people of Kansas; in construing the personal relations between master and servant to involve an unqualified property in persons; in its attempted enforcement, everywhere, on land and sea, through the intervention of Congress and of the federal courts, of the extreme pretensions of a purely local interest; and in its general and unvarying abuse of the power entrusted to it by a confiding people.

6. That the people justly view with alarm the reckless extravagance which pervades every department of the federal government; that a return to rigid economy and accountability is indispensable to arrest the systematic plunder of the public treasury by favored partisans; while the recent startling developments of frauds and corruptions at the federal metropolis, show that an entire change of administration is imperatively demanded.

7. That the new dogma, that the constitution, of its own force, carries slavery into any or all of the territories of the United States, is a dangerous political heresy, at variance with the explicit provisions of that instrument itself, with contemporaneous exposition, and with legislative and judicial precedent — is revolutionary in its tendency, and subversive of the peace and harmony of the country.

8. That the normal condition of all the territory of the United States is that of freedom; that as our republican fathers, when they had abolished slavery in all our national territory, ordained that "no person shall be deprived of life, liberty, or property, without due process of law," it becomes our duty, by legislation, whenever such legislation is necessary, to maintain this provision of the constitution against all attempts to violate it; and we deny the authority of Congress, of a territorial legislature, or of any individuals, to give legal existence to slavery in any territory of the United States.

9. That we brand the recent re-opening of the African slave trade, under the cover of our national flag, aided by perversions of judicial power, as a crime against humanity and a burning shame to our country and age; and we call upon Congress to take prompt and efficient measures for the total and final suppression of that execrable traffic.

10. That in the recent vetoes, by their federal governors, of the acts of the legislatures of Kansas and Nebraska, prohibiting slavery in those territories, we find a practical illustration of the boasted democratic principle of non-intervention and popular sovereignty, embodied in the Kansas-Nebraska bill, and a demonstration of the deception and fraud involved therein.

11. That Kansas should, of right, be immediately admitted as a state under the constitution recently formed and adopted by her people, and accepted by the House of Representatives.

12. That, while providing revenue for the support of the general government by duties upon imports, sound policy requires such an adjustment of these imports as to encourage the development of the industrial interest of the whole country; and we commend that policy of national exchanges which secures to the working men liberal wages, to agriculture remunerative prices, to mechanics and manufacturers an adequate reward for their skill, labor, and enterprise, and to the nation commercial prosperity and independence.

13. That we protest against any sale or alienation to others of the public lands held by actual settlers, and against any view of the homestead policy which regards the settlers as paupers or suppliants for public bounty; and we demand the passage by Congress of the complete and satisfactory home stead measure which has already passed the House.

14. That the Republican Party is opposed to any change in our naturalization laws, or any state legislation by which the rights of citizenship hitherto accorded to immigrants from foreign lands

shall be abridged or impaired; and in favor of giving a full and efficient protection to the rights of all classes of citizens, whether native or naturalized, both at home and abroad.

15. That appropriations by Congress for river and harbor improvements of a national character, required for the accommodation and security of an existing commerce, are authorized by the constitution and justified by the obligations of government to protect the lives and property of its citizens.

16. That a railroad to the Pacific ocean is imperatively demanded by the interest of the whole country; that the federal government ought to render immediate and efficient aid in its construction; and that as preliminary thereto, a daily overland mail should be promptly established.

17. Finally, having thus set forth our distinctive principles and views, we invite the co-operation of all citizens, however differing on other questions, who substantially agree with us in their affirmance and support.

Resolution Proposed by Joshua Giddings:

Resolved, That we deeply sympathize with those men who have been driven, some from their native States and others from the States of their adoption, and are now exiled from their homes on account of their opinions; and we hold the Democratic Party responsible for this gross violation of that clause of the Constitution which declares that the citizens of each State shall be entitled to all the privileges and immunities of citizens in the several States.

PART III: CHASE, THE ANTISLAVERY PUBLIC OFFICIAL

SPEECH ON THE RECAPTURE OF FUGITIVE SLAVES

31ST CONGRESS, AUGUST 23, 1850

MR. CHASE. I propose to vote for this amendment; but it will not, in my judgment, satisfy the people of the free States. It seems to be taken for granted that but one class of rights is to be regarded at all in this controversy—the rights of masters. Now, sir, I am one of those who believe that all the duties which arise from the Constitution, in regard to fugitives from labor, devolves upon the States, and upon the States exclusively.

The Senator from Massachusetts, [MR. WEBSTER] who originally introduced this amendment, has said that, in his judgment, these clauses were clauses of compact, binding upon the State. I suppose that that is a true description of their character. If that is the case, then, I do not see the source from which Congress derives its power of legislation upon this subject. But, if Congress has the power, it is by implication from these clauses of the compact, and it is to be exercised with a sound regard to the rights of all concerned.

It has been said that there is no danger to be apprehended by free persons of color, from the operation of the act now proposed; and we have been challenged to the production of a case where claimants have kidnapped any one, or have claimed the possession of any one when they were not entitled to his service. In the section in which I reside, cases of kidnapping have not unfrequently occurred. Not a few persons supposed to be free, and in some cases certainly free, have been kidnapped, and carried out of the State by force or fraud, without any process of law.

Nor is it true, as seems to be supposed by many here, that a person charged with this crime in Ohio or Indiana, who may escape into Kentucky, will be delivered up upon the demand of the Governor of Ohio, under the clause of the Constitution relating to fugitives from justice. A mere demand is not sufficient. It is not enough for an officer from the State of Ohio, commissioned by the Executive, to go into Kentucky and make a demand for the kidnapper. He must submit the charge to the Executive of Kentucky, who must refer the case to a judge; and if the evidence of the crime is not satisfactory, he is not surrendered. . . .

It seems to me very clear that this right—if it be a right under the Constitution—is to be placed upon the same footing as every other statutory right. It cannot safely be placed upon any other ground. Claims of right in the services of individuals found under the protection of the laws of a free State must be investigated in the same manner as other claims of right.

If the most ordinary controversy involving a contested claim to twenty dollars must be decided by a jury, surely a controversy which involves the right of man to his liberty should have a similar trial. And my objection to the amendment proposed by the Senator from New Jersey is, that it requires, as a condition to a jury trial, an affidavit of the party claimed that he is free. No such condition should be imposed. The defence to a claim of the custody and service of any man should be as free from every embarrassment as any other defence against any other claim.

One other word, sir. Difficulties have arisen in the free States in regard to the recovery of fugitives from labor; but have they not arisen in consequence of attempts to seize alleged fugitives without any process?

MR. MASON. It is perfectly lawful to do so.

MR. CHASE. I know that it has been so decided, but I think the decision wrong. I do not believe that a slave claimant can go into any State of this Union and take a person under this protection of its laws, and, upon his mere assertion that the person seized is a fugitive from labor, carry him off, without process, by private force. I deny utterly that any such proceeding is warranted by the Constitution.

The decision in the case of *Prigg*, I am aware, goes that length; but that decision never commanded the assent of my judgment. And, sir, just so long as the right to use private force without process in cases of this kind is insisted upon and acted upon, just so long will these difficulties continue. Upon that gentlemen may rely.

It will not do for any man to go into a State where every legal presumption is in favor of freedom and seize a person whom he claims as a fugitive slave, and say "this man is my slave, and by my authority under the Constitution of the United States I shall carry him off, and whoever interfered does so at his peril." He is asked where is your warrant, and he produces none; where is your evidence of claim, and he offers none. The language of his action is, "my word stands for law; the laws of your State stand for nothing against my claim."

In every case so far as I am aware, where excitement and

violence have occurred, it has been in consequence of the assertion of such a right as this. And you may rely upon it that so long as such a right is practically asserted, there will be excitement. You may rely upon it that so long as you send your agents in to the free States to seize and carry off this class of persons, without any trial, and upon no other authority that that of the claimant, so long you encounter difficulties and serious difficulties. A large share of all the trouble that has arisen is due to this case of *Pennsylvania vs. Prigg*. Before that decision, every State, I believe, had legislated upon the subject, and very little complaint had been made of difficulties in the reclamation of fugitives. Most of the States had very summary remedies. They had legislated quite as far as any one claimed they ought to legislate. . . .

MR. CHASE. I now move to strike out the second section of the amendment. The object of the motion is to restrict the operation of the act, in conformity with the provisions of the Constitution, to slaves escaping from one State into another.

The section which was proposed to be stricken out was then read, as follows:

> *And be it further enacted*, That the superior court of each organized Territory of the United States shall have the same power to appoint commissioners to take acknowledgements of bail and affidavit, and to take depositions of witnesses in civil causes, which is now possessed by the circuit courts of the United States; and all commissioners who shall hereafter be appointed for such purposes by the superior court of any organized Territory of the United States, shall possess all the powers and exercise all the duties conferred by law upon the commissioners appointed by the circuit courts of the United States for similar purposes; and shall, moreover, exercise and discharge all the powers and duties conferred by the third section of the act of Congress, approved February 12, 1793, in the preceding section of this act mentioned.

MR. CHASE. The object of the amendment is to conform the provisions of this bill to the provisions of the Constitution. The Constitution provides that "no person held to service or labor in one State, under the laws thereof, escaping into another, shall, in consequence of any law or regulation therein, be discharged from such service or labor, but shall be delivered up." The terms of the Constitution confine the right of reclamation to the taking of persons escaping from one State into another State. This section extends the remedy, or the right of reclamation where it does not exist, to the Territories. That is the reason why I desire that it may be stricken out.

MR. BERRIEN. I really hope this amendment will not prevail. It indicates a disposition, or it will indicate a disposition, in the view of the people at large, to do what is absolutely required by the letter of the Constitution, and refuse that spirit which renders the duty imperative.

The object of that provision of the Constitution was unquestionably to secure to southern slaveholders undisturbed possession of this property. The reason why the term "Territories" is not found in the clause of the Constitution is obvious; but the power of Congress to make such a provision for the Territories cannot be doubted.

In justice, and in accordance with the spirit of the Constitution, no possible reason can be assigned why the owners of slave property should be entitled to recover it if escaping into a State, and should be deprived of the same privilege if the slave escapes into a Territory. The only difference that can be pointed out in the two cases is, that, with regard to States, the obligation is rendered imperative by the Constitution; with regard to Territories, it is only imperative by the principles of justice, and by that obligation which the United States owes to its citizens, to protect them in the enjoyment of property which is lawfully held.

MR. BUTLER. I think there is a very obvious reason why Territories are not referred to in the Constitution. The framers of the Constitution knew very well the power of a State government to exclude slavery; but the very fact that Territories were not included presupposes that they were free for all the citizens of the United States without restriction. That is the reason nothing was said about Territories. The framers of the Constitution never dreamed that slavery would be excluded except by State governments. So far as relates to the Territories, they considered them free for all the citizens of the United States to settle in.

As regards the argument of the Senator from Georgia, I

acquiesce in it. Surely we have a right to include Territories; and the fact that nothing is said about Territories in the Constitution, is the strongest argument to show that Congress had no right to exclude citizens of the United States from the enjoyment of the rights in the Territories.

MR. UNDERWOOD. Here is a provision made in the act of 1793 that when persons held to service or labor in any of the States of the United States, or in any of the Territories on the north side of the Ohio river, under the laws thereof, shall escape into any of said States or Territories, he shall be delivered up on claim of the party to whom such service or labor may be due.

Now, the first exposition of the Constitution of the United States provided for the return of fugitive slaves from the Territories as well as from the States. We have exclusive jurisdiction over the Territories. No other power can interfere there. And shall we refuse to do in a Territory subject to our jurisdiction that which the Constitution requires us to do in a State?

Sir, I am surprised that the gentleman from Ohio should thus endeavor to change the principle of the law of 1793, which we have acted upon from that day down to this; that we should now endeavor to restrict the return of slaves when they have fled from a State to a Territory, and especially when we have exclusive jurisdiction over the Territories into which these slaves may escape.

MR. CHASE. I wish to say a few words in reply to suggestions made by different gentlemen. The Senator from Georgia thinks we ought to legislate in conformity with the spirit as well as the letter, of the Constitution; and although the letter of the Constitution does not authorize or bind the General Government to return fugitive slaves who have escaped into Territories, still we ought to assume a power beyond the Constitution, and legislate for that object.

I suppose the tribunals of almost every State in the Union, before which this question of slavery has come, have determined—so that it is not now a matter open to controversy—that slavery is a local institution, that the slave is reduced to the condition in which he is by force—force, legalized by the law of the State in which slavery exists—and that when the slave passes beyond the jurisdiction in which that force is legalized, he ceases to be a slave, simply because the power to detain him in slavery does not accompany him.

That is a doctrine which is held very generally, and which has been asserted throughout the northern States almost universally, as one of the grounds upon which it would be safe to withhold the application of the Wilmot proviso from the Territories. The argument has been, that if a slave passes from the jurisdiction of the State in which he is held as such under the municipal law of the State, he ceases to be a slave, because there is no authority by which he can be held.

If that be true, if that be a valid argument, and we yet legislate so as to recognize the continuance of the right of property in a slave, the right of absolute control over a slave in a Territory, as a matter of course it follows that we legislate to establish slavery in the Territories.

MR. UNDERWOOD. Will the gentleman allow me a moment?

MR. CHASE. I shall be through in a moment

THE PRESIDENT. The Senator must be permitted to conclude his remarks.

MR. UNDERWOOD. I wish to call his attention to the ordinance of 1787.

MR. CHASE. I was coming to that immediately.

MR. UNDERWOOD. That ordinance says: "There shall be neither slavery nor involuntary servitude in the said Territory, otherwise than in the punishment of crimes whereof the party shall have been duly convicted."

We have all heard that repeated so often that every child has it by heart. Listen to what follows: "*Provided, always,* That any person escaping into the same, from whom labor or service is lawfully claimed in any one of the original States, such fugitive may be lawfully reclaimed, and conveyed to the person claiming his or her labor or service aforesaid."

That is a part of that very celebrated ordinance of 1787, and a part of the same sentence that contains the provision which the gentleman is so anxious to apply to this bill. I think it all ought to go together. I am opposed to taking the first part and leaving the residue.

MR. CHASE. I am willing to compromise the matter with

the Senator from Kentucky, since compromises are so fashionable, and adopt the whole together. But I was saying when he interrupted me, that if we legislate so as to recognize slavery where the Constitution by its terms does not carry it, we do to that extent establish slavery in the Territories.

Non-intervention has been frequently asserted to be the doctrine of the Democratic party, and always justified to the people of the North upon this identical ground, that slavery could not go beyond the jurisdiction of the State which maintains it; that the Government of the United States has no power to establish slavery, and therefore that it cannot be introduced into the Territories.

Now, sir, let us act upon some principle. If slaveholding is right in itself—if the relation which it establishes is, as some say, a relation founded in the law of nature, like that of husband and wife, parent and child, guardian and ward—if, also, the Constitution confers the power and imposes the duty of legislation for its maintenance upon Congress—then let all the protection be given to the institution which southern gentlemen, however extreme, claim for it. Their claims, if these propositions be conceded to them, can hardly go beyond our duties.

But if, on the other hand, slaveholding is condemned by the law of nature, as the decisions, even of the slave States, declare it is; if slavery is a local institution, created by State law, and dependent upon State law for its existence and continuance, let us act upon this principle as if we believed in it, and declare that slavery cannot be extended beyond State jurisdiction, and deny its support the power of the National Government in the Territories.

No one contends that the fugitive servant clause of the Constitution applies to slaves escaped into Territories. If Congress legislates for the surrender of such persons, the power to do so must be sought elsewhere.

The Senator from Georgia [MR. BERRIEN] finds it in the power of Congress to "make all needful rules and regulations respecting the territory or other property of the United States." He claims that this clause confers on Congress an unlimited power of legislation over the Territories. Others maintain that it confers no power of legislation at all.

The correct opinion, I think, lies between these extremes.

Congress has the power of legislation over the Territories; not an arbitrary, unlimited power, but on fixed and limited by the general principles of the Constitution. It does not authorize Congress to reduce anybody to slavery, or to authorize slavery in any way or to any extent. If it did, there is no institution of arbitrary power which Congress might not establish in the Territories.

I deny, then, the existence of the unlimited power asserted for Congress. Of course I do not admit the inference deduced by the Senator from Georgia, from its assumed existence.

But the Senator from Kentucky [MR. UNDERWOOD] refers to the ordinance of 1787. A very slight examination will satisfy any thinking man that this ordinance gives no countenance to the claim of power over this subject now made for Congress.

The original policy of this Government was against the extension of slavery. The patriots who framed it and framed the ordinance—cotemporaneous acts—never anticipated the reclamation of slaves from Territories, under the Constitution. That instrument stipulated for the surrender of servants escaped from one *State* into *another*. The ordinance provided for the surrender of servants escaping from the original States into the only territory of the United States then existing. This provision was confined, it will be observed to servants escaped from the *original* States.

The Constitution and the ordinance covered the grounds intended to be covered. The Constitution provided for cases of escape from a State into a State; the ordinance for cases of escape from an original State into territory northwest of the Ohio. Escapes from States into other territories we left unprovided for.

The extinction of slavery itself was expected at no very remote period; and the last thing that the framers of the Constitution or the ordinance would have thought of would have been a provision looking to its perpetuity and indefinite extension. The ordinance, then, affords no evidence of the existence, and no countenance to the exercise of any such power as is now invoked.

The Senator from Kentucky also relies on the act of 1793 as a cotemporaneous exposition of the Constitution, and an authority in favor of the existence of the power. That act provides for the surrender of fugitives escaped into Territories; and the exercise of the power, at so early a period, proves—so runs the argument—

its constitutionality.

But it must be remembered that the same Congress, by the same act, conferred judicial power on State magistrates, and this the Supreme Court has decided could not constitutionally be done. This fact nullifies the authority of this act, as a cotemporaneous construction of the Constitution. The Congress which enacted it mistook their power as to State magistrates; they might as easily mistake their power as to the Territories. . . .

MR. BUTLER. Really, Mr. President, I am not surprised at anything in these days; but, if I understand the proposition of the gentleman from Ohio, it involves this: that a runaway slave may be reclaimed from a State, but that he cannot be reclaimed from a Territory; in other words, that a runaway slave is in a better condition in one of the countries or communities under the General Government of the United States than he is in a State where slavery is prohibited. . . .

On this question, sir, I shall ask for the yeas and nays, to see how far these perverse notions may prevail, and to see how many Senators entertain them, for I think this is—I will not say the most extravagant proposition, but, at all events, the indication of a disposition to torture the Constitution so as to make it an engine of oppression and exclusion.

Sir, our fathers who made this Constitution never contemplated that in the Territories there was any necessity for such a law as this, because it was supposed that these Territories were open to the possession and occupancy of all.

It is strange that we should buy Territories to make them the refuge for runaway negroes until they become States, and that the Constitution must apply afterwards. It is strange that in a transition state neither the provisions of the Constitution nor the legislation of Congress can prevail. When such an opinion prevails, I cannot believe it loyal.

I know that gentlemen who have their opinions regulated rather by the temper of the community in which they live are not apt to look at the Constitution through the medium of principle. The gentleman from Ohio asks for some principle; I only ask for the principle of honesty.

MR. BALDWIN. I differ, Mr. President, from the views which have been expressed by the honorable Senator from Ohio, on this question. Whatever constitutional obligation exists on the part of the United States in relation to the delivery of fugitives from service escaping into another State, does, in my opinion, exist equally in regard to a fugitive escaping into a Territory of the United States.

The reason why the Constitution itself was silent upon this subject is not, in my opinion, that which has been assigned by the honorable Senator from South Carolina, [Mr. Butler,] that the Constitution supposed that the Territories of the United States would be open to the settlement of slaveholders with their slaves in the same mannor [sic] as the Territories of the slave States themselves were.

I suppose, on the contrary, that the reason why there was no specific mention of territories in the constitution was, that provision had already been made, by the ordinance of 1787, in regard to the only territorial possession then in the contemplation of the Convention, and the reason why the provision was confined by the express language of the Constitution to the States then existing was because, no further territorial acquisitions being then in contemplation, and provision being made by the Constitution for the incorporation of new States from the territories to which the ordinance of 1787 applied, these States would of course come in as free States, and have no need of any provision for the security of slaves excepting therefrom into other States.

Therefore, as it was not in the contemplation of the Convention that there would be any new slave States, no specific provision was made or deemed necessary in the Constitution in regard to slaves escaping from any but the then existing States. . . .

MR. CHASE. If assertion were argument and denunciation proof, then, Mr. President, the positions I have taken might be affected in some degree by what has fallen from the Senator from South Carolina. It is quite easy to use epithets; but epithets prove nothing. It is very easy to say that a proposition is "extravagant" and "perverse;" but after a gentleman has gratified his taste by such an application of terms, the proposition remains just as it was before.

I should like to hear some argument in contravention of the position I maintain. I am, I trust, as open to conviction as any gentleman upon this floor—as little willing and as little likely to advance propositions which can justly be denominated "perverse" or "extravagant" as any other gentleman. . . .

Slavery is an institution of force, and not of right, as our law books teach—the private force of the master being made efficient and sufficient by the public force of the State. When, therefore, a person held as a slave passes beyond the jurisdiction within which public force can be invoked in aid of the private force which would subject him to slavery, he is no longer a slave. He is a man; and he is where the power which made him a slave cannot follow him. He is free, therefore.

That is all there is of it; and that, it seems to me, is sound logic. It is a legitimate deduction, from unquestionable premises. If gentlemen can show that the premises are unsound, or the conclusions erroneous, let them do so.

Now, sir, a few words in answer to the Senator from Connecticut. He thinks we may legislate for the extradition of slaves escaped into the Territories, although the clause of the Constitution under which we act does not extend to the Territories at all. Now, I ask the Senator where he finds constitutional power to enforce the surrender of slaves escaped into the Territories? What clause of the Constitution confers it?

Will the Senator say that slaves passing or taken from one of the States into the Territories remain slaves? If he says that, I understand him. That is the modern southern doctrine. Does he say that these persons, if fugitives from service, may be delivered up under the general power of Congress over the Territories? That, also, is a position which I understand.

The point of difference between us would then be this: I maintain that Congress has no power to authorize or sanction slavery in the Territories, and that, inasmuch as all territorial legislative power is derived from Congress, there can be, therefore, no territorial slavery; while the Senator insists that a qualified right of the master to the slave, the right of reclamation, may exist in the Territories.

The Senator denies, however, that the condition of the person thus liable to be surrendered is slavery. He denies that the Constitution continues the condition of slavery in the case of a slave escaping from one State into another. He insists that the fugitive is not property in the non-slaveholding State. In that, as a legal proposition, I agree with him; but this will furnish no warrant for the legislation contemplated by the section which I propose to strike out.

The opinion which the Senator and myself entertain has not yet received the sanction of the courts. Our opinion is not the law; quite otherwise. The Supreme Court, in the case of Pennsylvania vs. Prigg, decided that, as between States, the condition of the fugitive slave remains in all respects the same in the State into which he escapes as it was in the State from which he fled. This is the language of the Court:

> The clause contains a positive and unqualified recognition of the right of the *owner in the slave*-- * * * puts the right to the service or labor on the same ground and to the same extent in every other State as in the State from which the slave escaped, and in which he was held to service or labor. If this be so, *all the incidents* of the right attach also. The owner must, therefore, have the right to seize and repossess the slave, which the local laws of his own State confer upon him, as property.

Now, we are or should be practical men. We should legislate upon facts and laws as we find them. The power under which the Senate must act in passing a bill for the surrender of fugitives from service is nowhere expressly granted by the Constitution, but it is claimed by implication from this clause of compact, and the claim is sanctioned by a decision of the Supreme Court. We must take this whole decision together, if we desire to ascertain the consequences of the legislation which it asserts to be within the competency of Congress.

This decision asserts that Congress, in providing for the surrender of a slave escaped, must regard him as property. If, then, Congress shall exercise this same power in regard to slaves escaped into Territories—a case not provided for in the Constitution—it must recognize, or rather authorize, the continuance in the Territories of the property-relation between the master and the escaped slave.

In the absence of legislation by Congress, a slave escaped into the Territories is free. There is no slavery there for any man, whensoever or howsoever he may come. Congress intervenes; and there is slavery there—slavery unlimited in duration, unrestricted in extent, "with all the incidents" which attach to the condition as a property-relation in the State from which the slaves come. Now, this slavery gets into the Territories by the legislation of Congress. If not, will the Senator explain how it gets there?

Why, sir, the very woman whose seizure and abduction gave rise to the case of *Prigg vs. Pennsylvania*, had children by a free husband, who never escaped from Maryland, but were born in Pennsylvania. And yet, as the mother was an escaping slave, and "all the incidents" of slavery attached to her, her children were carried off with her and sold to the slave-dealer.

I do not say that this was lawful or constitutional—far from it; but it was sanctioned by the decision of the Supreme Court. That decision, though in my judgment wholly unwarranted by the Constitution, yet stands for law; and we must legislate as practical men, well knowing that, until reversed, it will stand for law.

If, then, Congress, by its legislation, creates the right of reclamation in a class of cases in which it is not given by the Constitution—if it continues the master's power over and his property in slaves escaped to the Territories, as that power and property are held by the Supreme Court to be continued by the Constitution in and over slaves escaped into the States, does not Congress introduce slavery into the Territories? It seems to me that there can be but one answer to this question. I would hope, therefore, that the Senator from Connecticut might reconsider his opinion.

MR. DAYTON. I desire to say a few words upon this amendment, inasmuch as the yeas and nays have been ordered. . . .

The Senator from Ohio assumes the legal position that slavery is controlled by the common law, except where the common law is overridden by the Constitution. There is no controversy about that; there is no controversy that if a slave escape from a slave State to free soil, even if it be a Territory, upon common law principles that slave is free.

But the only question is whether we, legislating in good faith, ought not to give to the South the fair benefit of this provision of the Constitution? Whether we ought not, in this matter, to override the common-law principle? It seems to me that we should; and that we should carry out the provisions of the Constitution in good faith, and only give the fugitive slave the benefit of a fair trial, and give him that anywhere and everywhere. . . .

MR. CHASE. Mr. President, the Senator from New Jersey admits the general principle for which I contend, that a slave escaping into free territory is free. But he says that we have, nevertheless, the right to legislate upon this subject, because we may establish slavery in the Territories if we choose, and if not, we may establish this qualified right in a slave. And he says that this is the principle upon which I have voted for the prohibition of slavery in the Territories. Not so.

I deny the right of the General Government to establish slavery. But it does not follow that because they cannot establish it, therefore they cannot prohibit it. The powers are quite different in their character. Legislation may be restrained from authorizing a particular act, and yet you may have the power to prohibit that act. And that is very often the case.

But the Senator says that good faith requires it. I trust I am not insensible to the obligations of good faith. But when I am asked to aid in reducing any person to slavery, then I ask for the power in the Constitution; I ask for the obligation imposed on me by the Constitution. If I do not find that obligation imposed, then it seems to me that I am under no obligation arising from good faith to exercise that power in favor of slavery which is not conferred. Let the Constitution be extended. But I am unwilling to make a supplement to the Constitution, for the sake of erecting a bulwark for slavery. I am unwilling to go beyond the Constitution, in legislation, for any such object as that, because I do not believe it to be right.

It is no matter in which we are at liberty to exercise discretion and taste. We are bound to do what we believe to be right, and we are not bound to go beyond the terms of the Constitution in any respect. Gentlemen on the other side of the Chamber admit that the propositions upon which I proceed are correct; but they think that we ought not to apply them in the case of the Territories. I have the misfortune to differ with them; I think that where a proposition is right it ought to be carried out. . . .

The simple question under consideration is, whether, as a part of this bill, we will provide for the surrender, as slaves, of persons escaping from the slave States into the Territories.

The question being taken on the amendment of Mr. Chase, it was rejected—yea 1, nays 44; as follow:

Yea—Mr. Chase—1.

Nays—Messrs. Atchison, Badger, Baldwin, Barnwell, Bell, Berrien, Bradbury, Butler, Cass, Clarke, Cooper, Davis of Massachusetts, Davis of Mississippi, Dawson, Dayton, Dodge of Wisconsin, Dodge of Iowa, Downs, Greene, Hamlin, Houston, Hunter, Jones, King, Mangum, Mason, Pearce, Rusk, Turney, Underwood, Wales, Walker, Winthrop, Whitcomb, and Yulee—41.

UNION AND FREEDOM, WITHOUT COMPROMISE SPEECH OF MR. CHASE CONCERNING A NEW FUGITIVE SLAVE ACT AND THE STATUS OF SLAVERY IN NEW MEXICO

IN THE SENATE, MARCH 26-27, 1850

The Senate having under consideration the resolutions submitted by MR. CLAY—

MR. CHASE said:

I rise, Mr. President, with unaffected diffidence, to offer to the Senate my views of the important questions presented by the resolutions of the honorable Senator from Kentucky. . . .

It has been said, Mr. President, and said in a tone of complaint, by southern gentlemen; that this Government is rapidly becoming a mere Government of the majority—becoming a great consolidated democracy. Now, sir, if by this it be meant that this Government of ours has become, or is to become, a Government of the American people, administered in conformity with the will of a majority of the people—if it be meant that the democratic principle is carried, or is likely to be carried, into practical application in it administration and legislation, I see in the fact, if fact it be, no ground of complaint, but rather ground of congratulation and satisfaction.

Why, sir, what is this democratic principle? Equality of

natural rights, guarantied and secured to all, by the laws of a just popular Government. For one, I desire to see that principle applied to every subject of legislation, no matter what that subject may be—to the great question involved in the resolutions now before the Senate, and to every other question.

But our responsibilities are limited by our powers; and however clear it may be that we are bound by allegiance to democratic principle to condemn, to mitigate, to abolish slavery wherever we can constitutionally do so, it is equally clear that we are not bound, and that we have no right to interfere with slavery by legislation beyond the sphere of our constitutional powers.

We have no power to legislate on the subject of slavery in the States. We have power to prevent its extension, and to prohibit its existence within the sphere of the exclusive jurisdiction of the General Government. Our duty, therefore, is to abstain from interference with it in the States. It is also our duty to prohibit its extension into national territories, and its continuance where we are constitutionally responsible for its existence. . . .

It has been said, in the course of this debate, that there was some understanding between Congress and the Convention in regard to the question of slavery. That may be so. There is, however, nothing in history which proves it, though circumstances do certainly seem to warrant such a conjecture.

But, if there was an understanding, to what did it relate? Not certainly to the whole subject of slavery; for, up to the time of the promulgation of the ordinance, no discussion had taken place in the Convention on that subject, except in respect to the question of representation and taxation. That question had been discussed with considerable heat; so much, indeed, that some members declared themselves ready to break up the Convention rather than consent to the representation of slaves.

The exclusion of slavery from the territories by the ordinance may have been intended to have, some influence upon this discussion. It may be that members from the free States, seeing slavery excluded from national territory, and supposing its extension to be thereby forever interdicted, were the more willing to consent to a representation of slaves as a temporary arrangement, which would cease of itself when slavery itself should cease or run out, at some period "not remote."

But there is not a particle of foundation for any supposition that there was any understanding between Congress and the Convention, based upon the idea that slavery and freedom were entitled to equal regard in the action of the Government. Far from it. Whatever understanding there was, if there was any, must have been based upon the idea of a slavery restriction; upon the fact that its extension was prohibited, and that its final disappearance was expected.

The framers of the Constitution acted under the influence of the general sentiment of the country. Some of them had contributed in no small measure to form that sentiment. Let us examine the instrument in its light, and ascertain the original import of its language. What, then, shall we find in it? The guarantees so much talked of? Recognition of property in men? Stipulated protection for that property in national territories and by national law? No, sir; nothing like it.

We find, on the contrary, extreme care to exclude these ideas from the Constitution. Neither the word "slave" nor "slavery" is to be found in any provision. There is not a single expression which charges the National Government with any responsibility in regard to slavery. No power is conferred on Congress either to establish or sustain it. The framers of the Constitution left it where they found it, exclusively within and under the jurisdiction of the States.

Wherever slaves are referred to at all in the Constitution, whether in the clause providing for the apportionment of representation and direct taxation, or in that stipulating for the extradition of fugitives from service, or in that restricting Congress as to the prohibition of importation or migration, they are spoken of, not as persons held as property, but as persons held to service or having their condition determined, under State laws. . . .

Unhappily, however, the original policy of the Government and the original principles of the Government in respect to slavery did not permanently control its action. A change occurred—almost imperceptible at first, but becoming more and more marked and decided, until nearly total.

The honorable Senator from Massachusetts in the course of his late speech noticed this change and ascribed it to the rapid increase in the production of cotton. Doubtless, sir, that was a leading course. The production of cotton, in consequence of the invention of the cotton gin, increased from 487,600 pounds in 1793, to 6,276,300 pounds in 1796, and continued to increase very rapidly afterwards. Of course the market value of slaves advanced, and masters were less inclined to emancipation.

But the increase of the cotton crop was not the only, nor, in my judgment, the chief cause of altered public sentiment and governmental action. The change in the structure of the Government which introduced into one branch of the Legislature, and into the electoral college, a representation for slaves, constituted, I think, a far more potent cause. I will sketch the progress of the power derived from this source, for I think it important that its practical operation should be understood. I admit that it is conferred by the Constitution; but—

MR. BORLAND. Will the honorable Senator allow me to ask him a question?

MR. CHASE. Certainly.

MR. BORLAND. I think I understood the Senator as giving a reason for adhering to the institution of slavery on the part of the southern statesmen, that the Constitution allowed the slave population to form a basis of representation. Does the Senator give that as a reason why they adhered to the institution of slavery, and became more attached to it?

MR. CHASE. I believe that was one of the reasons.

MR. BORLAND. Then I can say to the Senator that his argument, it seems to me, confutes itself; for the reason that if the slaves were liberated, each would be counted; whereas, being retained as slaves, only three-fifths of their number are brought into computation, and we lose two-fifths.

MR. CHASE. Undoubtedly, Mr. President, if the slaves were free they would be reckoned at their full number in the basis of representation; but the influence of their representation upon the character of the Government would be wholly changed. There would be no slave interest.

MR. BORLAND. Free negroes are represented.

MR. CHASE. I am obliged to the Senator from Arkansas for the information he gives me; I had learned the fact he states from the Constitution. Why, sir, is it not quite obvious that in a district where the number of slaves is considerable, even if suffrage be universal, the number of votes must be proportionally reduced? And, inasmuch as slaveholders are usually the chief landholders and property holders, and have a common interest, is it not quite obvious that they will generally be able to wield the political power of the district?

Destroy the slave representation, and their power is gone. Enfranchise the slaves, and there are no slaveholders, and of course no slave power. Enfranchisement will, doubtless, increase the political power of the State, but it will annihilate the slave power.

I repeat, Mr. President, and they who think me wrong may refute what I say, if they can, that there must have been some adequate cause or causes for the remarkable change of feeling and action in regard to slavery which began to manifest itself about this time, and that these causes, in my judgment, were—*first*, the political power derived by slaveholders of their slaves; and, *secondly*, the augmented value of slaves arising from the sudden increase of the cotton culture. The last of these causes requires no further consideration; but I wish to direct attention somewhat more particularly to the first.

The first apportionment was made by the Constitution Convention. Regard was had, doubtless, to the three-fifths rule in determining the number of Representatives assigned to each State; but we cannot now ascertain how many were allowed for the slaves. The census supplies the means of ascertaining the precise quantum of slave representative in each decennial period since the first apportionment. I now propose to submit to the Senate a table, which exhibits at one view each decennial period since the adoption of the Constitution; the number of slaves reckoned at three-fifths of their actual number; and the number of Representatives for slaves for each period. . . . From this table it appears that in the very first Congress, if the Convention based their original apportionment upon anything like a correct estimate of the population, there must have been at least ten representatives of slaves, and that in the second Congress there were thirteen. It was impossible that the influence of this representation should not be felt. It was natural, though it does seem to have been anticipated, that the unity of the slave interest, strengthened by this accession of political power, should gradually weaken the public sentiment and modify the national policy against slavery.

Well, sir, occasion was not long wanting to test the dispositions of Congress in this respect. At an early period of the second session of the first Congress, petitions were presented from the Society of Friends in Philadelphia and New York, and from the Pennsylvania Abolition Society, of which Benjamin Franklin was the President, praying Congress to take such measure as the Constitution would permit to discountenance and discourage slavery and the slave trade. A similar address had been made by a deputation of Friends to the Congress of the Confederation, in 1783, who were received and heard with great respect, though Congress, having no power over the subject, was obliged to decline taking such action as was desired. The petitions now presented were not treated with similar consideration. They were, however, received and referred, and in due time a report was made. . . .

It was apparent that there was a large majority in favor of the report; but a desire to satisfy even unreasonable objectors, induced the concession of one point after another, until the report was reduced to three propositions: *First*, that migration or importation could not be prohibited prior to 1808. *Second*, that Congress had not power to interfere in the emancipation or treatment of slaves in the States. *Third*, that Congress could prohibit the slave trade by the citizens of the United States for the supply of foreigners, and provide for humane treatment, on their passage, of those imported into the States. The last resolution of the original report, which pledged the Government, in conformity with its past policy and professed principles, to promote the objects of the memorialists, was stricken out altogether.

This was the first fruit of intimidation on the one side, and concession and compromise on the other. The majority of the House forbore to express their own settled convictions; forbore to pledge themselves to that course of disfavor to slavery and the slave trade, which consistency, honor, and humanity, required of them; yielded everything of substance, and retained little else than form. Could they have seen that this was but the first step in a long line of concessions, perhaps not yet ended, surely the patriotic men who composed that Congress would never have taken that first step.

What followed, sir? In that same year, North Carolina tendered to the United States a cession of the territory lying between the mountains which form her present western boundary and the Mississippi, and now constituting the State of Tennessee upon condition "that the inhabitants should have all the privileges, benefits, and advantages, of the ordinance of 1787, provided, always, that no regulations made or to be made by Congress should tend to emancipate slaves." Congress accepted this cession, and provided for the government of the ceded country as a slaveholding territory.

Hitherto Congress had never sanctioned slaveholding. Never hitherto had a single slave been held under any authority emanating from the Congress. On the contrary, as we have seen, in all the territory hitherto acquired, slavery had been promptly abolished, and impregnable barriers erected against its renewed introduction. The acceptance of the North Carolina cession reversed the policy of the Government, and was a step in the wrong direction. To preserve the dominion of a few masters over an inconsiderable number of slaves, established policy, settled principle, and safe precedent, were alike disregarded. It was a mischievous—an almost fatal error.

In 1802, Georgia ceded to the United States the country lying between her present western limit and the Mississippi, stipulating that the ordinance of 1787, in all its provisions, should extend to the ceded territory, "that article only excepted which forbids slavery." This cession was accepted, and the territory placed under a territorial government, restricted from all interference with slavery. This was the second chapter in the history of reaction.[20]

In 1803, we acquired Louisiana by purchase from the French Republic. There were at that time about forty thousand slaves held within its limits, under the French law. The treaty contained this stipulation:

The inhabitants of the ceded territory shall be incorporated

---

[20] More properly speaking the third, since the cession of the District of Columbia had been previously accepted, and the slave codes of Virginia and Maryland adopted and continued therein by act of Congress.

> in the Union of the United States and admitted as soon as possible, according to the principles of the Federal Constitution, to the enjoyment of all the rights, advantages, and immunities of citizens of the United States; and, in the mean time, they shall be maintained in the free enjoyment of their liberty, property, and the religion which they profess.

This stipulation, interpreted according to the plain sense of its terms, and carried into practical effect, would have enfranchised every slave in Louisiana; for no one, I apprehend, will venture to affirm that the slaves were not inhabitants. Independently of this stipulation, it was the duty of the Government—even more imperative than in 1787, for since then the whole country south of the Ohio and east of the Mississippi had been formed into slave States and slave territories—to establish freedom as the fundamental law of the new acquisition. But this duty was not performed. There was some feeble legislation against the introduction of slaves from foreign countries, and of slaves imported since 1798 from the other States; but that was all, and that was useless.

Then came the cession of Florida by Spain in 1820. The stipulation in the treaty was substantially the same as in the treaty with France; the duty of the Government in respect to the acquisition was the same; and there was the same failure to perform it.

Finally, Texas came in, in 1845, not as a territory, but as a State. Within her limits, slavery was never under the control of Congress. The existence of slavery there was an objection to her admission into the Union; but once admitted, and admitted as a State, her internal legislation on that subject was as much beyond the reach of the National Government as before. . . .

Let me now, sir, sum up the results of this policy of adding new slave territories and new slave States to the Union, which was substituted for the original policy of free territories and free States. . . .

[O]ut of territories ceded to the Union, and actually organized under national jurisdiction, since the adoption of the Constitution, seven slave States have been erected and admitted: Tennessee out of the cession of North Carolina; Alabama and

Mississippi out of the cession Georgia; Louisiana, Missouri, and Arkansas, out of the cession of France; and Florida out of the cession of Spain. Besides these States, we have annexed slaveholding Texas, vast in her undisputed limits, and with vast claims beyond them. Here are eight new slave States, created and admitted out of territories, not one foot of which had been ceded to the United States prior to the Constitution, and five of them out of foreign territory acquired by purchase or annexation since its adoption.

Well, sir, where are the free States which have come into the Union out of these territories? There is but one. Iowa is the single State yet admitted out of all the vast territories acquired since the organization of the Government.

Thus, sir, we see that while the original policy of the Government secured to freedom all the territory acquired before the Constitution, and all the States erected out of it, the reversal of that policy secured to slavery most of the territory subsequently acquired, and all the States formed out of it except one.

Now, sir, I desire to submit to the Senate a comparison of the areas which belonged respectively to freedom and to slavery at the date of the Constitution, and the areas which have been devoted to freedom and to slavery, respectively in States created out of territories, and admitted into the Union since that date. I have compiled from the reports of the Commissioner of the Land Office a statement exhibiting this comparison, which I will read. . . .

Upon inspection of this table, it will be seen that, had the original policy of the Government been perserved [sic] in, and no new slave States created out of territories, the difference of area in favor of freedom within the original limits of the Republic would have been 282,738 square miles; and all territory acquired beyond those limits would of course have been free. It will be seen, also, that the reversal of this policy reduced this difference to 18,905 square miles, and by acquisitions of foreign territory, changed the balance and created a difference in favor of slavery of 304,967 square miles, which will be increased, if the claims of Texas are allowed, to the enormous quantity of 431,918 square miles. Within these limits slavery suffers want of room—is "cabined, cribbed, confined," and seeks a wider sphere!

Sir, complaint from the slave States, under these circumstances, sound strangely to me. Why, sir, has not the policy of the Government been reversed in favor of their system? Has not slavery been extended to undreamed-of limits? Have not the slave States been more than doubled in number? Has not their area been almost tripled in extent? And yet they complain—complain of the aggressions of the North. They complain that the recapture of fugitive slaves is rendered difficult by free State legislation and free State sentiment; and that the subject of slavery is discussed and adverse opinions formed in the free States, which the electors ask us to embody in national legislation; that slavery has been already excluded from a portion of the national territories; and that a determination is manifested to prevent its further extension, and to restore the original policy of slavery restriction and discouragement.

Now, sir, so far as these complaints have reference to the action of the people, it is impossible to appease them. This is a Government of the people, and the voice of the people must be heard and respected in its administration. The States also are governments of the people, and must be administered in conformity with the popular will. If the settled judgment and conscientious convictions of the people are against slavery, legislation, within constitutional limits, must follow that judgment and those convictions.

And, so far as these complaints respect the former action of the National Government, they who make them complain of themselves. For where has resided the practical control of this Government? Let a few facts answer this question.

At the close of the current Presidential term, the slave States will have held the Presidency fifty-two years; the free States only twelve years. Of the gentlemen who have filled the Department of State, fourteen have been from slave States, and five only from the free.

Thirteen of the Judges of the Supreme Court have been taken from the slave States; from the free States, twelve. No northern man has filled the office of Chief Justice during this century; and, notwithstanding the population of the free States is more than double the free population of the slave States, the latter have always been represented by a majority of the Judges upon the Supreme Bench.

Of the Speakers of the House of Representatives, twelve have been from the slave States, and eight only from the free States; thus, giving to the salve States the control of the appointment of the committees, and, consequently, of the business of the House. Sir, it cannot be denied that the power of this Government, in all its departments, has been for many years, practically and substantially, in the hands of southern men, and has been used to advance the interests, real or supposed, of the slave section of the country.

These are not my assertions merely. They are the assertions of our public history, confirmed by the testimony of southern gentlemen . . . I have prepared a table showing at one view the circuits, the States composing them, and the aggregate free population in each, which I will now submit. . . .

From this it will be seen that in order to secure a majority from the slave States upon the bench, the circuits are so arranged that, with something less than half of the free population, the slave States have five circuits and five judges out of nine. The smallest of the slave State circuits contains little more than one-seventh of the free population of the smallest of the free State circuits; while the largest of the latter contains near twice the number of free inhabitants in the largest of the former. The four southwestern slave States, lying contiguous to each other, are divided into two circuits, while the four northwestern free States, with nearly four times the free population, compose but one. . . .

Freedom is national; slavery only is local and sectional. I do not complain at all that the offices of the country have been filled by southern gentlemen. Let them have the offices, if they will only administer the Government in conformity with its original principles. But I do complain that it has not been so administered; that its powers have been perverted to the support of an institution which those principles condemn; and that, in consequence of this perversion, we are involved in all the difficulties of the struggle between slavery and freedom, in the midst of which we now are. . . .

Without concluding, Mr. Chase gave way for a motion to adjourn; whereupon the Senate adjourned.

WEDNESDAY, MARCH 27, 1850

The Senate having under consideration the resolutions submitted by MR. CLAY—

MR. CHASE resumed: If, Mr. President, the views which I submitted to the Senate yesterday are correct, there can be no foundation whatever for the doctrine advanced, and somewhat boldly of late, that an equilibrium between the slaveholding and non-slaveholding sections of our country has been, is, and ought to be, an approved feature of our political system.

No such equilibrium, nothing looking towards such an equilibrium, can be found in the Constitution, nor in any early action under it. It was not thought of by anybody. On the contrary, the Constitution was formed for seven free States and six slave States, and with full knowledge, on the part of those who framed and those who adopted it, that provision had been made by the Ordinance for the erection of five additional free States out of the Northwestern Territory. . . . The truth is, sir, that this idea of an equilibrium was never started until after we began to create slave States out of territory acquired from foreign powers. It is alien to our original policy, and inconsistent with the interests and the duty of the country. . . .

It is true that each State, except where restrained by constitutional provisions, may form its domestic institutions according to its own pleasure[.]... Why, sir, slavery depends entirely for its existence and continuance on local law. Beyond the sphere of the operation of such law, no man can be compelled to submit to the condition of a slave, except by mere unauthorized force.

I come now, Mr. President, to consider, in the light of these general principles, the particular questions under the consideration of the Senate. The honorable Senator from Kentucky has submitted to us several propositions, which mark out a general plan for the settlement of all questions growing out of the subject of slavery. I am afraid, sir, that the plan will hardly prove comprehensive enough. If we were prepared to adopt the whole scheme, who can say that other questions and other difficulties will not arise from this prolific source of embarrassment and trouble. . . .

Mr. President, the fifth, sixth, and eighth resolutions of the Senator from Kentucky embrace three propositions, which I propose to consider together.

1. That slavery in this District should not be abolished, except with the consent of the District and of Maryland.
2. That the slave trade in this District ought to be abolished.
3. That Congress has no power to prohibit the salve trade among the states.

I concur fully in the second of these propositions, and thank the honorable Senators from Kentucky [MR. CLAY] and from Alabama [MR. KING] for the favor they have shown to this measure.

I cannot concur in the first proposition. I have already said that, in my judgment, the Constitution confers on Congress no power to enforce the absolute subjection of one man to the disposal of another man as property. It is my opinion that all legislation adopted or enacted by Congress for enforcing that condition ought to be repealed, whether in this District or elsewhere. . . .

Sir, I will give no vote for the perpetuation or continuance of slavery in this District. I deny any implied obligation to the people of Maryland to continue slavery here as long as it is continued there. No evidence can be produced of any such an understanding. The state of public sentiment in Maryland and in Virginia at the time of the cession warrants the belief that the understanding and expectation, if there was any, was very different from that supposed. But, whatever the understanding or expectation may have been, our duty seems to me plain. The power of exclusive legislation over this District is confided to us. We are bound to use it so as to establish justice and secure the blessings of liberty for all within its reach.

I was surprised, Mr. President, by the proposition that Congress has no power to prohibit the slave trade between the States. Why, sir, that slave trade between the States. Why, sir, that trade is prohibited now, except upon certain conditions.

It is prohibited in vessels of less capacity that forty tons.

Not a slave can be shipped coastwise without a permit from an officer of the United States; not a slave shipped can be landed without such a permit. Anyone who will take the trouble to consult the act of 1807 will see how this matter stands. I do not think that law unconstitutional.

The Constitution confers on Congress power "to regulate commerce among the several States." Congress exercised this power in enacting that law. If they might enact that, they may enact others. If they can prohibit the trade in vessels of less than forty tons, they can prohibit it in vessels of one hundred, five hundred—altogether. And why should not Congress prohibit this traffic?

We hear much of the cruelty of the African slave trade. Our laws denounce against those engaged in it the punishment of death. Is it less cruel, less deserving of punishment, to tear fathers, mothers, children, from their homes and each other, in Maryland and Virginia, and transport them to the markets of Louisiana or Mississippi? If there be a difference in cruelty and wrong, is it not in favor of the African and against the American slave trade? Why, then, should we be guilty of the inconsistency of abolishing *that* by the sternest prohibition, and continuing *this* under the sanction of national law?

The seventh proposition of the Senator from Kentucky contemplates more effectual provision for the extradition of fugitive slaves. . . . I know I shall be told that the Constitution provides that "no person held to service or labor in one State, under the laws thereof, escaping into another, shall, in consequence of any law or regulation therein, be discharged from such service or labor, but shall be delivered up on claim of the party to who such service or labor may be due."

But this clause contains no grant of legislative power to Congress. That power is conferred exclusively by special clauses, granting legislative power in respect to the first article, which, after enumerating the specific powers of Congress, proceeds to declare that Congress shall have power "to make all laws which shall be necessary and proper for carrying into execution the foregoing powers, and all other powers vested by this Constitution in the Government of the United States, or in any department or officer thereof."

Now, sir, what power is vested, by the clause, in relation to fugitives from service, in the Government, or in any department or officer of the Government? None at all; and if none, then the legislative power of Congress does not extend to the subject. The clause is a clause of compact. It has been so denominated by every Senator who has had occasion to speak of it. . . .

MR. BUTLER. I interrupt the Senator merely with a view to obtain what I regard as important to the consideration of this matter. If some of the States who are parties to this compact refuse to pass such laws as will fulfill their obligations, where is the remedy?

MR. CHASE. I know of no remedy. None has been provided by the Constitution. But let me put a question to the Senator from South Carolina. The Constitution provides among these articles of compact, of which the stipulation in regard to fugitives from service is one, that "the citizens of each State shall be entitled to all privileges and immunities of citizens in the several States." Now, I ask the Senator if he admits that, under that clause, Congress has power to provide penalties for the imprisonment of colored citizens of Massachusetts in the ports and under the laws of South Carolina?

MR. BUTLER. I take the broad ground that each State has a right to prescribe its own qualifications of citizenship. In all the old acts of Congress the class of persons referred to by the Senator are spoken of as persons of color as contradistinguished from citizens. I believe it is in the power of every State to make a full citizen of black man, but not to make him a full citizen of any other State. The definition of a citizen in South Carolina is not governed by what may be the definition of a citizen in another State.

I believe that each State can determine the qualifications of voters, and control as it pleases the rights of different classes of persons. But the Senator has not answered or met the question I have asked, and that is, in case a State refuses to carry out the provisions of the article in the Constitution, where is the power to compel it to do so?

MR. CHASE. I certainly answered the Senator distinctly and candidly. I said I knew of no remedy in case of the refusal of a State to perform its stipulations. The obligation of the compact, and the extent of the compact are, as in every other case of treaty stipulation, matters which address themselves exclusively to the good faith and sound judgment of the parties to it. But did the Senator answer my question?

He has not told us whether in his judgment, the General Government has power to enforce that constitutional compact which guaranties to the citizens of each State the rights of citizens in all the States.

He has told us that each State determines for itself who shall be its citizens. I grant it. He says one State cannot determine who shall be a citizen of another. That may be so.

But when a State has once determined who its own citizens shall be, the compact stipulates that they shall have the privileges of citizens in every other State. Not that they shall *be* citizens—not that they shall be admitted to the elective franchise, or be made eligible to office; but that they shall have those rights and immunities, that security and that protection to which citizens generally, male or female, minors or adults, are entitled. My question was, "Has the General Government, in the judgment of the Senator, power under the Constitution to enforce the performance of this stipulation in South Carolina"?

But I have been drawn aside from the line of argument I intend to pursue.

I repeat, Mr. President, that this clause in relation to fugitives from service is a clause of compact. For many years after the adoption of the Constitution it was so regarded. It was not much discussed, and the limits of the respective powers of the State and Federal Governments under it were not very accurately settled. But nearly all the States legislated under it, and provided such provisions for the extradition of fugitives as they deemed consistent with the security of the personal rights of their own inhabitants.

At length, however, the *Prigg* decision was made, which asserted the exclusive right and duty of Congress to legislate on this subject, and denied that right and duty to the States. The same decision suggested, what everyone here will admit, that Congress could not require State officers to intervene in the business of extradition. It need surprise no one that after this the States ceased to enact extradition laws, or that some of them repealed those they had before enacted, and prohibited the intervention of their officers.

But, sir, a decision of the Supreme Court cannot alter the Constitution. If Congress had no power to legislate on this subject before the decision, Congress has none now. The decision determined the case before the court. It established a precedent for the determination of such cases. It must stand till overruled. But I do not see how any Senator who finds himself unable, after the fullest consideration, to concur in the principle of the decision, can justify himself in the exercise of a power which he does not believe the Constitution has conferred.

What, sir, is the history of this clause and the clauses of like character which stand with it in the Constitution? This clause was taken from the ordinance of 1787. In the ordinance no one pretends that it was anything more than an article of compact. No power was derived from it to the Government.

Three other clauses of the same nature are found in the same article of the Constitution: one stipulating for the extradition of fugitives from justice; another stipulating that the citizens of each State shall have the immunities of citizens in all the other States; and a third stipulating that full faith and credit shall be given in each State to the public acts, records, and judicial proceedings of every other State. All these clauses are taken from the Articles of Confederation, where they stood as articles of compact, binding the good faith of the States, but conferring no power on the Government. Can a good reason be given by any one why they should have a different operation in the Constitution?

It seems evident that the framers of the Constitution did not suppose that the General Government could enforce the execution of these clauses, or any of them, without special provision. For, coupled with the clause respecting records, we find a special power conferred on Congress to "prescribe, by general laws, the manner in which the record shall be proved, and the effect thereof." This grant of a special power in respect to records, and this omission to grant any power in respect to the other subjects, afford the strongest possible implication that the Constitutional Convention did not design to grant any such power.

Had the grant of the special power as to records been omitted, that clause would have been a stipulation precisely like other clauses, and having the same effect; no more, no less; no narrower, no broader. It would have been binding on the States; but no power could have been derived from it to Congress. To enable Congress to legislate, a special grant was necessary. The omission of any special grant of power to legislate upon the subject-matter of the other clauses must, then, have been designed, and must have been intended as a denial of such power.

Are Senators prepared to adopt the broad proposition upon which the Supreme Court rested and were obliged to rest the assertion of the power to legislate on the extradition of fugitives, namely, that wherever the Constitution confers a right or enjoins a duty, a power arises to the Federal Government to enforce the right or compel the performance of the duty? Are they prepared to carry this doctrine into its practical results? Is it not obvious that it will open a new and very copious source of powers to the General Government; and that it must tend to the subversion of the rights of the States and the establishment of a consolidated central power, dangerous to their independence and sovereignty?

I have said, Mr. President, that the several clauses providing for the extradition of fugitives from justice, and fugitives from service, and for the security in all the States of the rights of the citizens for each State, are in the nature of treaty stipulations, to be carried into effect by the appropriate action of the State governments. What that action should be is for the State governments to determine. It is for them to ascertain the true import of the terms of the compact, and to provide for its execution by such legislation as will guard equally the just rights of all parties. But, sir, those States who claim the performance of the compact from their sister States must see to it that they perform it themselves. A State which imprisons, without pretense of crime, the citizens of another State, cannot demand, with a good grace, the surrender of fugitives.

But, sir, if it be granted that Congress has the power to legislate, are we bound to exercise it? . . . We are not prepared, I hope, and I trust we never shall be prepared, to give the sanction of the American Senate to the bill and the amendments now upon our table—a bill which authorizes and requires the appointment of two hundred and sixty-one commissioners, and an indefinite number of other officers, to catch runaway slaves in the State of

Ohio; which punishes humanity as a crime; which authorizes seizure without process, trial without a jury, and consignment of slavery beyond the limits of the State without opportunity of defence, and upon *ex parte* testimony. Certainly no such bill can receive my vote. . . .

But we are told that if Congress prohibits slavery in the territories, or abolish slavery in the slave trade in this District, or fail to provide adequate securities for the return of runaway slaves, the South will dissolve the Union! This cry, Mr. President, neither astonishes nor alarms me. I have never thought, nor do I now think, that any man should be deterred by it, from an honest, fearless discharge of his duty here. It is an old cry, not without profit to those who have used it. It was first heard in the Congress of 1774. . . .

Now we are threatened with the dissolution of the Union unless we will consent to what no republican Government ever did consent to; what is in direct opposition to the principles and spirit of our institutions, and is condemned by the earliest and best precedents of our history; namely, the extension of slavery into territories now free! Shall we yield to this outcry? For one, I say, never! In my judgment, it is time to pause. We have yielded point after point; we have crowded concession on concession, until duty, honor, patriotism, shame demands that we should stop.

But we are told, almost with tone of taunt, that the free States have had the majority all this time in one branch of Congress at last, and in the electoral college, and, therefore, that whatever responsibility there may have been in making these concessions to slavery, it is upon them. It is well to remind us of this. The free States have had the majority; and the victories of slavery have been won by their divisions. John Randolph said, long ago, "We of the South are always unified and can always unite; while you of the North divide. We have conquered you once, and we can and we will conquer you again." These two sentences make a history.

I do not say, and I do not mean to say, that there has been but one political party in the slave States; but that, in these States, fidelity to the interests of slavery has always been, in both parties, an indispensable condition of support for high public station; and that great numbers, in either party, have always been ready to support a candidate of opposite general politics, if undoubted on this question, rather than a candidate of like general politics at all suspected of disfavor to slavery. No candidate known to be in favor of placing the legitimate influence of this Government actively and decidedly on the side of freedom, could receive the support of either party. It is by this unity of sentiment and purpose, aided by appeals to groundless fears for the safety of the Union, and by a disposition growing out of these fears and part alliances to submit to the tests imposed by the slaveholding sections of each political party, that the slave States have "conquered." . . .

Mr. President, honesty is the best policy; justice, the highest expediency; and principle, the only proper basis of union in a political organization. Holding fast as I do to Democratic principles, believing firmly that all men are created equal, and are endowed by their Creator with inalienable rights to life and liberty, I desire to see those principles carried out boldly, earnestly, absolutely, in the practical administration of affairs.

I wish to see the powers of this Government exercised for the great objects which the Constitution indicates; for the perfection of our Union; for the establishment of justice; for the common defence; for the security of liberty. At the same time I do not desire to see this Government, under the influence of any zeal, however honorable, for freedom, transcend at all the sphere of its constitutional powers and duties.

While, therefore, I shall steadily support all proper legislation for the establishment and security of freedom in the territories and elsewhere within the sphere of exclusive national jurisdiction, I shall, as steadily, refuse my support to all legislation on the subject of slavery within the States. In this line of action I shall feel myself supported by the precepts of the sages of the revolutionary era, by the example of the founders of the Republic, by the original policy of the Government, and by the principles of the Constitution.

I cannot believe that there is danger in such a course. Least of all does the stale cry of disunion alarm me. Men, generally, adapt remedies to evils. But what evil that the slave States complain of will disunion cure? Will it establish slavery in the territories? Will it procure the return of fugitives? Will it suppress discussion? Will it secure slavery where it is? Sir, all men must see that disunion is no remedy for the slave States. Why then the cry, if not to alarm the timid, the sensitive, the unreflecting—to afford excuses for concession—and thus secure advantages which the sober judgment and enlightened conscience of the country would never yield?

Mr. President, I have never calculated the value of the Union. I know no arithmetic by which the computation can be made. We of the West are in the habit of looking upon the Union as we look upon the arch of heaven, without a thought that it can ever decay or fall. With equal reverence we regard the great Ordinance of Freedom, under whose benign influence, within little more than half a century, a wilderness has been converted into an empire.

Ohio, the eldest born of the Constitution and the Ordinance, cleaves and will cleave faithfully to both. And now that the time has come when vast accessions of free territory demand the application of those principles of the Ordinance, to which she is indebted for her prosperity and power, to guard them against the blighting influence of slavery, she will insist that the same protection shall be extended to the territories which was extended to her.

Nor are these sentiments of Ohio alone. They are the sentiments of the people throughout the free States. Here and there the arts or the fears of politicians or capitalists may suppress their utterance; but they live, and will live, in the hearts of the masses. There is no great and real change in those opinions and convictions which placed a majority pledged to free soil in the other wing of the Capitol.

It may be, however, that you will succeed here in sacrificing the claims of freedom by some settlement carried through the forms of legislation. But the people will unsettle your settlement. It may be that you will determine that the territories shall not be secured by law against the ingress of slavery. The people will reverse your determination. It may be that you will succeed in burying the Ordinance of Freedom. But the people will write upon its tomb, *Resurgam*;[21] and the same history which records its resurrection may also inform posterity that they who fancied they had killed the [Wilmot] proviso [barring slavery in the territories]

---

[21] "I shall rise again."

only committed political suicide.

APPEAL OF THE INDEPENDENT DEMOCRATS IN CONGRESS TO THE PEOPLE OF THE UNITED STATES SHALL SLAVERY BE PERMITTED IN NEBRASKA? WASHINGTON, JANUARY 19, 1854

Fellow Citizens: As Senators and Representatives in the Congress of the United States, it is our duty to warn our constituents whenever imminent danger menaces the freedom of our institutions or the permanency of our Union. Such danger, as we firmly believe, now impends, and we earnestly solicit your prompt attention to it.

At the last session of Congress, a bill for the organization of the Territory of Nebraska passed the House of Representatives with an overwhelming majority. That bill was based on the principle of excluding slavery from the new Territory. It was not taken up for consideration in the Senate, and consequently failed to become a law.

At the present session, a new Nebraska bill has been reported by the Senate Committee on Territories, which, should it unhappily receive the sanction of Congress, will open all the unorganized territory of the Union to the ingress of slavery.

We arraign this bill as a gross violation of a scared pledge; as a criminal betrayal of precious rights; as part and parcel of an atrocious plot to exclude from a vast unoccupied region immigrants from the Old World, and free laborers from our own States, and convert it into a dreary region of despotism, inhabited by masters and slaves.

Take your maps, fellow citizens, we entreat you, and see what country it is which this bill, gratuitously and recklessly, proposes to open to slavery. . . . You have traced the outline of an area of four hundred and eighty five thousand square miles; more than twelve times as great as that of Ohio.

This immense region, occupying the very heart of the North American continent, and larger, by thirty-three thousand square miles, than all the existing free States, excluding California—this immense region, well watered and fertile, through which the middle and northern routes from the Atlantic to the Pacific must pass—this immense region, embracing all the unorganized territory of the nation, except the comparatively insignificant district of Indian territory north of Red river and between Arkansas and Texas, and now for more than thirty years regarded by the common consent of the American people as consecrated to freedom by statute and by compact—this immense region, the bill now before the Senate, without reason and without excuse, but in flagrant disregard of sound policy and sacred faith, purposes to open to slavery.

We beg your attention, fellow-citizen, to a few historical facts.

The original settled policy of the United States, clearly indicated by the Jefferson proviso of 1781, and by the ordinance of 1787, was non-extension of slavery.

In 1803, Louisiana was acquired by purchase from France. At that time there were some twenty-five or thirty thousand slaves in this Territory, most of them within what is now the State of Louisiana; a few only, further north, on the west bank of the Mississippi. Congress, instead of providing for the abolition of slavery in this new Territory, permitted its continuance. In 1812 the State of Louisiana was organized and admitted into the Union with slavery.

In 1818, six years later, the inhabitants of the Territory of Missouri applied to Congress for authority to form a State constitution, and for admission into the Union. There were, at that time, in the whole territory acquired from France, outside of the State of Louisiana, not three thousand slaves.

There was no apology in the circumstances of the country for the continuance of slavery. The original national policy was against it, and, not less, the plain language of the treaty under which the territory had been acquired from France.

It was proposed, therefore, to incorporate in the bill authorizing the formation of a State government, a provision requiring that the constitution of the new State should contain an article providing for the abolition of existing slavery, and prohibiting the further introduction of slaves.

This provision was vehemently and pertinaciously opposed, but finally prevailed in the House of Representatives by a decided vote. In the Senate it was rejected, and, in consequence of the disagreement between the two Houses, the bill lost.

At the next session of Congress the controversy was renewed with increased violence. It was terminated, at length, by a compromise. Missouri was allowed to come into the Union with slavery; but a section was interested in the act for authorizing her admission excluding slavery forever from all the territory acquired from France, not included in the new State, lying north of 36°30. . . .

Nothing is more certain in history than the fact that Missouri could not have been admitted as a slave State had no certain members from the free States been reconciled to the measure by the incorporation of this prohibition in the act of admission. Nothing is more certain than that this prohibition has been regarded and accepted by the whole country as a solemn compact against the extension of slavery into any part of the territory acquired from France, lying north of 36°30, and not included in the new State of Missouri. The same act—let it be ever remember—which authorized the formation of a constitution for the State, without a clause forbidding slavery, consecrated, beyond question, and beyond honest recall, the whole remainder of the territory to freedom and free institutions forever.

For more than thirty years—during more than half the period of our national existence under our present Constitution—this compact has been universally regarded and acted upon as inviolable American law. In conformity with it, Iowa was admitted as a free State, and Minnesota has been organized as a free Territory.

It is a strange and ominous fact, well calculated to awaken the worst apprehensions, and the most fearful forebodings of future calamities, that it is now deliberately purposed to repeal this prohibition, by implication or directly—the latter certainly the manlier way—and thus to subvert this compact, and allow slavery in all the yet unorganized territory. . . .

In 1820 the slave States said to the free States: Admit Missouri with slavery and refrain from positive exclusion south of 36°30, and we will join you in perpetual prohibition north of that line." The free States consented. In 1854 the slave States say to the free States: "Missouri is admitted; no prohibition of slavery south of 36°30 has been attempted: we have received the full consideration of our agreement; no more is to be gained by adherence to it on our part; we therefore propose to cancel the compact." If this be not Punic faith, what is it? Not without the deepest dishonor and crime can the free States acquiesce in this demand.

We confess our total inability properly to delineate the character or describe the consequences of this measure. Language fails to express the sentiments of indignation and abhorrence which it inspires; and now vision less penetrating and comprehensive than that of the All-Seeing, can reach its evil issues.

To some of its more immediate and inevitable consequences, however, we must attempt to direct your attention.

What will be the effect of this measure, should it unhappily become a law, upon the proposed Pacific railroad? We have already said that two of the principal routes, the central and the northern, traverse this Territory. If slavery be allowed there, the settlement and cultivation of the country must be greatly retarded. Inducements to the immigration of free laborers will be almost destroyed. The enhanced cost of construction, and the diminished expectation of profitable returns, will present almost insuperable obstacles to building the road at all; while, even if made, the difficulty and expense of keeping it up, in a country from which the energetic and intelligent masses will be virtually excluded, will greatly impair its usefulness and value.

From the rich lands of this large Territory, also, patriotic statesmen have anticipated that a free, industrious, and enlightened population will extract abundant treasures, and enlightened population will extract abundant treasures of individual and public wealth. There, it has been expected, freedom-loving emigrants from Europe, and energetic and intelligent laborers from our own land, will find homes of comfort and fields of useful enterprise. If this bill shall become a law, all such expectation will turn to grievous disappointment. The blight of slavery will cover the land. The homestead law, should Congress enact one, will be cruel necessity, will not, and should not, work beside slaves. Labor cannot be respected where any class of laborers is held in abject bondage.

We earnestly request the enlightened conductors of

newspapers printed in the German and other foreign languages, to direct the attention of their readers to this important matter.

It is of immense consequence, also, to scrutinize the geographical character of this project. We beg you, fellow citizens, to observe that it will sever the East from the West of the United States by a wide slaveholding belt of country, extending from the Gulf of Mexico to British North America. It is a bold scheme against American liberty, worthy of an accomplished architect of ruin.

Texas is already slaveholding, and occupies the Gulf region from the Sabine to the Rio Grande, and from the Gulf of Mexico to the Red river. North of the Red river, and extending between our own country and the British possessions, stretching from west to east through more than eleven degrees of longitude, and from south to north through more than twelve degrees of latitude, extends the great Territory, the fate of which is now to be determined by the American Congress.

Thus you see, fellow-citizens, that the first operation of the proposed permission of slavery in Nebraska will be to stay the progress of the free States westward, and to cut off the free States of the Pacific from the free States of the Atlantic. It is hoped, doubtless, by compelling the whole commerce and the whole travel between the East and West to pass for hundreds of miles through a slaveholding region, in the heart of the continent, and by the influence of a Federal Government, controlled by the slave power, to extinguish freedom and establish slavery in the States and Territories of the Pacific, and thus permanently subjugate the whole country to the yoke of slaveholding despotism. Shall a plot against humanity and democracy so monstrous, and so dangerous to the interests of liberty throughout the world, be permitted to succeed?

We appeal to the people. We warn you that the dearest interests of the freedom and the Union are in imminent peril. Demagogues may tell you that the Union can be maintained only by submitting to the demands of slavery. We tell you that the safety of the Union can only be insured by the full recognition of the just claims of freedom and man. The Union was formed to establish justice, and secure the blessings of liberty. When it fails to accomplish these ends, it will be worthless; and when it becomes worthless, it cannot long endure.

We entreat you to be mindful of that fundamental maxim of Democracy—EQUAL RIGHTS AND EXACT JUSTICE FOR ALL MEN. Do not submit to become agents in extending legalized oppression and systematized injustice over a vast Territory yet exempt from these terrible evils.

We implore Christians and Christian ministers to interpose. Their divine religion requires them to behold in every man a brother, and to labor for the advancement and regeneration of the human race.

Whatever apologies may be offered for the toleration of slavery in the States, none can be urged for its extension into Territories where it does not exist, and where that extension involves the repeal of ancient law, and the violation of solemn compact. Let all protest, earnestly and emphatically, by correspondence, through the press, by memorials, by resolutions of public meetings and legislative bodies, and in whatever other mode may seem expedient against this enormous crime.

For ourselves, we shall resist it by speech and vote, and with all the abilities which God has given us. Even if overcome in the impending struggle, we shall not submit. We shall go home to our constituents, erect anew the standard of freedom, and call on the people to come to the rescue of the country from the domination of slavery. We will not despair; for the cause of human freedom is the cause of God.

S.P. CHASE, *Senator from Ohio.*
CHARLES SUMNER, *Senator from Mass.*
J.R. GIDDINGS, *Representative from Ohio.*
EDWARD WADE, *Representative from Ohio.*
GERRIT SMITH, *Representative from N. York.*
ALEX. DE WITT, *Representative from Mass.*

SPEECH OF THE HON. S. P. CHASE, OF OHIO IN THE SENATE, FEB. 3, 1854 "MAINTAIN PLIGHTED FAITH"

MR. CHASE said:

Mr. President, I had occasion, a few days ago, to expose the utter groundlessness of the personal charges made by the Senator from Illinois (MR. DOUGLAS) against myself and the other signers of the Independent Democratic appeal, I now move to strike from this bill a statement which I will today demonstrate to be without any foundation in fact or history. I intend afterwards to move to strike out the whole clause annulling the Missouri prohibition.

I enter into this debate, Mr. President, in no spirit of personal unkindness. The issue is too grave and too momentous for the indulgence of such feelings, I see the great question before me, and that question only.

Sir, these crowded galleries, these thronged lobbies, this full attendance of the Senate, prove the deep, transcendent interest of the theme.

A few days only have elapsed since the Congress of the United States assembled in this Capitol. Then no agitation seemed to disturb the political elements. Two of the great political parties of the country, in their national conventions, had announced that slavery agitation was at an end, and that henceforth that subject was not to be discussed in Congress or out of Congress. . . .

Now, sir, who is responsible for this renewal of strife and controversy? Not we, for we have introduced no question of territorial slavery into Congress—not we, who are denounced as agitators and factionists. No, sir: the quietists and the finalists have become agitators; they who told us that all agitation was quieted, and that the resolutions of the political conventions had put a final period to the discussion of slavery.

This will not escape the observation of the country. It is SLAVERY that renews the strife. It is Slavery that again wants room. It is Slavery, with its insatiate demands for more slave territory and more slave States.

And what does Slavery ask for now? Why, sir, it demands that a time-honored and sacred compact shall be rescinded—a compact which has endured through a whole generation a compact which has been universally regarded as inviolable, North and South—a compact, the constitutionality of which few have doubted, and by which all have consented to abide. . . .

The Senator from Illinois, in his speech the other day, made a general charge of gross ignorance of the history and geography of the country against the signers of the Independent Democratic

Appeal, and singled out several paragraphs of that Appeal for special reprehension.

It was rather adroit in the Senator to mix the defence of his own bill with an attack upon two Senators whose opinions on slavery questions are at variance with those most commonly received here. But this movement will not, I think, avail him much. I have no fears that he can refute any statement, or overturn any proposition of that address. Sir, he might as well attack Gibraltar. True in all its statements, and irrefragable, as I believe, in all its reasonings, it is impregnable to any assault by him, or any man. . . .

[T]he Senator charges the signers of the Appeal with misrepresentation of the original policy of the country in respect to slavery. The Senator says:

> The argument of this manifesto is predicated upon the assumption that the policy, of the fathers of the Republic was to prohibit slavery in all the territories ceded by the old States to the Union, and made United States territory for the purpose of being organized into new States. I take issue upon that statement.

The Senator then proceeds to attempt to show that the original policy of the country was one of indifferentism between slavery and freedom; and that, in pursuance of it, a geographical line was established reaching from the eastern to the western limit of the original States that is to say, to the Mississippi river. Sir, if anything is susceptible of absolute historical demonstration, I think it is the proposition that the founders of this republic never contemplated any extension of slavery. Let us for a few moments retrace the past.

What was the general sentiment of the country when the Declaration of Independence was promulgated? I invoke Jefferson as a witness. Let him speak to us from his grave, in the language of his memorable exposition of the rights of British America, laid before the Virginia Convention, in August, 1774. These are his words: "The abolition of domestic slavery is the greatest object of desire in these colonies, where it was unhappily introduced in their infant state."

In the spirit which animated Jefferson, the First Congress—

the old Congress of 1774—among their first acts, entered into a solemn covenant against the slave traffic.

In 1776, the Declaration of Independence, drafted by Jefferson, announced no such low and narrow principles as seem to be in fashion now. That immortal document asserted no right of the strong to oppress the weak, of the majority to enslave the minority. It promulgated the sublime creed of human rights. It declared that ALL MEN are created equal, and endowed by their Creator with inalienable rights to life and liberty.

The first acquisition of territory was made by the United States in 1784, three years before the adoption of the Constitution. Just after the country had emerged from the war of independence, when its struggles, perils, and principles, were fresh in remembrance, and the spirit of the Revolution yet lived and burned in every American heart, we made our first acquisition of territory. That acquisition was derived from I might, perhaps, better say confirmed by the cessions of Virginia, New York, and Connecticut. It was the territory northwest of the river Ohio. . . .

The territory was to be formed into States; the settlers were to receive authority from the General Government to form temporary governments. The temporary governments were to continue until the population should increase to twenty thousand inhabitants; and then the temporary were to be converted into permanent governments. Both the temporary and the permanent governments were to be established upon certain principles, expressly set forth in the ordinance, as their basis. Chief among those was the important proviso to which I now ask the attention of the Senate:

> After the year 1800 of the Christian era there shall be neither slavery nor involuntary servitude in any of the said States, otherwise than in the punishment of crimes whereof the parties shall have been duly convicted to have been personally guilty.

Let it be noted and remembered that this proviso applied not only to the territory which had been ceded already by Virginia and the other States, but to all territory ceded and to be ceded. There was not one inch of territory within the whole limits of the Republic which was not covered by the claims of one or another of the States. It was then the opinion of many statesmen Mr. Jefferson himself among them that the United States, under the Constitution, were incapable of acquiring territory outside of the original States. The Jefferson proviso, therefore, extended to all territory which it was then supposed the United States could possibly acquire.

Well, what was the action of Congress upon this proviso? Mr. Speight, of North Carolina, moved that it be stricken from the ordinance, and the vote stood, for the proviso, six States, New Hampshire, Massachusetts, Rhode Island, Connecticut, New York, and Pennsylvania; against it, three States, Virginia, Maryland, and South Carolina. Delaware and Georgia were not then represented in the Congress, and the vote of North Carolina being divided, was not counted; nor was the vote of New Jersey counted, one delegate only being present. But the Senate will observe that the States stood six to three.

Of the twenty-three delegates present, sixteen were for the proviso, and seven against it. The vote of the States was two to one, and that of the delegates more than two to one for the proviso. But under the provisions of the Articles of Confederation which then controlled the legislation of Congress, the votes of a majority of all the States were necessary to retain the proviso in the ordinance. It failed, consequently; precisely as a proviso in a treaty must fail unless it receive the votes of two-thirds of the members of the Senate.

Sir, if that doctrine of the rights of majorities, of which we hear so much and see in actual practice so little, had then been recognized if the wishes of a majority of the States, and of the majority of the delegates, had prevailed if the almost universal sentiment of the people had been respected, the question of slavery in this country would have been settled, that day, forever.

All the territory acquired by the Union would have been covered with the impenetrable aegis of freedom. But then, as now, there was a Slave Interest in the country; then, as now, there was a Slave Power. The Interest was comparatively small, and the Power comparatively weak; but they were sufficient, under the then existing government, to defeat the proviso, and transfer the great question of slavery to future discussion.

The facts which I have detailed, however, are sufficient to

show what was the general sentiment, and what was the original policy of the country in respect to slavery. It was one of limitation, discouragement, repression. What next occurred?

The subject of organizing this territory remained before Congress. Mr. Jefferson, in 1785, went to France. His great influence was no longer felt in the councils of the country, but his proviso remained, and in 1787 was incorporated into the ordinance for the government of the territory northwest of the river Ohio. I beg the Senate to observe, that this territory was, at that moment, the whole territory belonging to the United States.

I will not trouble the Senate by reading the proviso of the ordinance. It is enough to say that the Jefferson Proviso of 1784, coupled with a provision saving to the original States of the Union a right to reclaim fugitives from service, was incorporated into the ordinance, and became a fundamental law over every foot of national territory.

What was the policy indicated by this action by the fathers of the Republic? Was it that of indifferentism between slavery and freedom? That of establishing a geographical line, on one side of which there should be liberty, and on the other side, slavery, both equally under the protection and countenance of the Government? No, sir; the farthest thing possible from that. It was the policy of excluding slavery from all national territory.

It was adopted, too, under remarkable circumstances. The territory over which it was established was claimed by Virginia, in right of her charter, and in right of conquest. The gallant George Rogers Clarke, one of the bravest and noblest sons of that State, had, with a small body of troops, raised under her authority, invaded and conquered the territory. Slavery was already there, under the French colonial law, and also, if the claim of Virginia was well founded, under the laws of that State. These facts prove that the first application of the original policy of the Government converted slave territory into free territory.

Now, sir, what guarantees were given for the maintenance of this policy in time to come? I once, upon this floor, adverted to a fact, which has not attracted so much attention, in my judgment, as its importance deserves. It is this: While the Congress was framing this Ordinance almost the last act of its illustrious labors the Convention which framed the Constitution was sitting in

Philadelphia. Several gentlemen were members of both bodies, and at the time this Ordinance was adopted, no proposition in respect to slavery had been discussed in the Convention, except that which resulted in the establishment of the three-fifths clause.

It is impossible to say, with absolute certainty, that the incorporation of that clause into the Constitution, which gave the slave States a representation for three-fifths of their slaves, had anything to do with the unanimous vote by which the proviso was ingrafted upon the Ordinance; but the coincidence is remarkable, and justifies the inference that the facts were connected. At all events, the proviso can hardly fail to have been regarded as affording a guarantee for the perpetuation of the policy which it established.

Already seven of the original thirteen States had taken measures for the abolition of slavery within their limits, and were regarded as free States. Six only of the original States were regarded as slave States. The Ordinance provided for the creation of five new free States, and thus secured the decided ascendency of the free States in the Confederation. The perpetuation of slavery even in any State, it is quite obvious, was not then even thought of.

And now, sir, let me ask the attention of the Senate to the Constitution itself. That charter of our Government was not formed upon pro-slavery principles, but upon anti-slavery principles. It nowhere recognizes any right of property in man. It nowhere confers upon the Government which it creates, any power to establish or to continue slavery.

Mr. Madison himself records in his Report of the Debates of the Convention, his own declaration, that it was "wrong to admit in the Constitution the idea that there could be property in men." Every clause in the Constitution which refers in any way to slaves speaks of them as persons, and excludes the idea of property. In some of the States, it is true, slaves were regarded as property.

But the language of Mr. Justice McLean on this point is very striking. He says:

> That cannot divest them of the leading and controlling quality of persons by which they are designated in the Constitution. The character of property is given them by

> the local law. This law is respected, and all rights under it are protected by the Federal authorities. But the Constitution acts upon slaves as persons, and not as property.

Well, sir, not only was the idea of property in men excluded from the Constitution; not only was there no power granted to Congress to authorize or enable any man to hold another as property, but an amendment was afterwards ingrafted upon the Constitution, which especially denied all such power.

The history of that amendment is worth attention. The State which the Senators from Virginia so ably represent on this floor was one of those which immediately after the adoption of the Constitution proposed amendments of it. One of the amendments which she proposed was this: "No freeman ought to be taken, imprisoned, or deprived of his freehold, liberties, or franchises, or outlawed, or exiled, or in any manner deprived of his life, liberty, or property, but by the law of the land."

Did Congress adopt that amendment? No, sir; it adopted and proposed to the States a very different amendment. It was this: "No person * * * shall be deprived of life, liberty, or property, without due
process of law."

Now, sir, in my judgment, this prohibition was intended as a comprehensive guarantee of personal freedom, and denies absolutely to Congress the power of legislating for the establishment or maintenance of slavery. This amendment of itself, rightly interpreted and applied, would be sufficient to prevent the introduction of slaves into any territory acquired by the United States. At all events, taken in connexion with the Ordinance, and with the original provision of the Constitution, it shows conclusively the absence of all intention upon the part of the founders of the Government to afford any countenance or protection to slavery outside of State limits. Departure from the true interpretation of the Constitution has created the necessity for positive prohibition.

My general view upon this subject is simply this: Slavery is the subjection of one man to the absolute disposal of another man by force. Master and slave, according to the principles of the Declaration of Independence, and by the law of nature, are alike men, endowed by their Creator with equal rights. Sir, Mr. Pinckney was right, when, in the Maryland House of Delegates, he exclaimed, "by the eternal principles of justice, no man in the State has a right to hold his slave for a single hour." Slavery then exists nowhere by the law of nature. Wherever it exists at all, it must be through the sanction and support of municipal or State legislation.

Upon this state of things the Constitution acts. It recognizes all men as persons. It confers no power, but, on the contrary, expressly denies to the Government of its creation all power to establish or continue slavery. Congress has no more power under the Constitution to make a slave than to make a king; no more power to establish slavery than to establish the Inquisition.

At the same time the Constitution confers no power on Congress; but, on the contrary, denies all power to interfere with the internal policy of any State, sanctioned and established by its own Constitution and its own legislation, in respect to the personal relations of its inhabitants.

The States, under the Constitution, are absolutely free from all interference by Congress in that respect, except, perhaps, in the case of war or insurrection; and may legislate as they please within the limitations of their own constitutions. They may allow slavery if they please, just as they may license other wrongs. But State laws, by which slavery is allowed and regulated, can operate only within the limits of the State, and can have no extra territorial effect.

Sir, I could quote the opinions of southern judges ad infinitum, in support of the doctrine that slavery is against natural right, absolutely dependent for existence or continuance upon State legislation. I might quote the scornful rejection by Randolph of all aid from the General Government to the institution of slavery within the States. I might quote the decision of the celebrated Chancellor Wythe, of Virginia overruled afterwards, I know, in the court of appeals that slavery was so against justice that the presumption of freedom must be allowed in favor of every alleged slave suing for liberty, and that the onus of proving the contrary rested upon the master.

I think I have now shown that the Ordinance of 1787, and the Constitution of the United States, were absolutely in harmony one with the other; and that if the Ordinance had never been adopted, the Constitution itself properly interpreted, and administered, would have excluded slavery from all newly-acquired territory. But, sir, whatever opinion may be entertained in respect to the interpretation of the Constitution which I defend, one thing is absolutely indisputable, and that is, that it was the original policy of the country to exclude slavery from all national territory. . . .

Mr. President, three great Eras have marked the history of this country, in respect to slavery. The first may be characterized as the Era of ENFRANCHISEMENT. It commenced with the earliest struggles for national independence. The spirit which inspired it animated the hearts and prompted the efforts of Washington, of Jefferson, of Patrick Henry, of Wythe, of Adams, of Jay, of Hamilton, of Morris, in short, of all the great men of our early history. All these hoped, all these labored for, all these believed in the final deliverance of the country from the curse of slavery.

That spirit burned in the Declaration of Independence, and inspired the provisions of the Constitution, and of the Ordinance of 1787. Under its influence, when in full vigor, State after State provided for the emancipation of the slaves within their limits, prior to the adoption of the Constitution. Under its feebler influence at a later period, and during the administration of Mr. Jefferson, the importation of slaves was prohibited into Mississippi and Louisiana, in the faint hope that those Territories might finally become free States.

Gradually that spirit ceased to influence our public councils, and lost its control over the American heart and the American policy. Another Era succeeded, but by such imperceptible gradations that the lines which separate the two cannot be traced with absolute precision. The facts of the two Eras meet and mingle as the currents of confluent streams mix so imperceptibly that the observer cannot fix the spot where the meeting waters blend.

The second Era was the Era of CONSERVATISM. Its great maxim was: Preserve the existing condition. Men said, Let things remain as they are; let slavery stay where it is; exclude it where it is not; refrain from disturbing the public quiet by agitation; adjust all differences that arise, not by the application of principles, but by compromises. . . . It is something to the credit of the Era of Conservatism, uniting its influences with those of the expiring Era of Enfranchisement, that it maintained the ordinance of 1787 in the northwest.

The Era of CONSERVATISM passed, also by imperceptible gradations, into the Era of SLAVERY PROPAGANDISM. Under the influences of this new spirit we opened the whole territory acquired from Mexico, except California, to the ingress of slavery. Every foot of it was covered by a Mexican prohibition; and yet, by the legislation of 1850, we consented to expose it to the introduction of slaves. Some, I believe, have actually been carried into Utah and into New Mexico. They may be few, perhaps, but a few are enough to affect materially the probable character of their future governments.

Under the evil influences of the same spirit, we are now called upon to reverse the original policy of the Republic; to subvert even a solemn compact of the conservative period, and open Nebraska to slavery.

Sir, I believe that we are upon the verge of another Era. That Era will be the Era of REACTION. The introduction of this question here, and its discussion, will greatly hasten its advent. We, who insist upon the denationalization of slavery, and upon the absolute divorce of the General Government from all connexion with it, will stand with the men who favored the Compromise Acts, and who yet wish to adhere to them, in their letter and in their spirit, against the repeal of the Missouri prohibition.

But you may pass it here. You may send it to the other House. It may become law. But its effect will be to satisfy all thinking men that no compromises with slavery will endure, except so long as they serve the interests of slavery; and that there is no safe and honorable ground for non-slaveholders to stand upon, except that of restricting slavery within State limits, and excluding it absolutely from the whole sphere of Federal jurisdiction.

The old questions between political parties are at rest. No great question so thoroughly possesses the public mind as this of slavery. This discussion will hasten the inevitable reorganization of parties upon the new issues which our circumstances suggest.

It will light up a fire in the country which may, perhaps, consume those who kindle it.

I cannot believe that the people of this country have so far lost sight of the maxims and principles of the Revolution, or are so insensible to the obligations which those maxims and principles impose, as to acquiesce in the violation of this compact.

Sir, the Senator from Illinois tells us that he proposes a final settlement of all territorial questions in respect to slavery, by the application of popular sovereignty. What kind of popular sovereignty is that which allows one portion of the people to enslave another portion? Is that the doctrine of equal rights? Is that exact justice? Is that the teaching of enlightened, liberal, progressive Democracy? No, sir; no!

There can be no real Democracy which does not fully maintain the rights of man, as man. Living, practical, earnest Democracy imperatively requires us, while carefully abstaining from unconstitutional interference with the internal regulations of any State upon the subject of slavery, or any other subject, to insist upon the practical application of its great principles in all the legislation of Congress.

I repeat, sir, that we who maintain these principles will stand shoulder to shoulder with the men who, differing from us upon other questions, will yet unite with us in opposition to the violation of plighted faith contemplated by this bill. There are men, and not a few, who are willing to adhere to the compromises of 1850.

If the Missouri Prohibition, which those compromises incorporate and preserve among their own provisions, shall be repealed, abrogated, broken up, thousands will say, Away with all compromises; they are not worth the paper on which they are printed; we will return to the old principles of the Constitution. We will assert the ancient doctrine, that no person shall be deprived of life, liberty, or property, by the legislation of Congress, without due process of law. Carrying out that principle into its practical applications, we will not cease our efforts until slavery shall cease to exist wherever it can be reached by the constitutional action of the Government. . . .

Sir, I have faith in Progress. I have faith in Democracy. The planting and growth of this nation, upon this western continent, was not an accident. The establishment of the American

Government, upon the sublime principles of the Declaration of Independence, and the organization of the union of these States, under our existing Constitution, was the work of great men, inspired by great ideas, guided by Divine Providence. These men, the fathers of the Republic, have bequeathed to us the great duty of so administering the Government which they organized, as to protect the rights, to guard the interests, and promote the well-being of all persons within its jurisdiction, and thus present to the nations of the earth a noble example of wise and just self-government. Sir, I have faith enough to believe that we shall yet fulfil this high duty. . . .

Sir, we may fulfil this sublime destiny if we will but faithfully adhere to the great maxims of the Revolution; honestly carry into their legitimate practical applications the high principles of Democracy; and preserve inviolate plighted faith and solemn compacts. Let us do this, putting our trust in the God of our Fathers, and there is no dream of national prosperity, power, and glory which ancient or modern builders of ideal commonwealths ever conceived, which we may not hope to realize. But if we turn aside from these ways of honor, to walk in the by-paths of temporary expedients, compromising with wrong, abetting oppression, and repudiating faith, the wisdom and devotion and labors of our fathers will have been all ALL in vain.

Sir, I trust that the result of this discussion will show that the American Senate will sanction no breach of compact. Let us strike from the bill that statement which historical facts and our personal recollections disprove, and then reject the whole proposition which looks toward a violation of the plighted faith and solemn compact which our fathers made, and which we, their sons, are bound by every tie of obligation sacredly to maintain.

INAUGURAL ADDRESS OF SALMON P. CHASE GOVERNOR OF THE STATE OF OHIO DELIVERED BEFORE THE SENATE AND HOUSE OF REPRESENTATIVES JANUARY 14, 1856.

FELLOW-CITIZENS OF THE SENATE, AND HOUSE OF REPRESENTATIVES

It has pleased the people of Ohio to call me to their service in the capacity of Governor of the State.

Before entering upon the discharge of the duties to which I am thus summoned, I am required, by the fundamental law, to take an oath or affirmation to support the Constitution of the United States and of this State, and to take also an oath of office.

In compliance with a venerable usage, not established, indeed, by the Constitution, but recommended by the examples of all my predecessors, I now appear before you for the purpose of taking upon myself the solemn obligations which the Constitution imposes; of declaring, briefly, the general principles by which, in my judgment, the conduct of public affairs should be regulated, and of indicating some of their more obvious applications.

The constitutional duty of communicating to the General Assembly the condition of the State, and of recommending measures by him deemed expedient, devolved upon my predecessor, who has, accordingly, laid before you the reports of the several State officers, accompanied by such recommendations as seemed to him most likely to promote the public welfare.

The duty which usage imposes upon me, requires no detailed exposition or elaborate discussion. . . . The sovereignty of the people is the distinguishing characteristic of our institutions. The people constitute the State. Government is nothing but the administration of the affairs of the people by the agents of the people, selected in such manner, and invested with such powers, as are best adapted, in their judgment, to the security of their own rights, and the advancement of their own interests.

To the successful working of such institutions, two conditions are indispensable. This first is personal freedom; the second is official responsibility. Without personal freedom, inviolably secured to every individual, there may be a community of privileged superiors and degraded dependents; but there cannot be, in the true sense of the word, a people. Without responsibility, constantly exacted, and rigorously enforced, the servants of the people are but too apt to become their masters. Eternal vigilance, it has been well said, is the price of liberty.

In our own State, personal freedom is guaranteed by the fundamental law; and the responsibility of public servants is secured by the partition of governmental powers, by strict limitations of authority, and by frequent elections.

To you, Senators and Representatives, belongs exclusively the function of legislation. No part of this power, and no control whatever over your exercise of it, is confided to the Executive. To him belongs the duty of recommending to your consideration such measures as he may think best adapted to promote the public welfare; but there his duty ends. The rest is yours.

To secure individual rights against invasion; to furnish adequate remedies for the redress of injuries; to provide the means, and diffuse the benefits of education; to rescue from unhappy destinies those children of sorrow, the deaf, the dumb, the blind and the insane; to define the just course and limits of individual and associated action; to develop the resources, protect the interests, and defend the honor of the State; to maintain the public faith, and make provision for the discharge of the public obligations: these are some of the high duties which the Constitution of the State and the choice of the people devolve upon you. . . .

Your first and most earnest attention, gentlemen, will doubtless be directed to the important matters within the immediate sphere of your legislative powers; but you cannot forget that you represent a sovereign State of the American Union, third of the thirty-one, in wealth, and power, and population, and second to none in patriotic devotion to the welfare of the whole country. The appointment of a Senator to represent the State in one branch of the American Congress devolves upon you, and in making this appointment you will necessarily be required to consider the interests of Ohio as a member of the Union.

Foremost among these interests is the preservation of the Union itself. Established by the wisdom of our Fathers, for the sublimest and noblest political ends, it descends to us as a sacred trust. Under its benign influence, our country has steadily advanced from strength to strength, and from greatness to greatness, extending her borders, enlarging her resources, and augmenting her power, until the name of American citizen has become a nobler distinction than was the name of Roman citizen in the proudest days of the mightiest Republic of antiquity. To maintain the integrity of this Union; to defend the Constitution which is its bond; and to guard against all invasion, from whatever quarter, those American Institutions which the Union and the Constitution secure to us, have ever been, and I trust will ever be, acknowledged as sacred obligations by the people of Ohio. . . .

While in these and many other important details of administration, the interests of our own State are deeply affected by the action of the National Government, we are even more vitally concerned in the great principle by which that action and the progressive development of our country are regulated and controlled.

As man is more than his circumstances, as freedom is better than wealth, as rights are more important than institutions, it becomes us to look well to the fundamental ideas which determine the character of Government, and the course of its practical operation.

The basis of American Institutions is the democratic principle of equality among men. They rest upon the solid foundation of popular consent. The primary objects of their establishment are the defence and protection of personal rights. If they fail to secure these ends, it is the duty of the people who established, to amend or change them. To organize and administer Government upon these principles, is the true work of a republican people.

While the democratic idea thus constitutes the basis of American Institutions, various exceptions, under the pressure of real or supposed exigencies, have been admitted to its universal application. Among these, Slavery, the creature of despotism and the deadly opposite of democracy, claims baleful pre-eminence.

When our country asserted her independence, slavery existed in all the States. Its evil influences, social and political, were, however, well understood, and its irreconcilable antagonism to the rights of human nature and the principles of just government, was universally acknowledged.

The founders of the Republic, in framing our institutions, were careful to give no national sanction to this portentous anomaly; but they attempted no interference with its existence in the States. Outside of State limits, they allowed it no shelter. Within State limits, they left it to the exclusive disposition of the States immediately concerned. No fact is better established by the records of the past, than the prevalence, during the earlier period of our history, of an almost universal expectation that slavery, excluded, by positive prohibition, from all national territory, would gradually but certainly, and at no distant day, under the operation of the principles of the Declaration of Independence, and through the action of the State authorities, disappear wholly from every State of the Union. The foremost champions of freedom were citizens of slave States, and occupied the highest stations in the State and National governments.

In 1784, immediately after the partial adjustment of the conflict between the claims of the Union and the pretensions of the States in respect to the territory between the Alleghanies and the Mississippi, though the cession, by Virginia, of the territory northwest of the Ohio, Jefferson proposed to provide forever against the extension of slavery, by a positive prohibition of its existence after 1800, in any territory ceded, or to be ceded, or in any State to be created out of such territory.

This proposed prohibition received the votes of sixteen out of twenty-three delegates, and of six out of nine States in the Congress of the Confederation. It failed to become a law by reason of that provision of the Article of the Confederation which made the concurrence of at least seven States necessary to an affirmative decision of any question. The great majority in its favor indicates, however, the prevalent sentiment of the time.

Three years later, the Ordinance of 1787 impressed upon the soil of the territory northwest of the Ohio an indelible prohibition of slavery. That Ordinance was adopted by the unanimous votes of all the States in Congress. It covered every inch of territory subject to the exclusive regulation of the general government.

In the same year the National Constitution was framed. Mr. Madison declared it "wrong to admit in the Constitution the idea that there could be property in men." No such word as slave or slavery found place in any of its provisions. All recognition of the rightfulness of slaveholding, and all national sanction of the practice, was carefully excluded from the instrument.

In every clause which has been, or can be construed as referring to slavery, it is regarded as the creature of State legislation, and dependent, wholly, upon State legislation for its existence and continuance. There is no trace in the Constitution itself, or in the debates of its framers, of any expectation or apprehension of the institution or maintenance of slavery by national law, or in national territory. No one anticipated its extension beyond the limits of the existing States.

But the people required additional security. When, therefore, Virginia suggested an amendment of the Constitution, that "no freeman ought to be deprived of his life, liberty or property, *but by the law of the land*," Congress refused to sanction this restricted guaranty, but proposed, for the adoption of the States, an amendment, embracing a comprehensive and express interdict against all invasion of personal rights by the general government. That interdict, made part of the Constitution by the consent of the States, is in these words: "No person * * * shall be deprived of life, liberty, or property, without due process of law." So long as this provision remains unaltered, it is not easy to see how slavery can be constitutionally introduced anywhere or continued anywhere, by national legislation or in national territory.

This brief statement will suffice to show what was the policy and what was the anticipation of the founders of this Republic in respect to slavery. Their policy was one of repression, limitation, discouragement; they anticipated with confidence the auspicious result of universal freedom. Persistent adherence to their policy would doubtless have realized their anticipations.

I need not say to you that this policy has not been adhered to; nor need I trace the gradual process by which the Constitution has been wrested from its original purposes, and the government has been converted into an instrument for the maintenance and extension of slavery.

By cessions from original States, and by treaties with foreign governments, vast territories have been acquired, in all of which the original policy of the government required prohibition, but to none of which was prohibition actually applied, until resistance to the further increase of slavery and the slave power in the Republic, by the admission of Missouri as a slave State, led to the great contest between the extensionists and the restrictionists, which, in 1820, terminated in the adjustment generally known as the Missouri Compromise.

The terms of that compromise were these: that Missouri

should be admitted with slavery; that slavery should be forever prohibited in the territory acquired from France, north of 36 degrees 30 minutes, except Missouri; and that Congress should refrain, for the present at least, from legislative prohibition of slavery south of 36 degrees 30 minutes. This last term was only implied; it was not expressed.

This compromise, in substance and effect, was a compact between the slaveholding and non-slaveholding sections of the country, and was universally so regarded. It yielded to slavery absolutely the territory occupied by Missouri, and it left without the protection of prohibition all the residue of the territory, acquired under the French treaty, south of 36 degrees 30 minutes.

As the original policy of the country, and the true principles of the Constitution, required the exclusion of slavery from the whole of this territory, it was to be expected that this adjustment would be received with much dissatisfaction in the free States. It was so received; but after a time, for the sake of peace, and in the full belief that its stipulations in respect to the territory north of 36 degrees 30 minutes, would be faithfully observed, the people generally acquiesced in it.

Concession invites aggression. Having succeeded in establishing slavery in Missouri, the slave power soon insisted upon the implied term of the compromise as a positive stipulation for the allowance of slavery south of 36 degrees 30 minutes; not only in the territory acquired from France, but in all other territory, whenever and however acquired, in which slavery might exist at the time of acquisition. This interpretation was tacitly admitted; and under the compromise, thus interpreted, Arkansas, Texas, and Florida came into the Union as slave States, and the small remainder of the territory south of 36 degrees 30 minutes, was allotted to slaveholding Indian tribes.

All the territory south of the Missouri line, whether acquired before or after the date of the compromise, was thus incorporated into slave States, or otherwise appropriated to slavery under the slaveholding interpretation of the Compact. Nothing was left to freedom or settlement by non-slaveholding freemen, except the territory north of the Missouri line. The freedom of this territory, it was thought, was firmly secured. Guaranteed by the Constitution, protected by original policy, guarded by a compact in the fulfillment of which so much has been yielded that it seemed impossible for slavery itself to ask more, the people of the free States never dreamed that it could be invaded or endangered.

But this anticipation proved illusory. When the time arrived for the organization of government for this territory, with a view to open it for settlement and cultivation, the country was astounded by the demand of the slave power for the abrogation of the Missouri prohibition.

At first the demand was heard with incredulous amazement, and then with unavailing indignation. It availed nothing to appeal to plighted faith; nothing to appeal to ancient policy or constitutional guaranties. The great dominant power of slavery demanded the sacrifice of freedom, and the oblation must be made. The Missouri prohibition was repealed; the compromise of 1820, performed to the letter, and far beyond the letter, by the free States, was broken up and destroyed by the slave States, to avoid the fulfillment of its only stipulation in favor of freedom.

The pretences under which this wrong was perpetrated, give additional keenness to the sense of injury.

It was boldly asserted that the prohibition was unconstitutional. The power to prohibit territorial slavery had been exercised by the first Congress under the Constitution, in the act providing for continuing in full effect the ordinance of 1787. The Constitution in express terms, had conferred on Congress the power to make all needful rules and regulations concerning the Territory of the United States.

This provision had been uniformly regarded as authorizing all necessary territorial legislation. Almost every Congress had exercised the power, and almost every President had approved its exercise. The very persons who denied the power to prohibit slavery, asserted the power to establish territorial governments, and to define their departments and powers; and therefore, in denying the power of prohibition, were reduced to the necessity of denying that the greater includes the less.

Under these circumstances, after the prohibition had remained unquestioned for more than the third of a century, the denial of its constitutionality rather provoked indignation than excited doubt.

It was also insisted that the doctrine of popular sovereignty required the repeal of the prohibition. This was a mere abuse of terms. The true idea of popular sovereignty demands as a primary essential condition the recognition of inalienable personal rights. There can be no genuine popular sovereignty where a portion of the population is enslaved. The prohibition of slavery is therefore a necessary prerequisite to a real sovereignty of the people.

In the sense of the apologists for repeal, popular sovereignty signifies nothing but the right of a portion of the community to enslave the rest. It begins by the denial of the natural rights of man. It must end in the total subversion of the fundamental principles of American institutions. For a free and independent people, it would substitute a community of masters, dependents, and slaves.

Such is the repulsive theory. In practical operation, it has not proved more attractive. As embodied in the Nebraska-Kansas bill, it has been fruitful of nothing but evil. It has not conferred a single substantial benefit upon the settlers of either territory. In no respect are they distinguished from the settlers of Minnesota, where slavery is prohibited, except by exposure to its evils.

The sole, special effect of the Nebraska-Kansas act upon the territories organized under it is to open them to the introduction of slaves. In one of them it has led to desperate attempts to effect that object—to invasion, usurpation, violence, bloodshed—almost to civil war. Crimes like these are not the legitimate fruits of that doctrine of popular self-government, to the maintenance of which our fathers pledged their lives, their fortunes and their honor.

In all these things our own State has a deep and peculiar interest. Our own history furnishes the most complete vindication of the policy of slavery prohibition. We occupy, in part, the soil protected from the blight of slavery by the ordinance of 1787. For more than half a century the people of Ohio have been accustomed to regard that ordinance with mingled emotions of gratitude and pride.

Conspicuous among its provisions, and in fit companionship with its sacred guaranties of religious freedom, of liberality towards immigrants, of the inviolability of private contracts, of the security of private property, and of universal education, stands the great interdict against slavery, acknowledging and impartially protecting the rights of man as man. The words to which we always recur when seeking in the ordinance the peculiar springs of our wonderful prosperity and progress, are those which embody this prohibition.

Never did the noble pioneers who laid the foundations on which we now joyfully build, complain of that interdict as an abridgement of any rights, personal or political. On the contrary, they have ever spoken of it as the pillar of fire by night and of cloud by day, which guided and protected them in the wilderness.

More than any other State, Ohio, as the first-born of the ordinance, and indebted to the ordinance for her proud position, as the third State of the Confederacy and first among the new States, is bound to cherish and defend its great and beneficent principles. In so doing, we shall be fellow-workers with its illustrious framers, in their own declared policy and purpose of "extending the fundamental principles of civil and religious liberty whereon these republics, their laws and constitutions, are erected, and fixing and establishing those principles as the basis of all laws, constitutions, and governments which forever hereafter shall be formed in" American "territory."

No political duty appears to me more urgent than this.

The question of slavery, it is almost universally conceded, transcends in present importance all other political questions of a national character. The repeal of the Missouri Prohibition, abrogating the Missouri Compromise, opens anew the whole subject of the relations of slavery to the Union, to the States, and to the Territories.

In determining the true line of duty, under these circumstances, it seems to be the part of wisdom to recur to the acts of the founders of the Republic, and to the principles of the Constitution. To me these guides seem to indicate a plain path. It leads back to the original national policy.

That policy, I have already remarked, while it sanctioned no outside interference with slavery in slave States, contemplated no extension of it beyond State limits. It regarded slavery in all its relations as subject, exclusively, to State legislation, and absolved the General Government from all responsibility for its existence or continuance. Our return to that policy should be signalized by the restoration of the guaranty of freedom to the territories which have been deprived of it by the retrograde legislation of Congress.

Had the policy originally adopted been persistently pursued, the question of slavery would have ceased long since to vex our repose and disturb our councils. Should that policy be restored, may we not confidently expect the restoration also of those relations of harmony and good will which characterized the era of its adoption, and that, through repeal of all national legislation in support of slavery, and the constitutional action of State Governments, the ardent desire of our Fathers for the deliverance of the whole country from the great evil, may at length be fulfilled?

No worthier objects than these, in my judgment, can engage the united efforts of freemen. Frank and cordial co-operation for these noble ends excludes all invidious and unjust discrimination on account of birth or creed, endangers no right of any individual or any State, but promises the happy result of a more perfect Union established upon the solid foundations of exact justice, and equal rights.

I have thus submitted to you, gentlemen, my general views upon several things of public interest. Other important matters will doubtless engage your attention. You need no further assurance of my disposition to cooperate faithfully with you in whatever may promote the common welfare. Let us proceed, then, to the discharge of our respective duties.

With hearts full of gratitude to God for the liberty which we enjoy, and the prosperity which has attended us hitherto, let it be our constant endeavor, looking reverently to Him for guidance and direction, to ensure the transmission to those who are to come after us, of the noble heritage of free institutions which we have received from our fathers, not only unimpaired, but augmented and improved.

VOTE OF THANKS
SPEECH OF HON. SALMON P. CHASE
DELIVERED IN ODD FOLLOWS' HALL, COVINGTON, KENTUCKY
THURSDAY EVENING, OCT. 14, 1864

KENTUCKIANS — LADIES AND GENTLEMEN: Four years ago I stood where I now stand, and spoke to an audience in this hall upon the issues which were then before the country. Then, as now, I advocated the election of Abraham Lincoln to the Presidency of the United States, and I endeavored to show to my fellow citizens that the Republican plan — what we now know as the Union plan — for the settlement of the great controversy before the country, was the true plan.

Four parties then claimed the suffrage of American citizens. One supported Mr. Breckenridge and asserted as their fundamental principle that slavery should be extended throughout the Union; not only that it should be secure in the States where it existed under local constitutions and laws, but that it should be carried beyond those limits, into all the territories of the Union; not only so, but that under claims of transit and reclamation it should be established practically in all the States. I endeavored to show you at that time that upon this platform there could be no peace.

Another party supported Mr. Douglas, and their theory was, that subject to the construction of the Constitution by the Supreme Court, and to the action of the Federal Administration, slavery should be disposed of in the Territories of the Union, according to the will of the inhabitants of these Territories. The objection to this theory, which I deemed to be insuperable, and which I then stated to you was, that under the practical operations of the Government, and under judicial constructions of the Constitution by the Supreme Court, no practical liberty of choice was left to the people of the Territories.

Another party, of which Mr. Bell and Mr. Everett were the representatives, took for their, platform the simple motto, the Union, the Constitution, and the enforcement of the laws. That this was a good platform, I fully conceded; but maintained that, as all parties claimed alike to stand upon it, it could not form any substantial issue before the American people.

That no issue was, in fact, made by it, is plain enough, from the disposition which the rebellion has made of its candidates. Mr. Bell as you all know, is now among the rebels, and openly arrayed against the Constitution and Union, and the enforcement of the laws, while Mr. Everett in his vigorous age, (long may he live, the pride and ornament of his country,) upholds with all his energies the Constitution and the Union, and insists that throughout every foot of American soil, every constitutional law must be enforced by the whole power of the Government. [Applause.]

Having considered these plans of settlement and shown them to be impracticable and defective, I invoked your attention to that proposed by Mr. Lincoln and his friends. Its substance was simply this: That we should let slavery alone, in all the States which it existed, subject only and absolutely to the disposal of the people of those States; but that beyond State limits, where the Government of the United States and the people who make the Government, are directly responsible for the existence of slavery, there ought to be, and could be, no allowance of the institution.

I endeavored to show you that acquiescence in that simple proposition would give peace to the country. Slavery, except by the free action of the citizens of the State, would be disturbed in no State where it existed; it would simply be excluded from the territories and portions of the country under the exclusive jurisdiction of the Congress of the United States. In the States it would remain absolutely undisturbed. No guarantee of the rights of any State would be invaded or jostled. With this principle established, no just cause of complaint could remain. This I endeavored to show you on that occasion.

SECESSION

The result of the election was what I predicted at the time. Mr. Lincoln was chosen President of the United States. He was elected upon the platform of which I have been speaking. No sooner was the result ascertained, than it became evident that a very considerable body of the opponents of his election, and especially of the supporters of Mr. Breckenridge, in the Southern States, and more particularly in the Cotton States, had made up their minds that unless their candidate could be elected they would break up the Union.

South Carolina, almost immediately after the election of Mr. Lincoln, passed, as you know, what she called an ordinance of secession. That example was followed by State after State; and the Senators of State after State left the halls of Congress, until, in February, 1861, a revolutionary Government was organized at Montgomery, with Jefferson Davis, who had just been a Senator of the United States, at its head.

Here was organized secession. I endeavored to prove to you four years ago that secession was revolution. Somebody, I remember, on that occasion, sent up a written question to the stand, and wanted me to say what, in my judgment, Abraham Lincoln would do in case any State should endeavor to withdraw from the Union.

My reply was that I did not know what Abraham Lincoln would do, because he had not expressed himself on that subject; but that in my judgment there was no more noble utterance of Mr. Douglas upon record, than that which be pronounced at Norfolk, in Virginia, when he declared that "against all opposition the Federal Union must be preserved." [Applause.] I did not doubt that Mr. Lincoln would act in the spirit of that declaration of Mr. Douglas.

DISAPPOINTED HOPES

I have no doubt, however, that when secession organized itself in Montgomery, the revolutionists thought they were going to have a peaceable time of it. They counted upon large assistance here in Kentucky; upon large assistance, also, from certain friends over the river, and especially on large assistance in the city of New York.

Unfortunately for them, soon after rebellion had thus organized itself, as I have just stated, it found itself, or thought it found itself, under the necessity of lifting its sacrilegious hand against the flag. The bombardment of Sumter united the whole people of the loyal States.

You, in Kentucky, had a Governor who refused to furnish men. There was, also, a Missouri Governor who refused to furnish men to enforce the laws. But in due time, you disposed of your Governor, and the people of Kentucky responded to the call of the President. So the Missouri Governor was driven from the State disgraced, and the people of Missouri put a man in his place who kept his cath to the Constitution.

Shoulder to shoulder since have Kentuckians and Ohioans stood upon many a field of battle, fighting for the Union of the States. Shoulder to shoulder have the men of Missouri and the men of Massachusetts fought on many a bloody field, for the supremacy of the Constitution and constitutional laws. The rebels were greatly disappointed. They thought the people were going to acquiesce in the dismemberment of the country. They did not realize that of all political sentiments, the dearest to every American heart is the territorial integrity of the republic, the indivisible unity of the country. [Applause.]

MR. LINCOLN'S POLICY

My fellow-citizens, what is our country? It is our common land, inhabited by our folks. We cannot go into any part of it where we do not find our own blood relatives. Every foot of the soil is consecrated by thousands of precious memories. We see Washington everywhere — everywhere the spirit and influence of Jefferson. One law, one people, one destiny, one glorious past, one glorious future. No American can ever consent that this great country shall be broken up and ruined. [Applause.]

The rebels did not count on this. They thought that attachment to States was more than devotion to country. They forgot that States make country, and that country is just as much dearer than States as the whole is dearer than its parts. [Applause.]

But then, fellow citizens, arose a question for Mr. Lincoln to determine. How shall rebellion be dealt with. Mr. Lincoln thought the most concilatory and lenient policy the best policy. Kentucky, you remember, assumed a position of neutrality, and that position was respected at Washington, until it became evident that neutrality must end in secession.

Then William Nelson — a glorious Kentucky name — marched a little band of heroes which he had organized, under the authority of the President, to Camp Dick Robinson, and saved the State. Rousseau — another name dear to Kentuckians — organized his twenty companies at Louisville, and cooperated with Nelson. Thus, by Kentuckians was Kentucky saved. [Applause.]

Mr. Lincoln simply sanctioned this organization and action, and gave it such support as the law at that time allowed. It was the voluntary action of those gallant Kentuckians which kept the State from revolution and ruin. I happened to know a good deal about this matter. I was in constant conference with the Union men of Kentucky, and know I that whereof I speak. All honor, then, to William Nelson and Lovell Rouseau. They can never be forgotten while patriotism and heroism are held worthy of remembrance. [Applause.]

SLAVERY OR UNION?

But not alone in Kentucky was the action of Mr. Lincoln marked by this forbearance and patience. Every where he displayed the same spirit. It was only when events proved that it was impossible to get along with mild measures that he resorted to stronger measures. At length, it became necessary to touch the institution of slavery in the rebel States. That institution, it became evident, was the main support of rebellion.

Everybody knows that under rebel masters, every slave maintained a rebel in the field. Mr. Lincoln saw there was no use in trying to put down rebellion with one hand and to hold up slavery with the other, and he did what any wise man would have done in his place. He struck the main prop of the rebellion. [Applause.]

Some say Mr. Lincoln had no business to strike slavery. Mr. Lincoln did not want to do so. It became a question with him whether the Union or slavery was to be saved; and, when that question was made, he had no choice, and he did not hesitate. [Applause.] He gave the rebels fair warning, and plenty of time to repent and come back into the Union. They mocked at his warning and his invitation, and right. [Applause.]

There is, I suppose, no proposition better settled than this — that in time of war, he who controls and directs the military force of the nation, has the power to do whatever, within belligerent law, is necessary to the success of the war. The Constitution provided for raising armies, and made the President Commander-in-Chief. It gave him, therefore, full power to take all steps necessary to the effectual prosecution of the war.

The best statesmen in the land have said, and the proposition has passed unchallenged, that in case of insurrection or foreign war, the institution of Slavery must be subject to such disposal as the national interests shall require. In other words, that with insurrection in a slave State, the whole power over Slavery must pass to the National Government.

In my judgment, when insurrection gave the President power over Slavery, with the power came the duty to put an end to it. Mr. Lincoln was bound to do that which was necessary for the salvation of the Republic. [Applause.]

An old Roman maxim declares that, "The safety of the Republic is the supreme law." There is no law — there can be no law — higher than the safety of the country. [Applause.] Whatever is necessary to insure the safety of the country, is right and fit to be done, and must be done. [Applause.]

But we are not obliged to resort, to any extra constitutional views, for the Constitution, as I have said, provides for the case. When Congress authorized the raising and organization of armies for the suppression of the rebellion, the President, by its very terms became Commander-in-chief. The safety of the Republic is committed to him, and it is right, — nay more, it is his duty, to overcome and destroy whatever opposes itself to it. Under the Constitution he had authority to proclaim freedom to the slaves, and he simply performed a plain duty when he executed it. [Applause.]

Do the loyal men of the rebel States complain? I have seen many of them. In my position at Washington it was my duty to confer very frequently with them. I never yet found a single earnest loyal man from Louisiana, or Florida, or Texas, or Arkansas, or any other State in rebellion, who did not say "let slavery die that the Union may live." [Great applause.] My friend, Mr. Maynard, who will follow me, will tell you that that is the sentiment of the loyal men of Tennessee, and that their only regret is that the President did not include Tennessee in the proclamation; for had it been included one-half of the trouble that has occurred in Tennessee would have been avoided. [Applause.]

THE OBJECT OF THE WAR

But gentlemen tell us the President has changed the object of the war. "We went with him," they say, "as long as he was conducting the war exclusively for the restoration of the Union; but now that he is carrying it on for the destruction of slavery, we cannot go with him. He has changed the object of the war." Now is this true?

What was the object of the war? It was to bring back into the Union, as a loyal State, every State in which the standard of revolt had been raised. When every such State shall have received, one after another, to its place in the Union, the object of the war will be accomplished. Is that object changed? Not at all. But how and in what condition are those States to return? Must they not come back under such conditions as their loyal citizens approve?

Mr. Lincoln's proclamation was right. It was a right means to a right end, and I stand by it. [Applause.] But if no proclamation had ever been issued, who supposes that the thoroughly loyal citizens of rebel States, who have felt the grinding despotism of the slaveholding oligarchy, would ask a Union with slavery?

It was slavery which assailed the life of the nation. It was slavery which drove loyal citizens to caves and forests for shelter. When the Union armies came they brought deliverance from slavery. When the authority of the Union is restored, slavery dies by the decree of the loyal people. How many loyal men will you find in Louisiana who do not desire that slavery shall perish? They have adopted a Constitution within the last few weeks, and in it have abolished slavery.

But gentlemen may say: "Oh, yes, that is true enough in Louisiana, but it was the armed force of the Union that put an end to slavery, not the free will of the people." How was it in Maryland? There was very little armed force there, and none at all exerted to control the perfect freedom of elections. And what have we heard from Maryland? A majority of 7,000 in the City of Baltimore for the new Constitution, with this clause, "From and after the adoption of this Constitution, there shall be neither slavery nor involuntary servitude in Maryland."

Why did Maryland do that? Because free from the yoke of the slave oligarchy, the people can decide for themselves whether it is for their interest to have slavery or not, and they declare it is not for their interest to have Maryland any longer a slave State, and decree that slavery shall exist no longer. They act with perfect freedom.

In Louisiana, every loyal man acts in the same way. So will you find it through the South. Whenever they are ready to come back as loyal States, they will be ready to come back without a vestige of this institution. [Applause.]

Mr. Lincoln, then, has not changed the object of the war at all. He prosecutes the war for the Union, just as before. He finds slavery in the way, and he thrusts it out of the way. [Applause.] And the loyal people, in the midst of whom the authority of the Union is restored, all say amen. [Applause] They want it out of the way; and they will have it out of the way. They themselves are putting it out of the way. There will be no slavery left to trouble this country any longer in the rebel States, when this war comes to an end. [Applause.]

IS THE WAR A FAILURE?

But these gentlemen tell us, "you are vastly mistaken about this war. You are not succeeding in it. You ought to have done a great deal more with the men and money furnished to you, than you have done."

Well, I am not prepared to say that there is not some truth in this; but in every great war there must be mistakes; in every great war there must be more or less misapplication of the public funds; but if you have an honest man at the head of the Government, who does not want to make mistakes, and who does not want the public funds misapplied, is it not very certain that the more experience he gets, the less cause for complaint there will be? [Applause.]

So I feel that henceforward, as things have improved with experience hitherto, so they will continue to improve, until there is nothing, substantially, to be complained of. But, they say "the war is a failure. You have been prosecuting this war for four years, and have failed." Well, as I have had occasion to say elsewhere, in the first place that we have not prosecuted the war for four years; from the time when that assertion of failure was made, until the end of four years, eight months remain; give Grant, Sherman and Sheridan, eight months, and there won't be a great deal of talk among these gentlemen about the failure of the war. [Applause.]

But it has been a failure so far? Kentucky was neutral when the war began. Is she neutral today? I know there is a good many in Kentucky who do not sympathize with the Administration.

There are some, I am sorry to say, who sympathize with the rebellion, but the mass of the people in Kentucky are true and loyal men and women, and they have no more idea of deserting the old flag, than we in Ohio. [Applause.] You may have your choice about leaders — who shall uphold the flag; but then you have no difference among you as to the upholding the flag itself.

Kentucky is safe, Missouri is safe, Maryland is safe, West Virginia is safe, and a large portion of East Virginia is safe. Tennessee is in the Union, and a large portion of Louisiana is in the Union, and our flag floats in every State where rebellion displayed its standard four years ago. [Applause.] There is, then, progress — decided, unequivocal progress.

I shall never forget the state of things three years ago, last April, immediately after the firing on Fort Sumter. There was hardly a regiment at Washington. Our troops were scattered all over the Union, and the greater part of our little army was in Texas, where it was surrounded by a traitor General, to the rebel authorities of that State. There was no army under the command of the President — no navy. Our ships had been scattered all over the globe. There were but few guns in our arsenals, and we had but small means to equip armies, if we had them.

The railroad between Washington and Baltimore was in possession of the rebels. Baltimore itself was in possession of the rebels. They had seized the vessels in the harbor, and were preparing an attack upon Fort McHenry.

We were beleaguered in the capital, with no way out, except through West Virginia or Pennsylvania. The Ohio River was closed. Every light of commerce along the whole coast, from the Capes of Delaware to the mouth of the Rio Grande, had been extinguished. Instead of the accustomed greeting to foreign commerce entering our ports, all was darkness on our coasts.

All your forts were seized, with the exception of Fort Pickens and Fort Sumter. Fort Sumter itself fell. Such was the condition of things three years ago last April. Now, I have just told you what is the present condition. Is that a failure?

When the great armies of the Union, and, what is better still, the mighty people behind them, are advancing, step by step, resistlessly, certainly, to the consummation of the great work of the restoration of the Union, are we falling? There is no failure here.

What do you propose, who object to Mr. Lincoln? Do you say: Give the power into the hands of a General who will do the work better? But what assurance have you of that? Conceding all you claim for him — for argument's sake only — see how he is hampered by associations, by circumstances.

Even if his own heart were earnestly in his work, what can he do when he is required by the party he represents, as his first act, after election, to make earnest endeavors for an immediate cessation of hostilities? In that direction certainly lies failure.

Three great armies are advancing. Sherman at the head of one, Grant at the head of another, and Sheridan at the head of the third. They march toward the complete suppression of the rebellion. [Applause.] No failure there; but progress — a grand certainty of final success. [Applause.]

But suppose you go to these armies and say, cease hostilities, lay down your arms, resort to negotiations — would that be success? Would not that be failure, complete and most disastrous? How, then, can these gentlemen who propose that we shall cease to fight for the restoration of the Union, and resort to negotiation, the result of which every child can see must be dismemberment — how can these gentlemen ask the American people to trust them to do better, when they propose to do nothing? . . .

A WORD TO KENTUCKIANS

Now, what I want to impress upon you, Kentuckians, here tonight, is this: Four years ago I pointed out a plan which I think all will now admit, would, if adopted, have led to peace. If it had not been for the insane determination of the slave oligarchy, to impose the institution of slavery, not merely upon the States in which it exists, but upon all the Territories of the Union, we would have had none of this rebellion and civil war. You, in Kentucky, would have been at peace. The people of every other Slave State would have been at peace. The plan offered was rejected, and we are involved in war.

Now, let me say to you that, being involved in war, there is no way out of it, except by the complete suppression of the rebellion. No way but this one way, unless we are prepared to dismember the American Union; and we will fight forever before we will do that. [Great applause.]

There is no such thing; rely upon it, there is no such thing, as persuading our people to give up their country. They will not consent to see the sacred, venerable forms of our country hacked to pieces by rebel swords. [Applause.] So, then, you may count as certain that the country is to be preserved; and the only question is, will we be unanimous now? Will we profit by our past experience, and stand together now?

Mr. Lincoln is sure to be elected. [Applause.] Is it best for us to present the spectacle of a divided people? Will a vote against Mr. Lincoln do anything for the suppression of this rebellion? Everybody knows it will not. Everybody knows it; every rebel sympathizer, every rebel deserter, every man who wants the cause of the country to fall, the stock-jobbers of New York, who speculate upon the necessities of the people, in the rise of gold, every disloyal man of every shade of disloyalty knows it. Hence they are all against Mr. Lincoln.

Now, then, is it worthwhile to increase their number? Is it not a great deal better, inasmuch as Mr. Lincoln is sure to be elected, is it not a great deal better, as a matter of mere common sense and calculation, to stand by him, and make the rebels feel that this is a united people, and that they are determined that Mr. Lincoln shall finish the war which they began, by suppressing this rebellion. [Applause.]

Ask the men in the field; ask Grant! He tells you if the people will only be united in this war, he shall find no trouble in the front. Ask Sherman, and he tells you the same thing. Ask nearly every officer in the army, and they will tell you, "What we want is a united people at the ballot-box; we will take care of the rebels, if you will take care of their sympathizers. Make your ballots tell, and our bullets will not fail."

Now, then, if the men who conduct the war are thus unanimous; if it is a plain, common sense statement, that in Union is strength, safety and speedy peace, why should not Kentucky stand by the Union, and not merely by the Union, but by the only man through whom alone, under [existing circumstances, this Union can be preserved? [Applause.]

I speak as to wise men, judge ye what I say. Consider these things among yourselves. Determine for yourselves whether or not it is not better in every point of view for Kentucky and for Kentuckians to stand together with their brethren of Ohio, of Indiana, of Pennsylvania, and of all the other States which speak for Union and freedom, to be established and secured through the election of Mr. Lincoln — a great deal better than to go off into an opposition where all they can do can avail them nothing, just nothing. [Applause.]

PERORATION

Now, fellow-citizens, the time is short. In a very few days the issues of this election must be determined. I have already said how it is going to be determined. Abraham Lincoln, of Illinois, and Andrew Johnson, of Tennessee, are to be the next President and Vice-President of the United States. That is the way.

They will be supported, if not by the whole people, yet by such a body of the people that the power of the Government will come into their hands. The people will "rally round the flag." They will come to the rescue of their institutions. Grant's army, Sherman's army, Sheridan's army will be reinforced. The resistless march of the Union will prevail. Rebellion will fail.

State after State will haul down the rebel flag. Over State after State will the old Stars and Stripes float once more, resplendent in their original glory, until, at length, over the vast extent of the Republic shall again be "seen the gorgeous ensign of the Republic, once more full high advanced, its arms and trophies streaming in their original lustre, not a stripe erased or polluted, not a single star obscured — bearing for its motto no such miserable interrogatory as What is all this worth? but everywhere spread all over, in characters of living light, blazing on all its ample folds, as they float over the sea and over the land, and in every wind over the whole heavens, that other sentiment dear to every true American heart, Liberty and Union, now and forever, one and inseparable!" [Applause.]

PART IV: CHASE, THE RECONSTRUCTION CHIEF JUSTICE

IN RE TURNER
1 Abb. U. S. 84 (1867)
Circuit Court, D. Maryland

CHASE, CIRCUIT JUSTICE.

The petitioner in this case seeks relief from restraint and detention by Philemon T. Hambleton, of Talbot county, in Maryland, in alleged contravention of the constitution and laws of the United States. The facts, as they appear from the return made by Mr. Hambleton to the writ and by his verbal statement made in court, and admitted as part of the return, are substantially as follows:

The petitioner, Elizabeth Turner, a young person of color, and her mother, were, prior to the adoption of the Maryland constitution of 1864, slaves of the respondent. That constitution went into operation on November 1, 1864, and prohibited slavery. Almost immediately thereafter many of the freed people of Talbot county were collected together under some local authority, the nature of which does not clearly appear, and the younger persons were bound as apprentices, usually, if not always, to their late masters. Among others, Elizabeth, the petitioner, was indentured to Hambleton by an indenture dated November 3, two days after the new constitution went into operation.

Upon comparing the terms of this indenture (which is claimed to have been executed under the laws of Maryland relating to negro apprentices) with those required by the law of Maryland in the indentures for the apprenticeship, of white persons, the variance is manifest. The petitioner, under this indenture, is not entitled to any education; a white apprentice must be taught reading, writing, and arithmetic. The petitioner is liable to be assigned and transferred at the will of the master to any person in the same county; the white apprentice is not so liable. The authority of the master over the petitioner is described in the law as a "property and interest;" no such description is applied to authority over a white apprentice. It is unnecessary to mention other particulars.

Such is the case. I regret that I have been obliged to consider it without the benefit of any argument in support of the claim of the respondent to the writ. But I have considered it with care, and an earnest desire to reach right conclusions. For the present, I shall restrict myself to a brief statement of these conclusions, without going into the grounds of them. The time does not allow more.

The following propositions, then, seem to me to be sound law, and they decide the case:

1. The first clause of the thirteenth amendment to the constitution of the United States interdicts slavery and involuntary servitude, except as a punishment for crime, and establishes freedom as the constitutional right of all persons in the United States.

2. The alleged apprenticeship in the present case is involuntary servitude, within the meaning of these words in the amendment

3. If this were otherwise, the indenture set forth in the return does not contain important provisions for the security and benefit of the apprentice which are required by the laws of Maryland in indenture of white apprentices, and is, therefore, in contravention of that clause of the first section of the civil rights law enacted by congress on April 9, 1866, which assures to all citizens without regard to race or color, "full and equal benefit of all laws and proceedings, for the security of persons and property as is enjoyed by white citizens."

4. This law having been enacted under the second clause of the thirteenth amendment, in enforcement of the first clause of the same amendment, is constitutional, and applies to all conditions prohibited by it, whether originating in transactions before or since its enactment

5. Colored persons equally with white persons are citizens of the United States. The petitioner, therefore, must be discharged from restraint by the respondent.

The chief justice passed the following order: Ordered by the court, this 10th day of October, A. D. 1867, that Elizabeth Turner be discharged from the custody of Philemon T. Hambleton, upon the ground that the detention and restraint complained of is in violation of the constitution and laws of the United States; and it is further ordered that the costs of this proceeding be paid by the petitioner.

When Chief Justice Taney died in October of 1864, President Lincoln nominated Salmon P. Chase as the sixth Chief Justice of the United States. Chase administered the oath of office to Abraham Lincoln during his second inaugural. As Chief Justice, Chase agreed to the admission of the first black lawyer to be a member of the Supreme Court bar. Massachusetts attorney John Rock had been denied admission the previous year by the Taney Court on the basis of race. Now, upon the motion of Massachusetts Senator Charles Sumner, he was admitted with Chase's approval. *Harper's Weekly* observed that this event represented an "extraordinary reversal" of *Dred Scott*, and would "be regarded by the future historian as a remarkable indication of the revolution which is going on in the sentiment of a great people."[22]

When Lincoln was murdered by the Maryland-born actor, and Southern sympathizer, John Wilkes Booth on April 14, 1865, Chief Justice Chase administered the oath of office to Vice President Andrew Johnson, a Democrat from Tennessee. When Johnson was later impeached by the House of Representatives for resisting the efforts of the Republican Congress to "reconstruct" the South,[23] Chase presided over his trial in the Senate. In part because Chase established a judicial-style proceeding, Johnson escaped conviction and removal from office by a single vote.

TEXAS v. WHITE
74 U.S.700 (1868)

THE CHIEF JUSTICE delivered the opinion of the court.

This is an original suit in this court, in which the State of Texas, claiming certain bonds of the United States as her property, asks an injunction to restrain the defendants from receiving payment from the National government, and to compel the surrender of the bonds to the State.

It appears from the bill, answers, and proofs, that the United

---

[22] See DORIS KEARNS GOODWIN,TEAM OF RIVALS 681 (2006)

[23] His specific offence concerned the alleged violation of the Tenure in Office Act which provided that all federal officials whose appointment required Senate confirmation could not be removed without the consent of the Senate. The bill had been enacted over Johnson's veto, which was based on his objections to its constitutionality.

States, by act of September 9, 1850, offered to the State of Texas, in compensation for her claims connected with the settlement of her boundary, $10,000,000 in five per cent. bonds, each for the sum of $1000; and that this offer was accepted by Texas. One-half of these bonds were retained for certain purposes in the National treasury, and the other half were delivered to the State. The bonds thus delivered were dated January 1, 1851, and were all made payable to the State of Texas, or bearer, and redeemable after the 31st day of December, 1864. They were received in behalf of the State by the comptroller of public accounts, under authority of an act of the legislature, which, besides giving that authority, provided that no bond should be available in the hands of any holder until after indorsement by the governor of the State.

After the breaking out of the rebellion, the insurgent legislature of Texas, on the 11th of January, 1862, repealed the act requiring the indorsement of the governor, and on the same day provided for the organization of a military board, composed of the governor, comptroller, and treasurer; and authorized a majority of that board to provide for the defence of the State by means of any bonds in the treasury, upon any account, to the extent of $1,000,000. The defence contemplated by the act was to be made against the United States by war. Under this authority the military board entered into an agreement with George W. White and John Chiles, two of the defendants, for the sale to them of one hundred and thirty-five of these bonds, then in the treasury of the State, and seventy-six more, then deposited with Droege & Co., in England; in payment for which they engaged to deliver to the board a large quantity of cotton cards and medicines. This agreement was made on the 12th of January, 1865. On the 12th of March, 1865, White and Chiles received from the military board one hundred and thirty-five of these bonds, none of which were indorsed by any governor of Texas. Afterward, in the course of the years 1865 and 1866, some of the same bonds came into the possession of others of the defendants, by purchase, or as security for advances of money.

Such is a brief outline of the case. It will be necessary hereafter to refer more in detail to some particular circumstances of it.

The first inquiries to which our attention was directed by

counsel, arose upon the allegations of the answer of Chiles (1), that no sufficient authority is shown for the prosecution of the suit in the name and on the behalf of the State of Texas; and (2) that the State, having severed her relations with a majority of the States of the Union, and having by her ordinance of secession attempted to throw off her allegiance to the Constitution and government of the United States, has so far changed her status as to be disabled from prosecuting suits in the National courts.

The first of these allegations is disproved by the evidence. A letter of authority, the authenticity of which is not disputed, has been produced, in which J. W. Throckmorton, elected governor under the constitution adopted in 1866, and proceeding under an act of the State legislature relating to these bonds, expressly ratifies and confirms the action of the solicitors who filed the bill, and empowers them to prosecute this suit; and it is further proved by the affidavit of Mr. Paschal, counsel for the complainant, that he was duly appointed by Andrew J. Hamilton, while provisional governor of Texas, to represent the State of Texas in reference to the bonds in controversy, and that his appointment has been renewed by E. M. Pease, the actual governor. If Texas was a State of the Union at the time of these acts, and these persons, or either of them, were competent to represent the State, this proof leaves no doubt upon the question of authority.

The other allegation presents a question of jurisdiction. It is not to be questioned that this court has original jurisdiction of suits by States against citizens of other States, or that the States entitled to invoke this jurisdiction must be States of the Union. But, it is equally clear that no such jurisdiction has been conferred upon this court of suits by any other political communities than such States.

If, therefore, it is true that the State of Texas was not at the time of filing this bill, or is not now, one of the United States, we have no jurisdiction of this suit, and it is our duty to dismiss it.

We are very sensible of the magnitude and importance of this question, of the interest it excites, and of the difficulty, not to say impossibility, of so disposing of it as to satisfy the conflicting judgments of men equally enlightened, equally upright, and equally patriotic. But we meet it in the case, and we must determine it in the exercise of our best judgment, under the guidance of the Constitution alone.

Some not unimportant aid, however, in ascertaining the true sense of the Constitution, may, be derived from considering what is the correct idea of a State, apart from any union or confederation with other States. The poverty of language often compels the employment of terms in quite different significations; and of this hardly any example more signal is to be found than in the use of the word we are now considering. It would serve no useful purpose to attempt an enumeration of all the various senses in which it is used. A few only need be noticed.

It describes sometimes a people or community of individuals united more or less closely in political relations, inhabiting temporarily or permanently the same country; often it denotes only the country or territorial region, inhabited by such a community; not unfrequently it is applied to the government under which the people live; at other times it represents the combined idea of people, territory, and government.

It is not difficult to see that in all these senses the primary conception is that of a people or community. The people, in whatever territory dwelling, either temporarily or permanently, and whether organized under a regular government, or united by looser and less definite relations, constitute the state.

This is undoubtedly the fundamental idea upon which the republican institutions of our own country are established. . . . In the Constitution the term state most frequently expresses the combined idea just noticed, of people, territory, and government. A state, in the ordinary sense of the Constitution, is a political community of free citizens, occupying a territory of defined boundaries, and organized under a government sanctioned and limited by a written constitution, and established by the consent of the governed. It is the union of such states, under a common constitution, which forms the distinct and greater political unit, which that Constitution designates as the United States, and makes of the people and states which compose it one people and one country.

The use of the word in this sense hardly requires further remark. In the clauses which impose prohibitions upon the States in respect to the making of treaties, emitting of bills of credit, and laying duties of tonnage, and which guarantee to the States representation in the House of Representatives and in the Senate, are found some instances of this use in the Constitution. Others will occur to every mind.

But it is also used in its geographical sense, as in the clauses which require that a representative in Congress shall be an inhabitant of the State in which he shall be chosen, and that the trial of crimes shall be held within the State where committed.

And there are instances in which the principal sense of the word seems to be that primary one to which we have adverted, of a people or political community, as distinguished from a government.

In this latter sense the word seems to be used in the clause which provides that the United States shall guarantee to every State in the Union a republican form of government, and shall protect each of them against invasion.

In this clause a plain distinction is made between a State and the government of a State.

Having thus ascertained the senses in which the word state is employed in the Constitution, we will proceed to consider the proper application of what has been said.

The Republic of Texas was admitted into the Union, as a State, on the 27th of December, 1845. By this act the new State, and the people of the new State, were invested with all the rights, and became subject to all the responsibilities and duties of the original States under the Constitution.

From the date of admission, until 1861, the State was represented in the Congress of the United States by her senators and representatives, and her relations as a member of the Union remained unimpaired. In that year, acting upon the theory that the rights of a State under the Constitution might be renounced, and her obligations thrown off at pleasure, Texas undertook to sever the bond thus formed, and to break up her constitutional relations with the United States.

On the 1st of February, a convention, called without authority, but subsequently sanctioned by the legislature regularly elected, adopted an ordinance to dissolve the union between the State of Texas and the other States under the Constitution of the United States, whereby Texas was declared to be "a separate and sovereign State," and "her people and citizens' to be 'absolved from all allegiance to the United States, or the government thereof."

It was ordered by a vote of the convention and by an act of the legislature, that this ordinance should be submitted to the people, for approval or disapproval, on the 23d of February, 1861.

Without awaiting, however, the decision thus invoked, the convention, on the 4th of February, adopted a resolution designating seven delegates to represent the State in the convention of seceding States at Montgomery, "in order", as the resolution declared, "that the wishes and interests of the people of Texas may be consulted in reference to the constitution and provisional government that may be established by said convention."

Before the passage of this resolution the convention had appointed a committee of public safety, and adopted an ordinance giving authority to that committee to take measures for obtaining possession of the property of the United States in Texas, and for removing the National troops from her limits. The members of the committee, and all officers and agents appointed or employed by it, were sworn to secrecy and to allegiance to the State. Commissioners were at once appointed, with instructions to repair to the headquarters of General Twiggs, then representing the United States in command of the department, and to make the demands necessary for the accomplishment of the purposes of the committee. A military force was organized in support of these demands, and an arrangement was effected with the commanding general, by which the United States troops were engaged to leave the State, and the forts and all the public property, not necessary to the removal of the troops, were surrendered to the commissioners.

These transactions took place between the 2d and the 18th of February, and it was under these circumstances that the vote upon the ratification or rejection of the ordinance of secession was taken on the 23d of February. It was ratified by a majority of the voters of the State.

The convention, which had adjourned before the vote was taken, reassembled on the 2d of March, and instructed the delegates already sent to the Congress of the seceding States, to apply for admission into the confederation, and to give the adhesion of Texas to its provisional constitution.

It proceeded, also, to make the changes in the State constitution which this adhesion made necessary. The words 'United States,' were stricken out wherever they occurred, and the words 'Confederate States' substituted; and the members of the legislature, and all officers of the State, were required by the new constitution to take an oath of fidelity to the constitution and laws of the new confederacy.

Before, indeed, these changes in the constitution had been completed, the officers of the State had been required to appear before the committee and take an oath of allegiance to the Confederate States.

The governor and secretary of state, refusing to comply, were summarily ejected from office.

The members of the legislature, which had also adjourned and reassembled on the 18th of March, were more compliant. They took the oath, and proceeded on the 8th of April to provide by law for the choice of electors of president and vice-president of the Confederate States.

The representatives of the State in the Congress of the United States were withdrawn, and as soon as the seceded States became organized under a constitution, Texas sent senators and representatives to the Confederate Congress.

In all respects, so far as the object could be accomplished by ordinances of the convention, by acts of the legislature, and by votes of the citizens, the relations of Texas to the Union were broken up, and new relations to a new government were established for them.

The position thus assumed could only be maintained by arms, and Texas accordingly took part, with the other Confederate States, in the war of the rebellion, which these events made inevitable. During the whole of that war there was no governor, or judge, or any other State officer in Texas, who recognized the National authority. Nor was any officer of the United States permitted to exercise any authority whatever under the National government within the limits of the State, except under the immediate protection of the National military forces.

Did Texas, in consequence of these acts, cease to be a State? Or, if not, did the State cease to be a member of the Union?

It is needless to discuss, at length, the question whether the right of a State to withdraw from the Union for any cause, regarded by herself as sufficient, is consistent with the Constitution of the United States. The Union of the States never was a purely artificial and arbitrary relation. It began among the Colonies, and grew out of common origin, mutual sympathies, kindred principles, similar interests, and geographical relations. It was confirmed and strengthened by the necessities of war, and received definite form, and character, and sanction from the Articles of Confederation. By these the Union was solemnly declared to "be perpetual." And when these Articles were found to be inadequate to the exigencies of the country, the Constitution was ordained "to form a more perfect Union." It is difficult to convey the idea of indissoluble unity more clearly than by these words. What can be indissoluble if a perpetual Union, made more perfect, is not?

But the perpetuity and indissolubility of the Union, by no means implies the loss of distinct and individual existence, or of the right of self-government by the States. Under the Articles of Confederation each State retained its sovereignty, freedom, and independence, and every power, jurisdiction, and right not expressly delegated to the United States. Under the Constitution, though the powers of the States were much restricted, still, all powers not delegated to the United States, nor prohibited to the States, are reserved to the States respectively, or to the people. And we have already had occasion to remark at this term, that "the people of each State compose a State, having its own government, and endowed with all the functions essential to separate and independent existence," and that "without the States in union, there could be no such political body as the United States."[12] Not only, therefore, can there be no loss of separate and independent autonomy to the States, through their union under the Constitution, but it may be not unreasonably said that the preservation of the States, and the maintenance of their governments, are as much within the design and care of the Constitution as the preservation of the Union and the maintenance of the National government. The Constitution, in all its provisions, looks to an indestructible Union, composed of indestructible States.

When, therefore, Texas became one of the United States,

she entered into an indissoluble relation. All the obligations of perpetual union, and all the guaranties of republican government in the Union, attached at once to the State. The act which consummated her admission into the Union was something more than a compact; it was the incorporation of a new member into the political body. And it was final. The union between Texas and the other States was as complete, as perpetual, and as indissoluble as the union between the original States. There was no place for reconsideration, or revocation, except through revolution, or through consent of the States.

Considered therefore as transactions under the Constitution, the ordinance of secession, adopted by the convention and ratified by a majority of the citizens of Texas, and all the acts of her legislature intended to give effect to that ordinance, were absolutely null. They were utterly without operation in law. The obligations of the State, as a member of the Union, and of every citizen of the State, as a citizen of the United States, remained perfect and unimpaired. It certainly follows that the State did not cease to be a State, nor her citizens to be citizens of the Union. If this were otherwise, the State must have become foreign, and her citizens foreigners. The war must have ceased to be a war for the suppression of rebellion, and must have become a war for conquest and subjugation.

Our conclusion therefore is, that Texas continued to be a State, and a State of the Union, notwithstanding the transactions to which we have referred. And this conclusion, in our judgment, is not in conflict with any act or declaration of any department of the National government, but entirely in accordance with the whole series of such acts and declarations since the first outbreak of the rebellion.

But in order to the exercise, by a State, of the right to sue in this court, there needs to be a State government, competent to represent the State in its relations with the National government, so far as least as the institution and prosecution of a suit is concerned.

And it is by no means a logical conclusion, from the premises which we have endeavored to establish, that the governmental relations of Texas to the Union remained unaltered. Obligations often remain unimpaired, while relations are greatly changed. The obligations of allegiance to the State, and of obedience to her laws, subject to the Constitution of the United States, are binding upon all citizens, whether faithful or unfaithful to them; but the relations which subsist while these obligations are performed, are essentially different from those which arise when they are disregarded and set at nought. And the same must necessarily be true of the obligations and relations of States and citizens to the Union. No one has been bold enough to contend that, while Texas was controlled by a government hostile to the United States, and in affiliation with a hostile confederation, waging war upon the United States, senators chosen by her legislature, or representatives elected by her citizens, were entitled to seats in Congress; or that any suit, instituted in her name, could be entertained in this court. All admit that, during this condition of civil war, the rights of the State as a member, and of her people as citizens of the Union, were suspended. The government and the citizens of the State, refusing to recognize their constitutional obligations, assumed the character of enemies, and incurred the consequences of rebellion.

These new relations imposed new duties upon the United States. The first was that of suppressing the rebellion. The next was that of re-establishing the broken relations of the State with the Union. The first of these duties having been performed, the next necessarily engaged the attention of the National government.

The authority for the performance of the first had been found in the power to suppress insurrection and carry on war; for the performance of the second, authority was derived from the obligation of the United States to guarantee to every State in the Union a republican form of government. The latter, indeed, in the case of a rebellion which involves the government of a State, and for the time excludes the National authority from its limits, seems to be a necessary complement to the former.

Of this, the case of Texas furnishes a striking illustration. When the war closed there was no government in the State except that which had been organized for the purpose of waging war against the United States. That government immediately disappeared. The chief functionaries left the State. Many of the subordinate officials followed their example. Legal responsibilities were annulled or greatly impaired. It was inevitable that great confusion should prevail. If order was maintained, it was where the good sense and virtue of the citizens gave support to local acting magistrates, or supplied more directly the needful restraints.

A great social change increased the difficulty of the situation. Slaves, in the insurgent States, with certain local exceptions, had been declared free by the Proclamation of Emancipation; and whatever questions might be made as to the effect of that act, under the Constitution, it was clear, from the beginning, that its practical operation, in connection with legislative acts of like tendency, must be complete enfranchisement. Wherever the National forces obtained control, the slaves became freemen. Support to the acts of Congress and the proclamation of the President, concerning slaves, was made a condition of amnesty by President Lincoln, in December, 1863, and by President Johnson in May, 1865. And emancipation was confirmed, rather than ordained, in the insurgent States, by the amendment to the Constitution prohibiting slavery throughout the Union, which was proposed by Congress in February, 1865, and ratified, before the close of the following autumn, by the requisite three-fourths of the States.

The new freemen necessarily became part of the people, and the people still constituted the State; for States, like individuals, retain their identity, though changed to some extent in their constituent elements. And it was the State, thus constituted, which was now entitled to the benefit of the constitutional guaranty.

There being then no government in Texas in constitutional relations with the Union, it became the duty of the United States to provide for the restoration of such a government. But the restoration of the government which existed before the rebellion, without a new election of officers, was obviously impossible; and before any such election could be properly held, it was necessary that the old constitution should receive such amendments as would conform its provisions to the new conditions created by emancipation, and afford adequate security to the people of the State.

In the exercise of the power conferred by the guaranty clause, as in the exercise of every other constitutional power, a discretion in the choice of means is necessarily allowed. It is essential only that the means must be necessary and proper for carrying into execution the power conferred, through the restoration of the State to its constitutional relations, under a republican form of government, and that no acts be done, and no authority exerted, which is either prohibited or unsanctioned by the Constitution.

It is not important to review, at length, the measures which have been taken, under this power, by the executive and legislative departments of the National government. It is proper, however, to observe that almost immediately after the cessation of organized hostilities, and while the war yet smouldered in Texas, the President of the United States issued his proclamation appointing a provisional governor for the State, and providing for the assembling of a convention, with a view to the re-establishment of a republican government, under an amended constitution, and to the restoration of the State to her proper constitutional relations. A convention was accordingly assembled, the constitution amended, elections held, and a State government, acknowledging its obligations to the Union, established.

Whether the action then taken was, in all respects, warranted by the Constitution, it is not now necessary to determine. The power exercised by the President was supposed, doubtless, to be derived from his constitutional functions, as commander-in-chief; and, so long as the war continued, it cannot be denied that he might institute temporary government within insurgent districts, occupied by the National forces, or take measures, in any State, for the restoration of State government faithful to the Union, employing, however, in such efforts, only such means and agents as were authorized by constitutional laws.

But, the power to carry into effect the clause of guaranty is primarily a legislative power, and resides in Congress. "Under the fourth article of the Constitution, it rests with Congress to decide what government is the established one in a State. For, as the United States guarantee to each State a republican government, Congress must necessarily decide what government is established in the State, before it can determine whether it is republican or not."

This is the language of the late Chief Justice, speaking for this court, in a case from Rhode Island,[24] arising from the organization of opposing governments in that State. And, we think that the principle sanctioned by it may be applied, with even more propriety, to the case of a State deprived of all rightful government, by revolutionary violence; though necessarily limited to cases where the rightful government is thus subverted, or in imminent danger of being overthrown by an opposing government, set up by force within the State.

The action of the President must, therefore, be considered as provisional, and, in that light, it seems to have been regarded by Congress. It was taken after the term of the 38th Congress had expired. The 39th Congress, which assembled in December, 1865, followed by the 40th Congress, which met in March, 1867, proceeded, after long deliberation, to adopt various measures for reorganization and restoration. These measures were embodied in proposed amendments to the Constitution, and in the acts known as the Reconstruction Acts, which have been so far carried into effect, that a majority of the States which were engaged in the rebellion have been restored to their constitutional relations, under forms of government, adjudged to be republican by Congress, through the admission of their 'Senators and Representatives into the councils of the Union.'

...By the act of March 2, 1867, the first of the series, these governments were, indeed, pronounced illegal and were subjected to military control, and were declared to be provisional only; and by the supplementary act of July 19, 1867, the third of the series, it was further declared that it was the true intent and meaning of the act of March 2, that the governments then existing were not legal State governments, and if continued, were to be continued subject to the military commanders of the respective districts and to the paramount authority of Congress.

We do not inquire here into the constitutionality of this legislation so far as it relates to military authority, or to the paramount authority of Congress. It suffices to say, that the terms of the acts necessarily imply recognition of actually existing governments; and that in point of fact, the governments thus recognized, in some important respects, still exist.

What has thus been said generally describes, with sufficient

---

[24] Luther v. Borden, 7 Howard, 42.

accuracy, the situation of Texas. A provisional governor of the State was appointed by the President in 1865; in 1866 a governor was elected by the people under the constitution of that year; at a subsequent date a governor was appointed by the commander of the district. Each of the three exercised executive functions and actually represented the State in the executive department.

In the case before us each has given his sanction to the prosecution of the suit, and we find no difficulty, without investigating the legal title of either to the executive office, in holding that the sanction thus given sufficiently warranted the action of the solicitor and counsel in behalf of the State. The necessary conclusion is that the suit was instituted and is prosecuted by competent authority.

The question of jurisdiction being thus disposed of, we proceed to the consideration of the merits as presented by the pleadings and the evidence.

And the first question to be answered is, whether or not the title of the State to the bonds in controversy was divested by the contract of the military board with White and Chiles?

That the bonds were the property of the State of Texas on the 11th of January, 1862, when the act prohibiting alienation without the indorsement of the governor, was repealed, admits of no question, and is not denied. They came into her possession and ownership through public acts of the general government and of the State, which gave notice to all the world of the transaction consummated by them. And, we think it clear that, if a State, by a public act of her legislature, imposes restrictions upon the alienation of her property, that every person who takes a transfer of such property must be held affected by notice of them. Alienation, in disregard of such restrictions, can convey no title to the alienee.

In this case, however, it is said, that the restriction imposed by the act of 1851 was repealed by the act of 1862. And this is true if the act of 1862 can be regarded as valid. But, was it valid?

The legislature of Texas, at the time of the repeal, constituted one of the departments of a State government, established in hostility to the Constitution of the United States. It cannot be regarded, therefore, in the courts of the United States, as a lawful legislature, or its acts as lawful acts. And, yet, it is an historical fact that the government of Texas, then in full control of the State, was its only actual government; and certainly if Texas had been a separate State, and not one of the United States, the new government, having displaced the regular authority, and having established itself in the customary seats of power, and in the exercise of the ordinary functions of administration, would have constituted, in the strictest sense of the words, a *de facto* government, and its acts, during the period of its existence as such, would be effectual, and, in almost all respects, valid. And, to some extent, this is true of the actual government of Texas, though unlawful and revolutionary, as to the United States.

It is not necessary to attempt any exact definitions, within which the acts of such a State government must be treated as valid, or invalid. It may be said, perhaps with sufficient accuracy, that acts necessary to peace and good order among citizens, such for example, as acts sanctioning and protecting marriage and the domestic relations, governing the course of descents, regulating the conveyance and transfer of property, real and personal, and providing remedies for injuries to person and estate, and other similar acts, which would be valid if emanating from a lawful government, must be regarded in general as valid when proceeding from an actual, though unlawful government; and that acts in furtherance or support of rebellion against the United States, or intended to defeat the just rights of citizens, and other acts of like nature, must, in general, be regarded as invalid and void.

What, then, tried by these general tests, was the character of the contract of the military board with White and Chiles?

That board, as we have seen, was organized, not for the defence of the State against a foreign invasion, or for its protection against domestic violence, within the meaning of these words as used in the National Constitution, but for the purpose, under the name of defence, of levying war against the United States. This purpose was, undoubtedly, unlawful, for the acts which it contemplated are, within the express definition of the Constitution, treasonable. [I]t was insisted in argument on behalf of some of the defendants, that the contract with White and Chiles, being for the purchase of cotton-cards and medicines, was not a contract in aid of the rebellion, but for obtaining goods capable of a use entirely legitimate and innocent, and, therefore, that payment for those goods by the transfer of any property of the State was not unlawful. We cannot adopt this view. . . . [T]he enlarged powers of the board appear to us to have been conferred in furtherance of its main purpose, of war against the United States, and that the contract, under consideration, even if made in the execution of these enlarged powers, was still a contract in aid of the rebellion, and, therefore, void. . . .

It follows that the title of the State was not divested by the act of the insurgent government in entering into this contract. . . .

On the whole case, therefore, our conclusion is that the State of Texas is entitled to the relief sought by her bill, and a decree must be made accordingly.

The opinions in the next two cases were authored by Chief Justice Chase. Both address the scope of the enumerated powers of Congress.

UNITED STATES v. DEWITT
76 U.S. (9 Wall.) 41 (1869)

[In 1867, Congress enacted a law providing:

That no person shall mix for sale naphtha and illuminating oils, or shall knowingly sell or keep for sale, or offer for sale such mixture, or shall sell or offer for sale oil made from petroleum for illuminating purposes, inflammable at less temperature or fire-test than 110 degrees Fahrenheit; and any person so doing, shall be held to be guilty of a misdemeanor, and on conviction thereof by indictment or presentment in any court of the United States having competent jurisdiction, shall be punished by fine, &c., and imprisonment,...

"Under this section one Dewitt was indicted, the offence charged being the offering for sale, at Detroit, in Michigan, oil made of petroleum of the description specified."]

MR. CHIEF JUSTICE CHASE delivered the opinion of the court.

The questions certified resolve themselves into this: Has

Congress power, under the Constitution, to prohibit trade within the limits of a State?

That Congress has power to regulate commerce with foreign nations and among the several States, and with the Indian tribes, the Constitution expressly declares. But this express grant of power to regulate commerce among the States has always been understood as limited by its terms; and as a virtual denial of any power to interfere with the internal trade and business of the separate States; except, indeed, as a necessary and proper means for carrying into execution some other power expressly granted or vested.

It has been urged in argument that the provision under which this indictment was framed is within this exception; that the prohibition of the sale of the illuminating oil described in the indictment was in aid and support of the internal revenue tax imposed on other illuminating oils. And we have been referred to provisions, supposed to be analogous, regulating the business of distilling liquors, and the mode of packing various manufactured articles; but the analogy appears to fail at the essential point, for the regulations referred to are restricted to the very articles which are the subject of taxation, and are plainly adapted to secure the collection of the tax imposed; while, in the case before us, no tax is imposed on the oils the sale of which is prohibited. If the prohibition, therefore, has any relation to taxation at all, it is merely that of increasing the production and sale of other oils, and, consequently, the revenue derived from them, by excluding from the market the particular kind described.

This consequence is too remote and too uncertain to warrant us in saying that the prohibition is an appropriate and plainly adapted means for carrying into execution the power of laying and collecting taxes.

There is, indeed, no reason for saying that it was regarded by Congress as such a means, except that it is found in an act imposing internal duties. Standing by itself, it is plainly a regulation of police; and that it was so considered, if not by the Congress which enacted, it, certainly by the succeeding Congress, may be inferred from the circumstance, that while all special taxes on illuminating oils were repealed by the act of July 20th, 1868, which subjected distillers and refiners to the tax on sales as manufacturers, this prohibition was left unrepealed.

As a police regulation, relating exclusively to the internal trade of the State, it can only have effect where the legislative authority of Congress excludes, territorially, all State legislation, as for example, in the District of Columbia. Within State limits, it can have no constitutional operation. This has been so frequently declared by this court, results so obviously from the terms of the Constitution, and has been so fully explained and supported on former occasions, that we think it unnecessary to enter again upon the discussion....

HEPBURN v. GRISWOLD
75 U.S. 603 (1869)

[The Legal Tender Act of 1862 was enacted to issue paper money to finance the Civil War without raising taxes. The paper money or "greenbacks" depreciated in terms of gold and became the subject of controversy, particularly because debts contracted earlier could be paid in this cheaper currency. This lawsuit originated when a Mrs. Hepburn attempted to pay a debt due to Henry Griswold on a promissory note using paper notes issued by the United States. Griswold sued Hepburn in the Louisville Chancery Court on the note and refused Mrs. Hepburn's tender of U.S. notes to satisfy his claim. She then tendered the notes into the chancery court, which declared her debt satisfied. When the Court of Errors of Kentucky reversed the chancery court's judgment, Mrs. Griswold appealed to the U.S. Supreme Court, where Chief Justice Salmon P. Chase was called to pass upon the constitutionality of the legal tender laws he had, with considerable reluctance as he had long been an advocate of "hard money," supported as Treasury secretary.]

Mr. CHIEF JUSTICE CHASE delivered the opinion of the court.

The question presented for our determination by the record in this case is, whether or not the payee or assignee of a note ... is obliged by law to accept in payment United States notes, equal in nominal amount to the sum due according to its terms, when tendered by the maker or other party bound to pay it? . . . We are thus brought to the question, whether Congress has power to make notes issued under its authority a legal tender in payment of debts, which, when contracted, were payable by law in gold and silver coin. . . .

It is generally, if not universally, conceded, that the government of the United States is one of limited powers, and that no department possesses any authority not granted by the Constitution.

It is not necessary, however, in order to prove the existence of a particular authority to show a particular and express grant. The design of the Constitution was to establish a government competent to the direction and administration of the affairs of a great nation, and, at the same time, to mark, by sufficiently definite lines, the sphere of its operations. To this end it was needful only to make express grants of general powers, coupled with a further grant of such incidental and auxiliary powers as might be required for the exercise of the powers expressly granted. These powers are necessarily extensive. It has been found, indeed, in the practical administration of the government, that a very large part, if not the largest part, of its functions have been performed in the exercise of powers thus implied.

But the extension of power by implication was regarded with some apprehension by the wise men who framed, and by the intelligent citizens who adopted, the Constitution. This apprehension is manifest in the terms by which the grant of incidental and auxiliary powers is made. All powers of this nature are included under the description of "power to make all laws necessary and proper for carrying into execution the powers expressly granted to Congress or vested by the Constitution in the government or in any of its departments or officers."

The same apprehension is equally apparent in the tenth article of the amendments, which declares that "the powers not delegated to the United States by the Constitution, nor prohibited by it to the States, are reserved to the States or the people."

We do not mean to say that either of these constitutional provisions is to be taken as restricting any exercise of power fairly warranted by legitimate derivation from one of the enumerated or express powers. The first was undoubtedly introduced to exclude all doubt in respect to the existence of implied powers; while the words "necessary and proper" were intended to have a "sense," to use the words of Mr. Justice Story, "at once admonitory and directory," and to require that the means used in the execution of an express power "should be bona fide, appropriate to the end." [2 Story on the Constitution p.142 §1253] The second provision was intended to have a like admonitory and directory sense, and to restrain the limited government established under the Constitution from the exercise of powers not clearly delegated or derived by just inference from powers so delegated.

It has not been maintained in argument, nor, indeed, would any one, however slightly conversant with constitutional law, think of maintaining that there is in the Constitution any express grant of legislative power to make any description of credit currency a legal tender in payment of debts. We must inquire then whether this can be done in the exercise of an implied power.

The rule for determining whether a legislative enactment can be supported as an exercise of an implied power was stated by Chief Justice Marshall, speaking for the whole court, in the case of McCullough v. The State of Maryland; and the statement then made has ever since been accepted as a correct exposition of the Constitution. . . . It must be taken then as finally settled, so far as judicial decisions can settle anything, that the words "all laws necessary and proper for carrying into execution" powers expressly granted or vested, have, in the Constitution, a sense equivalent to that of the words, laws, not absolutely necessary indeed, but appropriate, plainly adapted to constitutional and legitimate ends; laws not prohibited, but consistent with the letter and spirit of the Constitution; laws really calculated to effect objects intrusted to the government.

The question before us, then, resolves itself into this: "Is the clause which makes United States notes a legal tender for debts contracted prior to its enactment, a law of the description stated in the rule?"

It is not doubted that the power to establish a standard of value by which all other values may be measured, or, in other words, to determine what shall be lawful money and a legal tender, is in its nature, and of necessity, a governmental power. It is in all countries exercised by the government. In the United States, so far as it relates to the precious metals, it is vested in Congress by the grant of the power to coin money. But can a power to impart these qualities to notes, or promises to pay money, when offered in discharge of pre-existing debts, be derived from the coinage power, or from any other power expressly given?

It is certainly not the same power as the power to coin money. Nor is it in any reasonable or satisfactory sense an appropriate or plainly adapted means to the exercise of that power. Nor is there more reason for saying that it is implied in, or incidental to, the power to regulate the value of coined money of the United States, or of foreign coins. This power of regulation is a power to determine the weight, purity, form, impression, and denomination of the several coins, and their relation to each other, and the relations of foreign coins to the monetary unit of the United States.

Nor is the power to make notes a legal tender the same as the power to issue notes to be used as currency. The old Congress, under the Articles of Confederation, was clothed by express grant with the power to emit bills of credit, which are in fact notes for circulation as currency; and yet that Congress was not clothed with the power to make these bills a legal tender in payment. . . . Indeed, we are not aware that it has ever been claimed that the power to issue bills or notes has any identity with the power to make them a legal tender. On the contrary, the whole history of the country refutes that notion. The States have always been held to possess the power to authorize and regulate the issue of bills for circulation by banks or individuals, subject, as has been lately determined, to the control of Congress, for the purpose of establishing and securing a National currency; and yet the States are expressly prohibited by the Constitution from making anything but gold and silver coin a legal tender. This seems decisive on the point that the power to issue notes and the power to make them a legal tender are not the same power, and that they have no necessary connection with each other. . . .

[T]here is abundant evidence, that whatever benefit is possible from that compulsion to some individuals or to the government, is far more than outweighed by the losses of property, the derangement of business, the fluctuations of currency and values, and the increase of prices to the people and the government, and the long train of evils which flow from the use of irredeemable paper money. It is true that these evils are not to be attributed altogether to making it a legal tender. But this increases these evils. It certainly widens their extent and protracts their continuance.

We are unable to persuade ourselves that an expedient of this sort is an appropriate and plainly adapted means for the execution of the power to declare and carry on war. If it adds nothing to the utility of the notes, it cannot be upheld as a means to the end in furtherance of which the notes are issued. Nor can it, in our judgment, be upheld as such, if, while facilitating in some degree the circulation of the notes, it debases and injures the currency in its proper use to a much greater degree. And these considerations seem to us equally applicable to the powers to regulate commerce and to borrow money. Both powers necessarily involve the use of money by the people and by the government, but neither, as we think, carries with it as an appropriate and plainly adapted means to its exercise, the power of making circulating notes a legal tender in payment of pre-existing debts....

But there is another view, which seems to us decisive, to whatever express power the supposed implied power in question may be referred. In the rule stated by Chief Justice Marshall, the words appropriate, plainly adapted, really calculated, are qualified by the limitation that the means must be not prohibited, but consistent with the letter and spirit of the Constitution. Nothing so prohibited or inconsistent can be regarded as appropriate, or plainly adapted, or really calculated means to any end. Let us inquire, then, first, whether making bills of credit a legal tender, to the extent indicated, is consistent with the spirit of the Constitution. [Discussion of the "cardinal principles" embodied in the Contracts, Takings, and Due Process Clauses omitted.] . . .

We confess ourselves unable to perceive any solid distinction between such an act and an act compelling all citizens to accept, in satisfaction of all contracts for money, half or three-quarters or any other proportion less than the whole of the value actually due, according to their terms. It is difficult to conceive what act would take private property without process of law if such an act would not.

We are obliged to conclude that an act making mere promises to pay dollars a legal tender in payment of debts previously contracted, is not a means appropriate, plainly adapted, really calculated to carry into effect any express power vested in Congress; that such an act is inconsistent with the spirit of the Constitution; and that it is prohibited by the Constitution.

It is not surprising that amid the tumult of the late civil war, and under the influence of apprehensions for the safety of the Republic almost universal, different views, never before entertained by American statesmen or jurists, were adopted by many. The time was not favorable to considerate reflection upon the constitutional limits of legislative or executive authority. If power was assumed from patriotic motives, the assumption found ready justification in patriotic hearts. Many who doubted yielded their doubts; many who did not doubt were silent. Some who were strongly averse to making government notes a legal tender felt themselves constrained to acquiesce in the views of the advocates of the measure. Not a few who then insisted upon its necessity, or acquiesced in that view, have, since the return of peace, and under the influence of the calmer time, reconsidered their conclusions, and now concur in those which we have just announced. These conclusions seem to us to be fully sanctioned by the letter and spirit of the Constitution. …

***

In 1869, Congress expanded the number of justices from eight to nine. Combined with the resignation of Justice Grier, this left two vacancies on the Court for President Ullyses S. Grant to fill. The same day the decision in *Hepburn v. Griswold* was announced, Grant nominated William Strong and Joseph Bradley to be associate justices. Strong had previously been on record as supporting the constitutionality of the Legal Tender Acts. Two days after joining the Court, Strong and Bradley joined with Justices Swain, Miller, and Davis to rehear the *Hepburn* case. After a long and very bitter struggle, that motion was denied. But the new majority quickly agreed to hear the new case of *Knox v.* Lee as a vehicle to reverse *Hepburn*. "It is I think a sad day for the [country]," Chase wrote in his diary after the reversal, "& for the cause of constitutional government. The consequences of the sanction this day given to irredeemable paper currency may not soon manifest themselves but are sure to come."

KNOX v. LEE
The Legal Tender Cases, 79 U.S. 457 (1870)

MR. JUSTICE STRONG delivered the opinion of the court….

If it be held by this court that Congress has no constitutional power, under any circumstances, or in any emergency, to make treasury notes a legal tender for the payment of all debts (a power confessedly possessed by every independent sovereignty other than the United States), the government is without those means of self-preservation which, all must admit, may, in certain contingencies, become indispensable, even if they were not when the acts of Congress now called in question were enacted. It is also clear that if we hold the acts invalid as applicable to debts incurred, or transactions which have taken place since their enactment, our decision must cause, throughout the country, great business derangement, widespread distress, and the rankest injustice....

A decent respect for a co-ordinate branch of the government demands that the judiciary should presume, until the contrary is clearly shown, that there has been no transgression of power by Congress—all the members of which act under the obligation of an oath of fidelity to the Constitution. Such has always been the rule.... It is incumbent, therefore, upon those who affirm the unconstitutionality of an act of Congress to show clearly that it is in violation of the provisions of the Constitution. It is not sufficient for them that they succeed in raising a doubt.

Nor can it be questioned that, when investigating the nature and extent of the powers conferred by the Constitution upon Congress, it is indispensable to keep in view the objects for which those powers were granted. This is a universal rule of construction applied alike to statutes, wills, contracts, and constitutions. If the general purpose of the instrument is ascertained, the language of its provisions must be construed with reference to that purpose and so as to subserve it. In no other way can the intent of the framers of the instrument be discovered. And there are more urgent reasons for looking to the ultimate purpose in examining the powers conferred by a constitution than there are in construing a statute, a will, or a contract. We do not expect to find in a constitution minute details. It is necessarily brief and comprehensive. It prescribes outlines, leaving the filling up to be deduced from the outlines. . . .

If these are correct principles, if they are proper views of the manner in which the Constitution is to be understood, the powers conferred upon Congress must be regarded as related to each other, and all means for a common end. Each is but part of a system, a constituent of one whole. No single power is the ultimate end for which the Constitution was adopted. It may, in a very proper sense, be treated as a means for the accomplishment of a subordinate object, but that object is itself a means designed for an ulterior purpose. Thus the power to levy and collect taxes, to coin money and regulate its value, to raise and support armies, or to provide for and maintain a navy, are instruments for the paramount object, which was to establish a government, sovereign within its sphere, with capability of self-preservation, thereby forming a union more perfect than that which existed under the old Confederacy.

The same may be asserted also of all the non-enumerated powers included in the authority expressly given "to make all laws which shall be necessary and proper for carrying into execution the specified powers vested in Congress, and all other powers vested by the Constitution in the government of the United States, or in any department or officer thereof." It is impossible to know what those non-enumerated powers are, and what is their nature and extent, without considering the purposes they were intended to subserve. Those purposes, it must be noted, reach beyond the mere execution of all powers definitely intrusted to Congress and mentioned in detail. They embrace the execution of all other powers vested by the Constitution in the government of the United States, or in any department or officer thereof. It certainly was intended to confer upon the government the power of self-preservation. . . .

That would appear, then, to be a most unreasonable construction of the Constitution which denies to the government created by it, the right to employ freely every means, not prohibited, necessary for its preservation, and for the fulfilment of its acknowledged duties. Such a right, we hold, was given by the last clause of the eighth section of its first article. The means or instrumentalities referred to in that clause, and authorized, are not enumerated or defined. In the nature of things enumeration and specification were impossible. But they were left to the discretion of Congress, subject only to the restrictions that they be not prohibited, and be necessary and proper for carrying into execution the enumerated powers given to Congress, and all other powers vested in the government of the United States, or in any department or officer thereof.

And here it is to be observed it is not indispensable to the existence of any power claimed for the Federal government that it can be found specified in the words of the Constitution, or clearly and directly traceable to some one of the specified powers. Its existence may be deduced fairly from more than one of the substantive powers expressly defined, or from them all combined. It is allowable to group together any number of them and infer from them all that the power claimed has been conferred. Such a treatment of the Constitution is recognized by its own provisions. This is well illustrated in its language respecting the writ of habeas corpus. The power to suspend the privilege of that writ is not expressly given, nor can it be deduced from any one of the particularized grants of power. Yet it is provided that the privileges of the writ shall not be suspended except in certain defined contingencies. This is no express grant of power. It is a restriction. But it shows irresistibly that somewhere in the Constitution power to suspend the privilege of the writ was granted, either by some one or more of the specifications of power, or by them all combined. And, that important powers were understood by the people who adopted the Constitution to have been created by it, powers not enumerated, and not included incidentally in any one of those enumerated, is shown by the amendments. The first ten of these were suggested in the conventions of the States, and proposed at the first session of the first Congress, before any complaint was made of a disposition to assume doubtful powers. The preamble to the resolution submitting them for adoption recited that the "conventions of a number of the States had, at the time of their adopting the Constitution, expressed a desire, in order to prevent misconstruction or abuse of its powers, that further declaratory and restrictive clauses should be added." This was the origin of the amendments, and they are significant. They tend plainly to show that, in the judgment of those who adopted the Constitution, there were powers created by it, neither expressly specified nor deducible from any one specified power, or ancillary to it alone, but which grew out of the aggregate of powers conferred upon the government, or out of the sovereignty instituted. Most of these amendments are denials of power which had not been expressly granted, and which cannot be said to have been necessary and proper for carrying into execution any other powers. Such, for example, is the prohibition of any laws respecting the establishment of religion, prohibiting the free exercise thereof, or abridging the freedom of speech or of the press.

And it is of importance to observe that Congress has often exercised, without question, powers that are not expressly given nor ancillary to any single enumerated power. . . . Under the power to establish post-offices and post-roads Congress has provided for carrying the mails, punishing theft of letters and mail robberies, and even for transporting the mails to foreign countries. Under the power to regulate commerce, provision has been made by law for the improvement of harbors, the establishment of observatories, the erection of lighthouses, breakwaters, and buoys, the registry, enrolment, and construction of ships, and a code has been enacted for the government of seamen. Under the same power and other powers over the revenue and the currency of the country, for the convenience of the treasury and internal commerce, a corporation known as the United States Bank was early created.... Its incorporation was a constitutional exercise of congressional power for no other reason than that it was deemed to be a convenient instrument or means for accomplishing one or more of the ends for which the government was established, or, in the language of the first article, already quoted, "necessary and proper" for carrying into execution some or all the powers vested in the government. Clearly this necessity, if any existed, was not a direct and obvious one. . . .

Happily the true meaning of the clause authorizing the enactment of all laws necessary and proper for carrying into execution the express powers conferred upon Congress, and all other powers vested in the government of the United States, or in any of its departments or officers, has long since been settled. . . . It was . . . in McCulloch v. Maryland that the fullest consideration was given to this clause of the Constitution granting auxiliary powers, and a construction adopted that has ever since been accepted as determining its true meaning. . . . Suffice it to say, in that case it was finally settled that in the gift by the Constitution to Congress of authority to enact laws "necessary and proper" for the execution of all the powers created by it, the necessity spoken of is not to be understood as an absolute one. On the contrary, this court then held that the sound construction of the Constitution must allow to the national legislature that discretion with respect to the means by which the powers it confers are to be carried into execution, which will enable that body to perform the high duties assigned to it in the manner most beneficial to the people. . . .

With these rules of constitutional construction before us, settled at an early period in the history of the government, hitherto universally accepted, and not even now doubted, we have a safe guide to a right decision of the questions before us. Before we can hold the legal tender acts unconstitutional, we must be convinced they were not appropriate means, or means conducive to the execution of any or all of the powers of Congress, or of the government, not appropriate in any degree (for we are not judges of the degree of appropriateness), or we must hold that they were prohibited.

This brings us to the inquiry whether they were, when enacted, appropriate instrumentalities for carrying into effect, or executing any of the known powers of Congress, or of any department of the government. Plainly to this inquiry, a consideration of the time when they were enacted, and of the circumstances in which the government then stood, is important. It is not to be denied that acts may be adapted to the exercise of lawful power, and appropriate to it, in seasons of exigency, which would be inappropriate at other times.

We do not propose to dilate at length upon the circumstances in which the country was placed, when Congress attempted to make treasury notes a legal tender. They are of too recent occurrence to justify enlarged description. Suffice it to say that a civil war was then raging which seriously threatened the overthrow of the government and the destruction of the Constitution itself. It demanded the equipment and support of large armies and navies, and the employment of money to an extent beyond the capacity of all ordinary sources of supply. Meanwhile the public treasury was nearly empty, and the credit of the government, if not stretched to its utmost tension, had become nearly exhausted. Moneyed institutions had advanced largely of their means, and more could not be expected of them. They had been compelled to suspend specie payments. Taxation was inadequate to pay even the interest on the debt already incurred, and it was impossible to await the income of additional taxes. The necessity was immediate and pressing. The army was unpaid. There was then due to the soldiers in the field nearly a score of millions of dollars. The requisitions from the War and Navy Departments for supplies exceeded fifty millions, and the current expenditure was over one million per day. The entire amount of coin in the country, including that in private hands, as well as that in banking institutions, was insufficient to supply the need of the government three months, had it all been poured into the treasury. Foreign credit we had none. We say nothing of the overhanging paralysis of trade, and of business generally, which threatened loss of confidence in the ability of the government to maintain its continued existence, and therewith the complete destruction of all remaining national credit.

It was at such a time and in such circumstances that Congress was called upon to devise means for maintaining the army and navy, for securing the large supplies of money needed, and, indeed, for the preservation of the government created by the Constitution. It was at such a time and in such an emergency that the legal tender acts were passed. Now, if it were certain that nothing else would have supplied the absolute necessities of the treasury, that nothing else would have enabled the government to maintain its armies and navy, that nothing else would have saved the government and the Constitution from destruction, while the legal tender acts would, could any one be bold enough to assert that Congress transgressed its powers? Or if these enactments did work these results, can it be maintained now that they were not for a legitimate end, or "appropriate and adapted to that end," in the language of Chief Justice Marshall? That they did work such results is not to be doubted. Something revived the drooping faith of the people; something brought immediately to the government's aid the resources of the nation, and something enabled the successful prosecution of the war, and the preservation of the national life. What was it, if not the legal tender enactments?

But if it be conceded that some other means might have been chosen for the accomplishment of these legitimate and necessary ends, the concession does not weaken the argument. It is urged now, after the lapse of nine years, and when the emergency has passed, that treasury notes without the legal tender clause might have been issued, and that the necessities of the government might thus have been supplied. Hence it is inferred there was no necessity for giving to the notes issued the capability of paying private debts. At best this is mere conjecture. But admitting it to be true, what does it prove? Nothing more than that Congress had the choice of means for a legitimate end, each appropriate, and adapted to that end, though, perhaps, in different degrees. What then? Can this court say that it ought to have adopted one rather than the other? Is it our province to decide that the means selected were beyond the constitutional power of Congress, because we may think that other means to the same ends would have been more appropriate and equally efficient? That would be to assume legislative power, and to disregard the accepted rules for construing the Constitution. The degree of the necessity for any congressional enactment, or the relative degree of its appropriateness, if it have any appropriateness, is for consideration in Congress, not here. . . .

It is plain to our view, however, that none of those measures which it is now conjectured might have been substituted for the legal tender acts, could have met the exigencies of the case, at the time when those acts were passed. We have said that the credit of the government had been tried to its utmost endurance. Every new issue of notes which had nothing more to rest upon than government credit, must have paralyzed it more and more, and rendered it increasingly difficult to keep the army in the field, or the navy afloat. It is an historical fact that many persons and institutions refused to receive and pay those notes that had been issued, and even the head of the Treasury represented to Congress the necessity of making the new issues legal tenders, or rather, declared it impossible to avoid the necessity....

It may be conceded that Congress is not authorized to enact laws in furtherance even of a legitimate end, merely because they are useful, or because they make the government stronger. There must be some relation between the means and the end; some adaptedness or appropriateness of the laws to carry into execution the powers created by the Constitution. But when a statute has proved effective in the execution of powers confessedly existing, it is not too much to say that it must have had some appropriateness to the execution of those powers. The rules of construction heretofore adopted, do not demand that the relationship between the means and the end shall be direct and immediate....

We are accustomed to speak for mere convenience of the express and implied powers conferred upon Congress. But in fact the auxiliary powers, those necessary and appropriate to the execution of other powers singly described, are as expressly given as is the power to declare war, or to establish uniform laws on the subject of bankruptcy. They are not catalogued, no list of them is made, but they are grouped in the last clause of section eight of the first article, and granted in the same words in which all other powers are granted to Congress....

[In holding] the acts of Congress constitutional as applied to contracts made either before or after their passage. . . , we overrule so much of what was decided in Hepburn v. Griswold, as ruled the acts unwarranted by the Constitution so far as they apply to contracts made before their enactment. That case was decided by a divided court, and by a court having a less number of judges than the law then in existence provided this court shall have. These cases have been heard before a full court, and they have received our most careful consideration. The questions involved are constitutional questions of the most vital importance to the government and to the public at large. We have been in the habit of treating cases involving a consideration of constitutional power differently from those which concern merely private right. We are not accustomed to hear them in the absence of a full court, if it can be avoided. Even in cases involving only private rights, if convinced we had made a mistake, we would hear another argument and correct our error. And it is no unprecedented thing in courts of last resort, both in this country and in England, to overrule decisions previously made. We agree this should not be done inconsiderately, but in a case of such far-reaching consequences as the present, thoroughly convinced as we are that Congress has not transgressed its powers, we regard it as our duty so to decide and to affirm both these judgments.

THE CHIEF JUSTICE, dissenting:

We dissent from the argument and conclusion in the opinion just announced. . . .

The rule by which the constitutionality of an act of Congress passed in the alleged exercise of an implied power is to be tried is no longer, in this Court, open to question. It was laid down in the case of *McCulloch v. Maryland*, by Chief Justice Marshall, in these words: "Let the end be legitimate, let it be within the scope of the Constitution, and all means which are appropriate, which are plainly adapted to that end, which are not prohibited but consistent with the letter and spirit of the Constitution, are constitutional."

And it is the plain duty of the Court to pronounce acts of Congress not made in the exercise of an express power nor coming within the reasonable scope of this rule, if made in virtue of an implied power, unwarranted by the Constitution. Acts of Congress not made in pursuance of the Constitution are not laws.

Neither of these propositions was questioned in the case of *Hepburn v. Griswold.* The judges who dissented in that case maintained that the clause in the Act of February 25, 1862, making the United States notes a legal tender in payment of debts, was an appropriate, plainly adapted means to a constitutional end, not prohibited but consistent with the letter and spirit of the Constitution. The majority of the court as then constituted, five judges out of eight, felt obliged to conclude that an act making mere promises to pay dollars a legal tender in payments of debts previously contracted is not a means appropriate, plainly adapted, really calculated to carry into effect any express power vested in Congress, is inconsistent with the spirit of the Constitution, and is prohibited by the Constitution.

In the case of the *United States v. De Witt,* we held unanimously that a provision of the internal revenue law prohibiting the sale of certain illuminating oil in the states was unconstitutional, though it might increase the production and sale of other oils, and consequently the revenue derived from them, because this consequence was too remote and uncertain to warrant the court in saying that the prohibition was an appropriate and plainly adapted means for carrying into execution the power to lay and collect taxes.

We agree, then, that the question whether a law is a necessary and proper means to execution of an express power, within the meaning of these words as defined by the rule — that is to say, a means appropriate, plainly adapted, not prohibited but consistent with the latter and spirit of the Constitution — is a judicial question. Congress may not adopt any means for the execution of an express power that Congress may see fit to adopt. It must be a necessary and proper means within the fair meaning of the rule. If not such it cannot be employed consistently with the Constitution. Whether the means actually employed in a given case are such or not, the court must decide. The court must judge of the fact, Congress of the degree of necessity.

A majority of the Court, five of four, in the opinion which has just been read, reverses the judgment rendered by the former majority of five to three, in pursuance of an opinion formed after repeated arguments, at successive terms, and careful consideration, and declares the legal tender clause to be constitutional.... And this reversal, unprecedented in the history of the Court, has been produced by no change in the opinions of those who concurred in the former judgment. One closed an honorable judicial career by resignation after the case had been decided, after the opinion had been read and agreed to in conference, and after the day when it would have been delivered in court had not the delivery been postponed for a week to give time for the preparation of the dissenting opinion. The Court was then full, but the vacancy caused by the resignation of Mr. Justice Grier having been subsequently filled and an additional justice having been appointed under the act increasing the number of judges to nine, which took effect on the first Monday of December, 1869, the then majority find themselves in a minority of the Court, as now constituted, upon the question.

Their convictions, however, remain unchanged. We adhere to the opinion pronounced in Hepburn v. Griswold. Reflection has only wrought a firmer belief in the soundness of the constitutional doctrines maintained, and in the importance of them to the country....

We perceive no connection between the express power to coin money and the inference that the government may, in any contingency, make its securities perform the functions of coined money, as a legal tender in payment of debts. We have supposed that the power to exclude from circulation notes not authorized by the national government might perhaps be deduced from the power to regulate the value of coin, but that the power of the government to emit bills of credit was an exercise of the power to borrow money, and that its power over the currency was incidental to that power and to the power to regulate commerce....

The opinion of the then minority affirmed the power on the ground that it was a necessary and proper means, within the definition of the Court in the case of *McCulloch v. Maryland*, to carry on war, and that it was not prohibited by the spirit or letter of the Constitution, though it was admitted to be a law impairing the obligation of contracts and notwithstanding the objection that it deprived many persons of their property without compensation and without due process of law.

We shall not add much to what was said in the opinion of the then majority on these points.

The reference made in the opinion just read, as well as in the argument at the bar to the opinions of the Chief Justice when Secretary of the Treasury, seems to warrant, if it does not require, some observations before proceeding further in the discussion.

It was his fortune at the time the legal tender clause was inserted in the bill to authorize the issue of United States notes and received the sanction of Congress, to be charged with the anxious and responsible duty of providing funds for the prosecution of the war. In no report made by him to Congress was the expedient of making the notes of the United States a legal tender suggested. . . . In his report of December, 1862, he said that . . . "The Secretary recommends, therefore, no mere paper money scheme, but on the contrary a series of measures looking to a safe and gradual return to gold and silver as the only permanent basis, standard, and measure of value recognized by the Constitution."

At the session of Congress before this report was made, the bill containing the legal tender clause had become a law. He was extremely and avowedly averse to this clause, but was very solicitous for the passage of the bill to authorize the issue of United States notes then pending. He thought it indispensably necessary that the authority to issue these notes should be granted by Congress. The passage of the bill was delayed, if not jeoparded, by the difference of opinion which prevailed on the question of making them a legal tender. It was under these circumstances that he expressed the opinion, when called upon by the Committee of

Ways and Means, that it was necessary, and he was not sorry to find it sustained by the decisions of respected courts, not unanimous indeed, nor without contrary decisions of state courts equally respectable. Examination and reflection under more propitious circumstances have satisfied him that this opinion was erroneous, and he does not hesitate to declare it. . . .

It is unnecessary to say that we reject wholly the doctrine, advanced for the first time, we believe, in this Court by the present majority that the legislature has any "powers under the Constitution which grow out of the aggregate of powers conferred upon the government or out of the sovereignty instituted by it." If this proposition be admitted, and it be also admitted that the legislature is the sole judge of the necessity for the exercise of such powers, the government becomes practically absolute and unlimited. . . .

Until recently, no one in Congress ever suggested that that body possessed power to make anything else a standard of value.

Statesmen who have disagreed widely on other points have agreed in the opinion that the only constitutional measures of value are metallic coins, struck as regulated by the authority of Congress....

The present majority of the Court say that legal tender notes "have become the universal measure of values," and they hold that the legislation of Congress substituting such measures for coin by making the notes a legal tender in payment is warranted by the Constitution.

But if the plain sense of words, if the contemporaneous exposition of parties, if common consent in understanding, if the opinions of courts avail anything in determining the meaning of the Constitution, it seems impossible to doubt that the power to coin money is a power to establish a uniform standard of value, and that no other power to establish such a standard, by making notes a legal tender, is conferred upon Congress by the Constitution.

My brothers CLIFFORD and FIELD concur in these views, but in consideration of the importance of the principles involved, will deliver their separate opinions. My brother NELSON also dissents.

JUILLIARD v. GREENMAN
110 U.S. 421 (1884)

JUSTICE GRAY....

The constitutional authority of congress to provide a currency for the whole country is now firmly established. . . . The power, as incident to the power of borrowing money, and issuing bills or notes of the government for money borrowed, of impressing upon those bills or notes the quality of being a legal tender for the payment of private debts, was a power universally understood to belong to sovereignty, in Europe and America, at the time of the framing and adopting of the constitution of the United States. The governments of Europe, acting through the monarch or the legislature, according to the distribution of powers under their respective constitutions, had and have as sovereign a power of issuing paper money as of stamping coin....

The power of issuing bills of credit, and making them, at the discretion of the legislature, a tender in payment of private debts, had long been exercised in this country by the several colonies and states; and during the revolutionary war the states, upon the recommendation of the congress of the confederation, had made the bills issued by congress a legal tender. The exercise of this power not being prohibited to congress by the constitution, it is included in the power expressly granted to borrow money on the credit of the United States. . . .

Such being our conclusion in matter of law, the question whether at any particular time, in war or in peace, the exigency is such, by reason of unusual and pressing demands on the resources of the government, or of the inadequacy of the supply of gold and silver coin to furnish the currency needed for the uses of the government and of the people, that it is, as matter of fact, wise and expedient to resort to this means, is a political question, to be determined by congress when the question of exigency arises, and not a judicial question, to be afterwards passed upon by the courts. To quote once more from the judgment in McCulloch v. Maryland: "Where the law is not prohibited, and is really calculated to effect any of the objects intrusted to the government, to undertake here to inquire into the degree of its necessity would be to pass the line which circumscribes the judicial department, and to tread on legislative ground."

In 1873, the gravely ill Chase joined three other justices in dissenting from the Court's decision in *The Slaughter-House Cases*, which effectively gutted the Privileges and Immunities Clause from the Fourteenth Amendment. That same day, the Chief Justice was the only dissenting vote in *Bradwell v, Illinois*, a case in which the other *Slaughter-House* dissenters joined with the *Slaughter-House* majority to uphold the denial to women by the state of Illinois of the right to practice law. Chase was too weak and ill to write opinions in either case and one wonders if their outcomes might have been changed had he retained his previous vitality. Three weeks later, a second stroke took his life.

BRADWELL v. ILLINOIS

83 U.S. 130 (1872)

Mrs. Myra Bradwell, residing in the State of Illinois, made application to the judges of the Supreme Court of that State for a license to practice law. She accompanied her petition with the usual certificate from an inferior court of her good character, and that on due examination she had been found to possess the requisite qualifications. . . . On Mrs. Bradwell's application first coming before the court, the license was refused, and it was stated as a sufficient reason that under the decisions of the Supreme Court of Illinois, the applicant "as a married woman would be bound neither by her express contracts nor by those implied contracts which it is the policy of the law to create between attorney and client." After the announcement of this decision, Mrs. Bradwell, admitting that she was a married woman . . . filed a printed argument in which her right to admission, notwithstanding that fact, was earnestly and ably maintained. The court having thus denied the application, Mrs. Bradwell brought the case here as within the twenty-fifth section of the Judiciary Act. . . .

MR. JUSTICE MILLER delivered the opinion of the court.

The record in this case is not very perfect, but it may be fairly taken that the plaintiff asserted her right to a license on the grounds, among others, that she was a citizen of the United States, and that having been a citizen of Vermont at one time, she was, in the State of Illinois, entitled to any right granted to citizens of the latter State. . . .

As regards the provision of the Constitution that citizens of each State shall be entitled to all the privileges and immunities of citizens in the several States, the plaintiff in her affidavit has stated very clearly a case to which it is inapplicable. . . . [C]ounsel for the plaintiff in this court truly says that there are certain privileges and immunities which belong to a citizen of the United States as such; otherwise it would be nonsense for the fourteenth amendment to prohibit a State from abridging them, and he proceeds to argue that admission to the bar of a State of a person who possesses the requisite learning and character is one of those which a State may not deny.

In this latter proposition we are not able to concur with counsel. We agree with him that there are privileges and immunities belonging to citizens of the United States, in that relation and character, and that it is these and these alone which a State is forbidden to abridge. But the right to admission to practice in the courts of a State is not one of them. This right in no sense depends on citizenship of the United States. It has not, as far as we know, ever been made in any State, or in any case, to depend on citizenship at all. Certainly many prominent and distinguished lawyers have been admitted to practice, both in the State and Federal courts, who were not citizens of the United States or of any State. But, on whatever basis this right may be placed, so far as it can have any relation to citizenship at all, it would seem that, as to the courts of a State, it would relate to citizenship of the State, and as to Federal courts, it would relate to citizenship of the United States.

The opinion just delivered in the *Slaughter-House Cases* renders elaborate argument in the present case unnecessary; for, unless we are wholly and radically mistaken in the principles on which those cases are decided, the right to control and regulate the granting of license to practice law in the courts of a State is one of those powers which are not transferred for its protection to the Federal government, and its exercise is in no manner governed or controlled by citizenship of the United States in the party seeking such license.

It is unnecessary to repeat the argument on which the

judgment in those cases is founded. It is sufficient to say they are conclusive of the present case.

JUDGMENT AFFIRMED.

MR. JUSTICE BRADLEY:

I concur in the judgment of the court in this case, by which the judgment of the Supreme Court of Illinois is affirmed, but not for the reasons specified in the opinion just read.

The claim of the plaintiff, who is a married woman, to be admitted to practice as an attorney and counsellor-at-law, is based upon the supposed right of every person, man or woman, to engage in any lawful employment for a livelihood. . . . [This claim] assumes that it is one of the privileges and immunities of women as citizens to engage in any and every profession, occupation, or employment in civil life.

It certainly cannot be affirmed, as an historical fact, that this has ever been established as one of the fundamental privileges and immunities of the sex. On the contrary, the civil law, as well as nature herself, has always recognized a wide difference in the respective spheres and destinies of man and woman. Man is, or should be, woman's protector and defender. The natural and proper timidity and delicacy which belongs to the female sex evidently unfits it for many of the occupations of civil life. The constitution of the family organization, which is founded in the divine ordinance, as well as in the nature of things, indicates the domestic sphere as that which properly belongs to the domain and functions of womanhood. The harmony, not to say identity, of interest and views which belong, or should belong, to the family institution is repugnant to the idea of a woman adopting a distinct and independent career from that of her husband. So firmly fixed was this sentiment in the founders of the common law that it became a maxim of that system of jurisprudence that a woman had no legal existence separate from her husband, who was regarded as her head and representative in the social state; and, notwithstanding some recent modifications of this civil status, many of the special rules of law flowing from and dependent upon this cardinal principle still exist in full force in most States. One of these is, that a married woman is incapable, without her husband's consent, of making contracts which shall be binding on her or him. This very incapacity was one circumstance which the Supreme Court of Illinois deemed important in rendering a married woman incompetent fully to perform the duties and trusts that belong to the office of an attorney and counsellor.

It is true that many women are unmarried and not affected by any of the duties, complications, and incapacities arising out of the married state, but these are exceptions to the general rule. The paramount destiny and mission of woman are to fulfil the noble and benign offices of wife and mother. This is the law of the Creator. And the rules of civil society must be adapted to the general constitution of things, and cannot be based upon exceptional cases.

The humane movements of modern society, which have for their object the multiplication of avenues for woman's advancement, and of occupations adapted to her condition and sex, have my heartiest concurrence. But I am not prepared to say that it is one of her fundamental rights and privileges to be admitted into every office and position, including those which require highly special qualifications and demanding special responsibilities. In the nature of things it is not every citizen of every age, sex, and condition that is qualified for every calling and position. It is the prerogative of the legislator to prescribe regulations founded on nature, reason, and experience for the due admission of qualified persons to professions and callings demanding special skill and confidence. This fairly belongs to the police power of the State; and, in my opinion, in view of the peculiar characteristics, destiny, and mission of woman, it is within the province of the legislature to ordain what offices, positions, and callings shall be filled and discharged by men, and shall receive the benefit of those energies and responsibilities, and that decision and firmness which are presumed to predominate in the sterner sex.

For these reasons I think that the laws of Illinois now complained of are not obnoxious to the charge of abridging any of the privileges and immunities of citizens of the United States.

MR. JUSTICE SWAYNE and MR. JUSTICE FIELD concurred in the foregoing opinion of MR. JUSTICE BRADLEY.

THE CHIEF JUSTICE dissented from the judgment of the court, and from all the opinions.

Acknowledgements

We would like to thank Françoise Djoukeng and Elana Quint for their assistance with preparing this publication.

Made in the USA
Monee, IL
06 November 2026

68010592R00177